GET YOUR CHILD TO THE TOP

MEGAN
LISA
JONES

meganmail@gmail.com/310-890-6798

ISBN: 0615763340
ISBN 13: 9780615763347

TABLE OF CONTENTS

Acknowledgements and Thanks...ix
Foreword by Richard J. Riordan xi
Part One 1
  Two Very Different Children and Circumstances.............. 1
  David 1
  Sam 4
  Introduction.. 8
  A Note on Surveys and Studies 15
  The Schools They Are a Failing (Our Children) 17
  Side Note: Interview with Arthur Levine,
  Education Expert 24
  Los Angeles: A Case Study 28
  Jobs of the Future...30
  A Brief History of Education 37
  Our Children's World 44
  Alejandra 51
  Boot camp: Basics of the American Educational
  System Today...53
  Overview...53
  State Versus Federal 53
  No Child Left Behind and Testing 54
  The Common Core...55
  Standards in General 55
  Learning Styles 56
  Charter Schools...57
  Magnet Schools...59
  Catholic Schools...59
  Home Schools 61
  Vouchers 61
  Private Schools 61
  After School Programs..62
  Blended Learning..65

Innovative Schooling 66
Parental Impact 67
Redefine Literacy 70
Evaluating Your Child...73
A Simple Assessment Test.......................................78
Quiz: Where Do I Belong in Life?............................79
Motivation 101...83

Part Two 91
Subjects to be Studied.. 91
Early Influences; to Preschool and Beyond 95
The Three R's Defined Today................................... 98
Math.. 98
English..103
History...113
Science...118
Financial Literacy 124
Creativity...132
Entrepreneurship, Innovation and Risk Taking.............137
Technology..150
World Focus and Globalization 157
Arts and Music 161
Leadership and a Civic Mind (right purpose)................165
Ethics...172
A Civic Mind...173
Life Lessons..175
A Balanced Person..177
Health and Wellness (Food and Exercise)................179
Faith & Spirituality 181
Yoga and Meditation..183
Gifted Children...187
Failing or the Threat of it..190
Bullies and Mean Girls 193
Drugs, Alcohol, Sex, Pregnancy, Crime and
Even Gangs..199

College: Getting in and Paying for it..................................206
Callie..215

Part Three 219
Technology and the Future of Education.........................219

Part Four 237
Introduction...237
Daily Practice...237
Homework...238
Study Skills 239
Standardized Tests 242
Summers..243
Bad Schools 244
Conclusions 250
17 things You Should Take From This Book
(if Nothing Else) 250
And Three Things That Matter Most...............................252
Books to Read Before You're 18.......................................252
Video Sites..254

Sources 257

This book is dedicated to Lauren, Jason and Dick

ACKNOWLEDGEMENTS AND THANKS

THIS BOOK WAS WRITTEN WITH A LOT OF HELP.

Richard (Dick) J. Riordan helped shape it from early concept through the end, adding insight and helping refine the ideas. Dick founded a law firm, two private equity firms and a number of non-profits. He was also Mayor of Los Angeles and California Secretary of Education. Dick always helps me see the world where it is going and not where it has been, kindly and patiently.

Brigitte Bren kept the book different, compelling and sane; she kept me sane. Maria Gersh and Terri Ott supported me in too many ways to name. Suzanne Nora Johnson helped craft my global perspective, which started out lacking. Frank Baxter provided perspective, insight and understanding.

The list of further helpers is long and includes: Renee LeBran, Hathaway-Sycamores: Simon Gee and Ron Myers, the Gershs, Jack Davis, Tim Draper, Terry Moe, Marty Albertson, Chris Lewis, David Johnson, Jessica Flores, Jill Newhouse Calcaterra, Ari Engelberg, Andy Mazzarella, Kathleen Anderson, Theresa Fragoso, Laird Malamed, Leslie Stokes, Julie Butcher, Chad Keck, John Prior, Mark Suster, Kris Duggan, Arthur Levine, Tom Morley, Steve Ross, David Dwyer, Alejandra Negrete, Jack Nassar, Dee Menzies, Tim Kusserow, Pat Yanhke, Rita Cornyn, USC , the Hartmeiers, Carlthorp, Shannon Rotenberg and everyone at J.K. Liven. Peter Thiel for helping me learn how to think. Neil Morganbesser for helping me learn. Some people asked not to be named and others I forgot to mention. Double thanks.

And most of all, Lauren and Jason, who listened and answered when I kept discussing education until their ears burned. I love you both.

FOREWORD BY RICHARD J. RIORDAN

WHAT MAKES A COUNTRY GREAT? Is it outward looking through military might, the highest national income or the most prizes in whatever competition you value? Or is it inward looking via low child mortality, few citizens living below the poverty line and minimal unemployment?

I was born during the Great Depression and benefited in that my parents were in the minority able to provide me with a college education and because boys slightly older had been disproportionately winnowed out by World War II. But I also grew up at a time when hard work, strong values and family were emphasized. We had to work and care for our families so we did. I found success as a result.

But I also loved to read and continued my personal education and evolution long after I'd closed my last textbook. I worked as a lawyer, investor and founder, the latter of a law firm and two private equity firms. Then I became Mayor of Los Angeles. I've tried to stay engaged in the local community and do what I can to help those less fortunate. My mission in life has always been to help poor children, and indeed I remind myself of it each morning when I drink my morning black coffee and before I read the newspaper.

In 1983, I read the groundbreaking report on education, A Nation At Risk, and woke up to the dismal realities that some of our American children were facing in our educational system. Our schools then and today fail too many children, leading to a cycle of poverty and lacking hope. And the problem has only trickled up into the more fortunate in our society, making even the elite less competitive on a global basis as the world has flattened.

In the ensuing years I've put time and money into helping fix our domestic educational system and have had numerous inspiring partners also thus engaged. Working with charter schools, afterschool programs and even local school boards I've focused on empowering those so motivated to help one child or one school at a time. But I've also engaged at a systemic level through donating computers or other technology to school districts or even partnering to bring lawsuits to protect our children's fundamental right to a good education.

Technology has now leveled the playing field and made providing a good education to all children a reality, and at little to no cost, regardless of how bad, or good, a school is. The needed resources are all online but parents, children and teachers need a better way to find and use them.

Our world has also evolved greatly over the past century and children need to be educated recognizing the implications of those vast changes. What passed for the best education before no longer passes muster, especially when contemplating the jobs of the future. This book provides the first step in an ideal outcome, that all children can have a great education and chance to excel.

For when I look back at my years lived and the related experiences, I must conclude that what makes a country great is that it provides all with an equal opportunity to succeed, rich or poor, native born or immigrant, and irrespective of race or orientation. And education for our young is the first step in that equation. What can you do to get your child, or yourself, to the top? It turns out that you can do quite a lot. And this reality transcends demographics and even IQ.

I succeeded in life because I was given opportunities and worked hard to maximize them. Let's continue providing that great American ideal, which does set us apart globally and is well known as the American dream, to all, regardless of circumstance. And we'll do it one child at a time, if necessary, or together if possible.

Richard J. Riordan, *former Mayor of Los Angeles and California Secretary for Education, 2013*

PART ONE

TWO VERY DIFFERENT CHILDREN AND CIRCUMSTANCES

David

AT 6'5, WITH AN ATHLETIC PHYSIQUE AND ENGAGING PERSONALITY, David presents well. He has brown eyes and short sandy blonde hair, chats easy and smiles. David also exudes that special confidence which attaches to kids who have grown up in more sophisticated households as you can find in Los Angeles.

Living with his two sisters, brother, mom, dad and two dogs high in the hills above UCLA, David's house is a gated oasis above the clamor of the city below. Showing the family priorities, they have a pool, teepee and trampoline but otherwise live comfortably but somewhat modestly. David is an example of good parenting's effects on a family. One of David's sisters goes to school with my daughter; his brother with my son. Thus, I know the family well.

David's father is in finance and his mother left a busy career to focus on their four children. Birthday parties happen only once every four years and foreign travel is a valued and regular occurrence.

My parents gave me the gift of travel.

Listening to David talk requires some analysis. His thought process seems simple but upon reflection is very mature. Sixteen, he goes to a local private high school ranked among the top in the nation. Athletic, he typically plays football from 3:00 to 6:00 pm every day, then four days a week does club volleyball from 8:00 to 10:00 pm. And he gets very good grades in a tough school. David is social and his friends characterize him as "a big 5 year old" due to his sense of fun and goofy humor. Yet he also calls himself a hard personality in that he can be very judgmental.

Morality is important to David and his parents have instilled solid values of hard work and integrity. Thus he can be intolerant of those making bad decisions and veering into drugs, alcohol or other self-destructive behaviors. And he judges his friends strictly on such standards, being mature enough to recognize that his time is better spent with those more grounded, and quite frankly, with better character. He does judge people on whether they choose to do bad or good. Not tempted by intoxicants he also expressed that with his passion for sports he really can't otherwise indulge, as it will impact his on field or in practice performance, thus reinforcing good choices and making them easier.

A Catholic, David also values his religion. With four children and busy sports schedules the family often misses church so he hopes to more develop that part of his life in the future and may perhaps choose a college with a religious orientation.

David's favorite subject is history, especially American history, and a recent teacher helped ignite that interest. He also likes English and when younger, with more time, read a lot. Recent favorite books include *1984*, *The Picture of Dorian Grey* and *The Road*. Analytical, morality driven and politically aware, his book preferences reflect the sophistication of his thoughts. He's also learning Mandarin Chinese and has a community service requirement before he graduates.

His school offers classes like Criminal Law, Middle Eastern Studies and Philosophy of Art. The pressure both from the school and other students can be noticeable and homework averages 3 hours per night. The students do get empty periods during the day to complete homework as many kids have extracurricular activities every day after school. Comprised of mostly affluent children and some on full scholarship, it's a self-selected bunch. Most students who transfer out do so for economic or academic, not social, reasons. Offering resources too vast to list, children can pursue and develop passions if they're willing to work for them. About 30 percent of each graduating class goes to top schools such as those in the Ivy League or Stanford.

It's a scary world out there

In the upcoming school year David is currently planning to take 3 advanced placement classes and one honors class, though he may drop the easiest one. He'll also likely drop club volleyball and just play for his school team to juggle the academic load. Eventually, he'd like to attend college in the mid-west or east coast to experience something new. His mother has declared a 200-mile rule, essentially stating that she wants all of her children to go away to school though they are welcome to return upon graduation.

David lives in the high pressure, high performance world we all read about with respect to affluent and overachieving youth. He claims that, a competitive person by nature, most of his pressure is internal. Both parents are grounded and supportive, and his mother is very active and present for all her children, picking up the slack when her husband travels. Yet David's dad is active and engaged when in town and the family tries to all eat together each evening when possible.

David's classmates aren't always so lucky, much as most are likewise growing up in affluent households. Indeed, grades, college and careers loom over many peers, with a varying degree of pressure from their parents. Many of the classmates with the best grades work exceptionally hard at maintaining that level of excellence, eschewing a social life or most extracurricular activities. David feels like he could break that inner circle and achieve even better grades but would need to give up sports and his social life and so has settled for almost perfect grades. His parents support his choices but he admits that many other of his classmates get pressure to do better.

His conflicts are admittedly those of an elite and he claims that most of the problems his peers face aren't big. An example he gave was that of a friend getting a C on a test and fearing facing parents who'd be upset. Yet, David acknowledges that he doubts he'll get into an Ivy League school because, though his schedule is brutal, most other kids applying will have like challenges and perhaps better grades (remember, his are very good). However, he's accepted that possibility, with his parents support, and has decided to pick a college where he can play sports and have a social life, while not sacrificing much on the academic front.

He also feels pressure regarding whether or not he'll succeed after college. Politically astute and interested, to the point of debating politics and related philosophy with other students during a myriad of classes, David is well aware of the troubles facing our country today, from high employment to the debt burden. Willing to work hard, indeed already doing so, he also acknowledges that parts of life are outside our control. Feeling that he's been given much he feels pressure to use those gifts wisely and make an impact.

Asked where he wants to be in 20 years David talks about going into investment banking like his dad, and is interested in the international aspects of the career. He's also intrigued by law and politics. Marriage and family are also priorities.

David is a good example of a child raised by parents who provide acceptance, support and resources specific to their child's interest. The workload he carries is reflected in his maturity and thoughtful attitude. Presenting well, David has mastered more than he yet knows.

Sam

Heading to downtown Los Angeles from the Westside one cruises down the 10 Freeway; sometimes the drive takes fifteen minutes while other times two hours. All of life in Los Angeles is subject to traffic. Downtown is lovely, a cluster of tall steel buildings set off against the misty hills that too often fade gently into fog or smog. Graceful City Hall and other stately landmarks create that mix of modern and almost modern distinctive to California.

Turning left of downtown and nestled next to traditional Pasadena, with its wide green lawns and quant downtown, is a location of the non-profit Hathaway-Sycamores. The organization provides a comprehensive range of services for the local community including the tough ones, such as addressing domestic violence and gangs, all the way to providing a computer lab and homework help. Open until 8:00 P.M. most evenings they also offer an alternative to the streets, rife with gangs and other challenges. This community reaches out with such varying resources and guidance to an array of local children who want to better themselves.

Simon Gee is in charge of children's programs and has a wonderful way of engaging across issues and individuals. Wise and caring, he's also willing to push children to do better while also praising them for their efforts when appropriate. His program aims to help children move forward despite the challenges they face, often including family issues, and ensure they get an education.

Here in the Hathaway-Sycamore gardens I interviewed a young man who lives just outside downtown Los Angeles after Gee introduced us. Sam enrolled in numerous of the non-profits programs beginning when he was eight and continued attending, and helping out, almost until his recent high school graduation. A technology and science nut, Jack was active in the group's computer lab. Gee had been a mentor and guiding hand while Hathaway-Sycamores itself provided Jack with an alternative to going home after school for years.

The center is located in a quiet neighborhood of small but neat houses. Soft yellow hills provide a sheltered and hazy backdrop for the burning hot streets, and all looked calm. Mere blocks away are dueling rival gangs, both Hispanic. As someone said when asked about the guns, *they aren't carrying squirt guns around*. But while some of the children who avail themselves of Hathaway-Sycamores are in gangs, the center is a gang free zone and respected as such. It shelters a few jungle gyms, grassy areas and classrooms among other resources.

Sam just graduated from a local magnet school program at Marshall High School. He terms himself a geek but presents differently with an engaging personality and outgoing nature. Attractive and considerate, Sam is a fun conversationalist. Sam was able to distinguish himself in many ways but one thing that particularly impressed many was his dragging a few close friends back into the school system to ensure that they graduated. Asked about why he did it his response *was why wouldn't I?* That thought process shows real leadership, compassion and dedication to helping others. Asked how, he admitted to pushing and badgering but felt that risking their wrath was worth the effort. In response to local crime levels, one wants to eventually perhaps work for a sophisticated organization such as the FBI and Sam pointed out that he'd never get hired without a good education. His two good friends were at the lower end academically but not outright failing, which made his success possible. They did both graduate.

And his own story is not without its bumps. His parents are both originally from the Middle East, with his mother having expected more ambition from her future spouse as when she met him he was already "American". She'd been raised in a poorer suburb of their foreign capital, while he grew up in a village. They had two boys a year after each other but then split as they grew emotionally farther apart. She has worked two jobs, day and evening, to provide for her boys while he was less focused. Sam's brother spent some time living with their father but seemingly the lack of discipline in the household negatively impacted his schooling. He's now moving back with his mother and will be attending a local school that in the past has managed to graduate fewer than 40 percent of its students.

Sam is engaging when you sit down to speak. He's also remarkably humble, initially neglecting to tell me that his "goofing off" in high school, which lowered his grades to an acceptable but not stellar level, included a job busing tables for a trendy Las Feliz restaurant.

A science fiction and space nut he has focused his attention over the years on various science disciplines and now wants to be an engineer. While his grades weren't bad he also didn't rank high in his class, which if you grow up in a poorer neighborhood condemns you to a small or community college. Regretting that he didn't study more he now plans to work twice as hard at a local community college so he can eventually transfer to a better school. Unfortunately, due to budget cuts and overcrowding he's finding that getting necessary classes will be impossible during his first semester. Nonetheless, he's lined up a job at a local fast food restaurant and intends to both work and study.

His passion is space. Growing up Sam didn't always like the world around him and space really did offer the ultimate new frontier where he could imagine leaving everything behind. Ray Bradbury's *The Martian Chronicles* is his favorite book and he watches Space X and the Rover landing on Mars in fascination. Perhaps someday he'd like to go into space, for example with Space X's declared ambition of sending people to Mars. Ultimately, he's like to graduate in an engineering field that will let him develop a career in this discipline.

A runner, he also likes superheroes, especially Spiderman, a fellow science buff and nerd. Sam undersells his natural presence and likability but has had a huge positive impact on his many friends and others around him. Upbeat and interested in so much, he really only needs the right opportunities to soar.

Never tempted by gangs or drugs, and of Arab descent, unusual in the area, Sam is friendly and grounded. Somehow the surrounding chaos taught him to get along, not to fight. Slim, with dark eyes and hair, he carries himself with confidence.

Will he make it into space within the next 20 years? We'll see.

David and Sam are both smart and mostly well-behaved children, and a credit to their parents. All of the children interviewed herein were recommended as exceptional and inspiring, though each in their own distinctive way, so the above comparison isn't meant to rank one of the young men against another. These boys have however grown up under very different circumstances yet both have parents, or a mother in the latter case, that made sacrifices for their wellbeing.

Are they on very different paths? For these two, both of whom I suspect will do very well, the aimed for paths seem achievable, given their characters and commitment. But for many others the way is less clear. Why is that reality seemingly so prevalent in today's America? Is the defining feature economic, with vastly different resources and opportunities provided to a minority while the balance of children struggle to get a good education which in turn will lead to a great job and long term economic prosperity? Or is causation a deeper reality, with a mix of both controllable and uncontrollable factors? Let's find out, and also provide specific solutions for those families willing to make a slight effort to get their child to the top.

INTRODUCTION

Adults are just obsolete children.
DR. SEUSS

Whether a mother or a father, our children inspire deep love and protectiveness within us. We hold them for the first time right after they enter the world: red, screaming and with eyes looking every which way until they focus on ours in wonder. We hold their hand as they smile for the first time or venture from the comfort of a wall taking that first step. We lunge to catch them when they tumble, be it from a ledge or emotionally higher up.

Laughing over ice cream, digging through sand and venturing forth without us, they continue looking back to make sure we're still there (and we are). "I love you," they say with a smile before running off again to explore and build a world of their own. But we love them more though it takes years for our children to realize so.

Days pass in but a whisper of a second, from the first day of school, through homework then sports practice and play dates without us. We let them go. Suddenly our babies are dating or entering college and like all parents we learn to smile as the door closes behind them while we pray for their good time and safe return.

All parents want what's best for their children, even if sometimes deducing that outcome can be perplexing to impossible. Well, one day I realized that I was failing mine in preparing them for the world of the future.

Perhaps I'm an overachiever but I want what's best for my kids. Sometimes I just feel overwhelmed with the choices presented in that quest and unsure what decisions to make. Should my kids attend public or private school? What activities will shape them into a future American President or at least productive and functioning member of society? How do I meet their expectations and my own as they look at me with round eyes and absolute trust and I have no answer?

What if I'm not an overachiever but rather a normal parent and thus others are subject to the same conflicts or realities that gosh, we're also busy trying to provide our children with the basics – housing, food, a school and some love (let's leave out toys and iPads for now) that we don't really have time for conceptual debates about ultimate right choices?

We all have hopes and dreams for our children, starting from an ultrasound picture then continuing to the first day of school through college acceptance and beyond. And don't we hope that they will grow up to get a good (or excellent), stable job; avoid addiction or misfortune; and have a happy family of their own? Yet how many of us feel confident raising and advising the precious little people with whom we're entrusted, especially in this day and age of rapid global change, huge budget deficits, mixed record schools and high unemployment? Personally, I question my qualifications daily but am determined to rise above my own self-doubts to find the answers for my children (and yours). I'm a very determined person.

Confession one: I've never been a school person.

Every book starts with a story and this one has a long genesis. When I started learning about schools I was working in finance and more concerned with the declining literacy and functional literacy in our country, especially but not exclusively in low income communities. Estimates regarding Los Angeles, where I live, are that of the kids entering our kindergartens here less than fifty percent will graduate from high school; just over fifty percent graduate now. Recent published local high school dropout rates in some schools top forty percent per year with a slew of other high schools hitting well over twenty percent annually (the poverty rate in the local area correlates directly with the drop out rate). Los Angeles is the second largest school district in the country and as I write has proposed lowering course requirements for high school graduation to avoid an increased drop out rate going forward. Of the high school class that graduated in 2011 only 15 percent were eligible for admission to the University of California or California State University system.

Nationwide about 75 percent of students are estimated to graduate high school in four years but some school districts only count in that number the kids who start their senior year and not those who dropped out beforehand. Yet the jobs of the future increasingly require a high school education and basic literacy. Arts, history, science and language programs have been cut dramatically in schools across America. Our children are growing up both less proficient and less multidimensional.

Learning these facts, I was horrified for the future of our country and disappointed that these poor kids were having their future professional options so destroyed at such an early age. Who will support them if they are uneducated and unskilled! My kids meanwhile are in private school so I didn't feel a direct impact but rather an indirect one. Other people's problems....

In my neighborhood I had been more worried about the perfect, involved helicopter moms who drive their kids around town from activity to activity and started building their child's resume pre-birth event. I work and can't be so diligent since my obligations are more varied (my kids still love me and mostly tell me I'm a great mom anyway).

How wrong I was! As I read more I started to realize that my children are at risk too, as are all children. The world really is flat now and our kids will be competing on a global stage when they build their lives upon whichever graduation level they achieve, and some of those competitors are both hungrier and better educated.

Unpleasant fact: American schools (as run today) don't exist to provide children with an excellent education or maximize their long-term career possibilities and options. Rather, (we and) our government fund schools for public policy reasons including to build a community and socialize children, to impart basic knowledge and to provide employment (for adults). Educating children is a secondary goal. Thus parents, children and teachers must supplement the existing education infrastructure if they want a (my or your) child to reach the top of his/her class and be prepared for the challenges of our ever changing and knowledge enabled world. What constitutes an exemplary education has changed since our educational system was put in place, and doesn't account for massive innovation in areas including technology, psychology and science.

The reality is that our school system is antiquated and was designed to follow the crop seasons; teaches basic literacy to mostly factory or other manual workers; largely ignores the impact of technology, psychology, neurology and scientific progress; teaches to tests not to jobs of the future and is in decline relative to a steady percentage of other developed and even less developed nations. According to the Milken Institute, we underspend relative to many Asian nations when it comes to tutoring or supplemental education and overspend on schools that aren't educating well. Americans spend about 2 percent of their household budget on supplemental education for their children while many Asian nations average about 15 percent. Below I'll detail how much better the education children in many countries are getting when contrasted with our own, which used to be the best globally but now lags.

To me, at one level, the last paragraph reads like a big "so what". I'm not an educator and don't want to take on our school system. Yet practically speaking those words mean that our kids, even my kids, are truly not being prepared for the jobs and opportunities of the future and really will be competing with better-educated kids for them. So, if I don't help guide my children now I might be supporting them.

Meanwhile, I was just sending my kids to school and showing up when required, leaving the educating to the experts, blissfully unaware that my modest efforts aren't enough. Indeed, according to a McKinsey and Company study done in April 2009, "lagging achievement in the United States is not merely an issue for poor children attending schools in poor neighborhoods; instead, it affects most children in most schools."

Trickle up illiteracy?

Being proactive, I started reading stacks of books on education and honestly, one person's opinion, they didn't help me find answers as to how I can best prepare my kids to thrive in our ever changing and challenged world. I learned a lot about child psychology, behavioral issues and responses and even how to run a school (I have no intention of running a school) but I found little meaningful guidance on preparing my children to go to college and get a good job after they graduate. This book will tell you what I found that did help and provide a proactive plan so you likewise can guide your children.

One example, William Bennett, the ex-US Secretary of Education, wrote a best seller in 1999 called *The Educated Child*. At well over 600 pages the book was a great resource for parents then who wanted to ensure that their kids got an amazing education and were college ready. But the book is pre-Internet (widespread adoption of), Harry Potter and Facebook. Additionally, parents in the late 1990's had fewer options outside traditional schools such as charter schools or the Khan Academy.

So I kept reading. I love to read and do so at an amazingly fast pace (or so I'm told) with mostly good comprehension. Reading about education ranks up there with my civil procedure textbooks during law school which induced the first naps I've taken on a regular basis since toddlerhood. Let me explain what bored me: I don't want to be a teacher, not even for my two kids whom I love more than anything in the world and I don't want to do homework (theirs or mine). I don't want to learn teaching! What I do want is a solution for fixing my problem: giving my kids the training they need to face a complex and ever-changing world so they can thrive in it. I want an easy answer.

Another proactive example? I love *Outliers* by Malcolm Gladwell and lecture my children about it constantly! In my opinion, the book is one of the best education and parenting books I've ever read. Why? Because it explains in simple terms how to make my kids successful at something in a practical way that I can actually understand and implement. The message, in quick, is that time and effort add up to mastery, which leads to success. In contrast, making me learn adverbs again isn't constructive for anyone (my son still insists I should learn second grade math so I don't need to cheat with a calculator when I check his homework). The basic truth is that education is boring but learning is fun.

And there is an answer in that truism.

Kids love to learn; adults do too. But education itself is an inherently deep topic thus gets boring quickly as it requires constant and ongoing mental effort to stay engaged. Was I slowly on to the beginnings of an answer?

Still left with the basic question of what my children should be learning if they are to be a success in the world going forward, I turned to Aristotle and Reid Hoffman (Linkedin). The former founded early academies, which focused on shaping the balanced person and the right purpose of a life; the latter was similarly focused on the person but more on crafting those aspects that lead to long-term professional success now that traditional career paths no longer work. I'll discuss both concepts later but here want to address why this idea of the entire person is so important: people are much more complex than the sum of their academic knowledge and the data to shape our children and guide them exists. However, it's just scattered in a lot of different places and often not education or child focused but rather aimed at a self-curious person, usually an adult. This book applies what some of these innovative thinkers have discovered but with a game plan as how to use that information to guide your child, supplementary to their school while not replacing it.

My own academic history is complex and made me determined to do better for my own children. At six and seven I was in all advanced classes and doing well. Then my parents started moving my brother and me from place to place, and school to school. I went to three elementary schools, three junior high schools and three high schools, often moving in the middle of a school session. I was able to hold my grades up for a while but eventually, going to three schools my junior year of high school and missing almost the first four weeks as my parents battled in a bitter divorce, they suffered. I still managed college and even law school but not the ivy leagues by far.

I ended up becoming an investment banker and counseling mostly younger, innovative companies. A big lesson I learned was that success doesn't come from nowhere or luck: those companies that grasp their market within the larger global realities and provide something proprietary and of value do the best. Doesn't that conclusion apply to people as well?

My ex-husband, in contrast, moved once as a toddler, then stayed on a consistent school schedule with a very involved ex-teacher mother and was rewarded with Harvard then Stanford. He's obviously a smart guy but I have to suspect that his stable environment with a very active parent played a part in his academic success. So - lesson learned - how do we thus aid our children in less stable circumstances and with little control over the quality of the school they attend?

When I was growing up most kids did well under a theory of benign neglect. I spent a lot of time riding my bike with other neighborhood kids and playing in a variety of backyards, only returning home for dinner. The world today is more competitive and this generation of children can no longer expect, as has become a recent American reality, to out earn their parents. Chatting with my kids' tennis coach, our one dedicated sport, he touched on what it takes to be tennis pro today and the lesson applies to all education. Our coach trained some big names and did the junior circuit back when California was funneling prodigies into the top levels of the pros. He said it's different today and you can't just support a child who loves and excels at tennis but rather need to make the decision for them, and earlier, otherwise you'll get left behind. Tennis isn't alone in requiring more active parents and a focus on the end game. What do you want for your kids and do you wànt to leave it to chance?

Doing otherwise has arguably never been easier as the right tools and insights are more broadly available and we know more. I weighed very heavily whether to go wide and shallow or narrow and deep with this book and decided to do the first. This guide is meant to be a starting point that explains the current school realities, the worlds our children inhibit and are growing up to face and provides suggestions and simple solutions for addressing their needs so that they can excel in life. The right foundation isn't everything but it helps. Technology, the Internet and gaming are huge variables shaping our children and I'll address the related implications. I will also provide additional resources in each chapter so that parents can further develop depth in any specific area. Online are deeper resources, which can be more easily updated. Please go to www.laernn.com to suggest topics for coverage and utilize the other information there.

A note on how the book is organized: I start with some education related background information and supporting statistics though I will avoid the deeper school debates and conflicting arguments. This book isn't meant to convince but rather to aid children, parents and teachers thus my assumption will be that those reading aren't looking for policy but constructive advice to benefit kids. Next, I'll address specific academic topics and issues. Social, health and cultural issues will then be defined and explained. I'll close with conclusions, daily action plans and a few basic suggestions that someone without the time or resources to implement the wider options can use as an easier starting point.

And, this book is aimed at a broad range of parents since we all face similar challenges as our world continues to evolve, and hopes to maximize our children's options. American or living elsewhere, private or public school, hoping your child is the first in the family to graduate high school or the next to attend a legacy school, we all in today's world need to supplement what our schools can provide. They are too burdened with the basics to expect them to enable our kids to soar. I plan on getting my kids to the top. Do you? Are you willing to take a few simple steps to get them there?

Only the paranoid survive.
ANDY GROVE

A NOTE ON SURVEYS AND STUDIES

Data is not information, information is not knowledge, knowledge is not understanding, understanding is not wisdom.
CLIFFORD STOLL

This book is derivative. I'm a mother, not an educator, who wanted answers so I read and interviewed extensively. Looking for the impact of these books, articles and studies I pondered their implications with respect to real individual children and their circumstances. Then I synthesized and drew conclusions. I asked people more knowledgeable or wiser than me then revised my conclusions when what they said made more sense than my own. The data I reviewed stacks to my ceiling!

But the analysis is more complex than you'd expect.

For a parent the conclusions drawn in most of the surveys and studies I referenced here don't count. Or, I'll temper that statement and say that they don't count much. Reading extensively through well-documented studies and books I quickly noted that intelligent and knowledgeable people can draw very different conclusions from the same data or they can select to pull data from only those sources that support their thesis. What matters to a parent is their child not the mean or average.

Step back and understand the process that many of these academics and experts face: they only get published or noticed if they state something new or distinctive thus they are incented to support their position, even if extreme, and very often build careers on building this related "new" expertise.

Working as an investment banker I've always had a saying, "the numbers don't lie" and they never do. But you need to understand the numbers before you can interpret them. For example, an increase in payables can mean a company is cash short and drawing out the payment of its liabilities or it could mean that production has ramped rapidly and the company needed to increase raw material purchases quickly. A drop in revenue is never a good sign but is understandable in a cyclical business such as toys after Christmas. Whether children are born in January or July is irrelevant, especially if your child is born in November.

In one book I read a reviewer noted that all the data used by the author to support a point was over 40 years old and numerous recent studies done within the past twenty years were ignored.

Additionally, many studies comment on a population or group and not an individual. Debated for years is whether minorities do relatively poorly in school due to race (and lower IQ scores within that ethnic group) or due to socioeconomic and cultural realities (higher poverty rates, worse schools and less educated parents). Regardless of whether which point is true or neither the actual answer has no impact on your child – who is a person not a range of numbers. While forming a group, those numbers contain the full range of smart to less intelligent kids. Let the theorists argue such controversial topics and get the related press while you focus on evaluating the person who most matters to you, your child.

One further note here is that the debate over whether intelligence is based more on genetics or environmental factors is a heated one! Yet almost all experts agree that genetics is a factor in intelligence with most willing to concede that it's at least 50 percent. The extreme position tops out at around 85 percent and the numbers are mostly culled from studies done on twins and a variety of other children relative to adopted or biological parents. Do you really care what the exact percentage is when more important is that virtually all experts agree that environmental factors can make people more intelligent? Aren't us parents better focused on that proactive possibility of increasing our child's IQ?

Thus I'll site numerous studies as they provide a baseline from which we can use common sense guidelines to help our children not because they are assumed to be completely accurate or always applicable to your situation. No one thus far has been able to create a foolproof study when human beings are involved.

THE SCHOOLS THEY ARE A FAILING (OUR CHILDREN)

America is the best half-educated country in the world
NICHOLAS M. BUTLER

Please note, we're starting the brief data heavy section of the book. Later, we'll have an action plan with concrete suggestions but for a short while are going to define the issues. Child specific objectives for solving this problem will benefit from its being clarified upfront.

I hate this chapter. Below I'll add the raw data but just a preview, it isn't pretty. When I was growing up in California my state's schools ranked yearly at number one or two nationwide. Currently, 2011 data puts them at 41. The United States as a whole isn't doing much better on a global comparison.

The raw facts are actually quite simple.

Three main tests are used to compare global scores of different school systems by country. The PISA test (of OECD countries) is the most often cited one. In 1961 the Organization for Economic Co-operation and Development (OECD) was founded with a mandate of promoting economic growth and world trade. One related effort it sponsors is the Programme for International Student Assessment, or PISA, which is administered every three years to between 4,500 and 10,000 fifteen year olds. The tests were launched in 2000, cover a vast and detailed list of topics and in 2003 a problem solving skill section was added. School systems and students in 70 countries that account for nine-tenths of the world's economic output are evaluated.

Relatively speaking, US performance has not changed much over the past twenty years while numerous other countries have greatly improved, leaving us to drop to average performance (from high performance) over that time period.

For the year 2009 (the test is scored every three years) our basic US PISA OECD Country scores are:

14 for Reading (after Estonia, Iceland and Poland)

31 for Math (after Slovenia, the Slovac Republic and New Zealand)

17 for Science (after Ireland, Slovenia and Hungary)

Worse, American students overall did not rank well in comparison to students in countries competing for the same service sector and higher valued added jobs upon which the US future is reliant.

In the PISA 2009 results the three top performing countries in overall results, Finland, Korea and the partner economies of Hong Kong-China and Shanghai-China, also had among the lowest variance of students scores, proving that good results can be replicated across a population. The US had among the highest variance among student scores.

Top students also show a marked difference in performance when US students are ranked against top performing countries. We have the smallest proportion of 15 year olds at the highest level of math proficiency. Belgium, the Czech Republic, Finland, Korea and Switzerland all have five times the number of top performers (many of whom are also bilingual!).

Factors such as whether the child came from an immigrant family, an economically disadvantaged family or other variables did have a negative impact, and more so in the US than in many other countries. Girls, who tend to read more, scored slightly higher in reading, boys slightly higher in math and were about equal in science. Students who enjoy reading and did it frequently for pleasure scored higher across the board. Reading fiction helped, but reading more broadly, even including emails or online research, did the best.

Across the OECD countries 37% of students said they did not read for enjoyment at all. Those students that were socio-economically disadvantaged were especially weak in reading proficiency, even more so the boys. If these boys had the same awareness of effective reading and summarizing strategies as more advantaged boys their proficiency performance would have risen 28 points, and had they matched the girls it would have risen 35 points.

Parents also had an impact on test scores with those who regularly read to younger children or discussed political or social issues with older children having children who scored noticeably higher.

In the problem solving tests launched in 2003, only 20 percent of students in participating countries were deemed "reflective, communicative problem solvers" (PISA term) and can manage multiple issues simultaneously, grasp underlying relationships, use systematic thinking to resolve a challenge and then communicate the result. The US ranked 29 overall and almost 25 percent of its students scored at level one (one being the lowest). In four countries, Finland, Hong Kong-China, Korea and Japan, 30 percent of students scored at a three level, the top, while only 12 percent of US students got a like score. To be in the top 10 percent of US students a score of 604 was required; in Japan a like ranking required 675. Thus, not only did American students not score well on problem solving overall, our top scorers tended to a much lower average than those in numerous other countries.

Other outside influences also impact outcomes. PISA found that with children whose schooling was "tracked" based on ability, performance suffers and the earlier the division the worse the overall student impact. Students who attended pre-primary school did noticeably better on subsequent tests. The study noted that the United States also gives disadvantaged children larger classes, worse teachers and a less demanding curriculum, in contrast to higher performing countries.

Addressing the same topic but outside PISA, McKinsey and Company stated, "On average, black and Latino students are roughly two to three years of learning behind white students of the same age. This racial gap exists regardless of how it is measured, including both achievement (e.g. test score) and attainment (e.g. graduation rate)". Test scores show that 48 percent of blacks and 43 percent of Latinos rank below basic, while only 17 percent of white fall into this designation. Results vary some by state but the racial divide is a constant. Blacks and Latinos also fall more into the low scoring groupings and are only lightly sprinkled into the narrow band of students at the very top.

Rarely even having access to advanced placement options, under 4 percent of black students score a 3 or more on an AP high school test, as compared to 15 percent nationwide (still not high enough). Currently, California, Texas, New Mexico and Hawaii are the only states with under 50 percent of students coming from a European ancestry (thus over 50 percent are designated minority) but the country as a whole will reach that demographic breakdown by 2023. This demographic shift will have profound implications on our nation going forward. Not only are minority students currently underperforming they are also less likely to attend and graduate college, with only about 10 percent attaining a like degree.

The poverty gap also has important implications. According to McKinsey, students eligible for lunch programs (federally subsidized program for poor children) are two years behind other kids in schooling regardless of race. Meanwhile, in our country's top 120 colleges, the Tier One with an enrollment of about 170,000 students, only 9 percent of any entering class is from the bottom HALF of the country's income distributions.

But not only our poor and disadvantaged children are at risk of underperformance as the PISA results demonstrate. Even our higher performing students aren't attaining on a global basis, beyond the disheartening PISA results.

Indeed, a different study shows that students in wealthy United States public schools rank in the 50th percentile in math, even lower than in PISA.

And, according to McKinsey in 2009, "the longer American children are in school, the worse they perform compared to their international peers. In recent cross-country comparisons of fourth grade reading, math and science, United States students scored in the top quarter or top half of advanced nations. By age 15 these rankings drop to the bottom half. In other words, American students are farthest behind just as they are about to enter higher education or the workforce."

Thus to compensate, the study found that fifth-grade teachers spent 37 percent of instruction time on basic literacy skills, 25 percent on math, 11 percent on science and 13 percent on social studies.

In *That Used to be Us*, by Thomas Friedman and Michael Mandelbaum, their chapter on education begins with the results of a recent IBM sponsored competition known as the "Battle of the Brains" (the 2011 Association for Computing Machinery International Collegiate Programming Contest). Of the top twelve teams, only one is American and the winner is Chinese. To quote the authors, *that used to be us.*

What makes a difference in quality of education? Not surprisingly the most important factor is teacher quality. Yet teacher quality is a variable over which most parents have no control. Much quoted research from Tennessee data shows that if two average eight-year-old students are placed one with a high performing teacher and the other with a low performing one their performance will diverge by over 50 percentile points in three years. Also quoted by McKinsey, a Dallas study shows that "the performance gap between students assigned three effective teachers in a row and those assigned three ineffective teachers in a row was 49 percentile points". Reducing class size had little impact.

Moreover, there is a logic in these results beyond the obvious. In high performing school systems (judging globally) teachers were culled from the top of their class; top 5 percent in South Korea, top 10 percent in Finland and top 30 percent in Singapore and Hong Kong. In the United States only a few entities (such as Teach for America) do the same. Most public school teachers come from the bottom 30 percent of their class. Many teachers for courses such as math or science, or other hard to fill subjects, not only didn't major in these topics but also may not be even basically proficient in them (nor are they required to be).

And early success in school has shown across many studies to have a measurable impact on later success and eventual earnings. Lagging performance by many, though not all, students by fourth grade is a predictor of high school and college graduation rates as well as lifetime income. A study in England showed that students failing at age 11 had only a 25 percent chance of passing by age 14, and the likelihood that student would graduate was only 6 percent.

Results in fourth grade are (unfortunately) a good metric according to studies quoted by McKinsey. "For example, 87 percent of fourth grade students scoring in the bottom quartile of New York City math achievement tests remained in the bottom half in eight grade. Students who scored in the top quartile in math in eight grade had a 40 percent higher median income 12 years later than students who scored in the bottom quartile." Failure compounds, like that proverbial snowball rolling down a hill. The study also notes that those results aren't set in stone and kids, being resilient, can improve with the right efforts and support.

I was surprised to learn that student performance within a school in our country varies more than performance between schools. The good news for parents in this fact is that your efforts can overcome the impact of a bad school or teacher.

Forty years ago the United States had the highest high school graduation rate in the world but now we rank 18th out of 24 industrialized countries. Overall enrollment also lags, falling to 22nd in school enrollment of 5 to 14 year olds and 23rd in enrollment of 15 to 19 year olds among OECD member nations.

The lack of rigorous school programs extracts a greater toll the older children get and into adulthood. The Department of Education confirms that about a third of students entering college must take a remedial class in math, writing or reading, with the number being higher for black and Hispanic students. The corresponding number is about 40 percent at two-year colleges. Only 22 percent of high school students meet college ready standards (in English, math, science and reading) while only 3 percent of blacks do. Of those headed to college the number only jumps to 43 percent. Dismal.

And our students are also no longer completing higher education at the rates of the past. According the a report issued by the National Governors Association in 2008, in 1995 America still tied for first in university and college graduation rates but dropped to 14th by 2006 while also having the second highest drop out rates (among 27 countries). We had 30 percent of global college students in 1970 but now have less than half that as of 2008. Over the next decade, India and China will have more secondary and postsecondary graduates.

Meanwhile, other countries are making aggressive strides in educating well-rounded higher education students. "A July 2008 study found that the University of California, Berkeley had been displaced by not one but two Chinese universities as the top undergraduate feeder institutions for American Ph.D. programs."

Other spiraling factors? College graduates are 50 percent more likely to vote. People with less education don't eat as healthy or exercise as much, and are more likely to smoke. They are thus more likely to be obese and less likely to buy health insurance.

Lately we've all heard of education reform yet what does that mean? According to a McKinsey and Company study from 2007, education spending per student in the United States increased by 73 percent from 1980 to 2005 and class sizes were reduced. Numerous other initiatives to improve education from a myriad of sources were launched. Actual student outcomes, measured by the Department of Education, stayed about the same.

By the way, our government spends over $600 billion dollars a year on Kindergarten through twelfth grade (K-12) education so we deserve to see some solid returns for that investment, beyond poor test scores, high drop out rates and the broad need for remedial courses in college.

I want to bring in one more McKinsey quote: "In our observation, parents in poor neighborhoods are all too aware that their schools are not performing well; but middle class parents typically do not realize that their schools are failing to adequately prepare their children for the age of global competition. Our findings suggest this middle-class complacency is unjustified and should be challenged." Overall, as go our schools so goes our nation and all of our children are at risk for not meeting the competitive needs of our global economy. "Avoidable shortfalls in academic achievement impose heavy and often tragic consequences, via lower earnings, poorer health, and higher rates of incarcerations." Unfortunately, thus far we aren't actively addressing the broad depth of the education challenges within all 50 of our states, with a long-term impact only guessed at but broader than most likely expect.

The Council on Foreign Relations recently identified our (lacking) educational system as a national security issue. Our students not only aren't being prepared for the jobs of the future they are unfit for the military and the tasks required to protect our country. Schools, all schools, in the report are also noted for their lack of innovation

Parents can no longer rely on schools to educate their children if they expect them to be prepared for a global and knowledge based future.

An education isn't how much you've committed to memory, or even how much you know. It's being able to differentiate between what you know and what you don't.
ANATOLE FRANCE

Side Note: Interview with Arthur Levine, Education Expert

Arthur Levine is the President of the Woodrow Wilson National Fellowship Foundation and an education expert. He's written many books and articles on the topic, including a book series on the defining features of each successive generation of college students (based on extensive surveys). The most recent is titled *Generation on a Tightrope*, and is a worthwhile read for all. Levine was kind enough to discuss his insights into the current state of American education and confirmed my research cited above.

I'll quote Levine later in the section on schools of the future but he initially caught my attention in a Wall Street Journal editorial entitled *The Suburban Education Gap*. In the article, Levine details the two education gap problems we have in the United States, and as discussed above. The first is the substandard education offerings in the inner city, a civil rights issue which is increasingly starting to be pressed in the court system. Within these heavily minority neighborhoods the children are not graduating from high school, let alone college, and only a small percentage perform at grade level on standardized tests.

The other problem is that even in our affluent neighborhoods, he cites Gross Point, Mich., Scarsdale, N.Y. and Greenwich, Conn. as examples, the students are scoring well below those in countries such as Finland and Singapore. Even our best and most supported American students aren't doing well on a relative basis internationally. Overall, we're educating based on zip codes and race, yet all groups are falling increasingly behind.

So, why?

I asked Levine about this problem and he shared many important insights. He harkened back to when our educational system was much younger and focused on the analog problems of providing the 99 percent with an education that trained them to do rote work, or tasks, in a factory. We haven't revisited the education provided to address our new digital and international world. So how can our children not be left behind? They aren't being educated to keep up.

Indeed, all of our institutions are failing to meet the demands of our new realities and we're seeing people withdraw from these institutions, be they schools or government, finance or healthcare. At a time when our citizens need to be most involved they are being pushed away, even alienated. So people have disengaged.

Before children were batch processed; now they're being evaluated on what they've learned and whether they can apply those lessens productively. Being trained to do as told and not to reason through solutions or get creative, very often our children can't. This dynamic is reinforced through helicopter parents who control ever more of their children's realities. Levine has done extensive studies showing that parents really are much more engaged and present in their kid's lives, even during the college years. And the involvement isn't just a concern but rather often interferes, preventing children from learning independence.

Meanwhile, our kids aren't standing still, as Levine points out. Rather they're self-educating online and engaging in the fresher digital content that peers or those only slightly older are creating. I asked Levine about whether current teachers can adapt and teach these new empowered students. He said that there may be some skipping of generations within the teacher community, with the young adding such value that children gravitate to their offerings (note; on this point I'm interpreting his words). Thus, whether children ultimately do the bulk of their learning in schools or out, they will find content creators to meet their interests. I see this happening with my own children. Google is their best friend. YouTube is a close second. The result?

Well, Levine quotes the George W. Bush Presidential Center:

The problem America faces, then, is that its urban school districts perform inadequately compared with their suburban counterparts, and its suburban districts generally perform inadequately compared with their international counterparts. The domestic achievement gap means that the floor for student performance in America is too low, and the international achievement gap signals that the same is true of the ceiling. America's weakest school districts are failing their students and the nation, and so are many of America's strongest.

Thus, our inner city children can't compete against those in the suburbs and those latter kids aren't competitive internationally. Further clarifying the why behind the problem, Levine pointed to the lowered expectations we accept now. He even wrote a book about it. Looking into his South Bronx neighborhood, Levine contrasted the expectations of his youth, where the children were expected to work hard and do better than their parents with the realities of today. Now, the kids get little education and aren't pushed to learn more, facing violence and the possibility of early death instead.

And Levine also notes that low expectations aren't just a problem in the inner city. Grade inflation has become an ever-present reality, perhaps even more so in the "better" schools where these inflated grades enable acceptance into prestigious universities. I personally see coddled kids in my private school, who are told that everything they do is perfect and aren't taught to strive but rather are just given. Life isn't all As and field trips.

According to Levine, schools need to have one foot in the library and one in the streets. Practically speaking, this means we should be studying our human history as we look at the realities around us, and how they're impacting progress.

Parents have many choices, be it on a per child level or that of changing the educational system, which would benefit us all. The most important step is recognizing that experts like Levine are seeing the situation for what it is and providing due warning. Don't lose your child in an outdated system. Engage and help them do better.

One note, I have recounted my conversation with Levine based on my notes, a reading of his pieces and a slight writer's interpretation regarding the implications of his words. Levine is a thoughtful and fair expert; any emotional opinions are my own. Unfortunately, he confirmed my research on how our children truly are falling behind, at all levels of society, and he's done the surveys to prove it.

LOS ANGELES: A CASE STUDY

Los Angeles has a distinctive light, casting a soft focus on the littered scenery, perfect when seen through a camera lens. On a clear day the details of a far away hillside are striking and the exact blue of the ocean waves is discernable. Our weather is almost always a perfect balminess, utterly lacking in humidity. And thus the film industry claimed the yellow hillsides and vast valleys early in its infancy, and studio buildings still litter otherwise uneventful streets.

The city has a storied past, and celebrities compete for headlines with scandals, riots and earthquakes. Life is never calm in a city of almost 4 million people, making it the most populous in California and the second in the nation. The greater Los Angeles area contains about 18 million people. With notoriously clogged freeways these people mostly move slowly. Indeed, the local traffic was ranked the most congested in the United States in the 2005 edition of the *Urban Mobility Report*. Thus sometimes Los Angeles ends up being viewed as less ambitious or focused than other large cities. Yet who really controls world opinion given our blockbuster movies and evergreen television series?

And Los Angeles is nothing if not diverse. People from over 140 countries speaking over 240 languages live in the region. Recorded population is about 29 percent whites, 9 percent African Americans, 1 percent Native Americans, 11 percent Asians, 49 percent Latino, with the balance being scattered widely.

Even the topography has expanded beyond the famously golden hills that fade quickly from green to yellow summer brush. Our neighborhoods house towering palm trees and vast expanses of well-watered emerald gardens. The area gets little rain, with its fall concentrated in January and February, while random sprinkles arrive unpredictably during other months. Angelinos are notoriously skittish rain drivers, and we're also famous for our high-speed chases that capture local television programming (puzzling visitors who can't seem to understand why we watch mesmerized as police cars speed after some truant across vast freeways and through crowded grey neighborhoods).

An average day is 70 degrees, spiking up during the warmer summer months (though typically not June) and dropping into the 50s or even 40s during winter. January can revisit summer highs, thus the concept of dressing for the seasons takes on a new meaning.

The arts are a huge local driver, with the legendary status of Hollywood as the center of films and entertainment. One in six people work in a creative industry, the highest in the world. That old joke about the guy in the cap and glasses looking like George Clooney and really being Clooney is true. A lot of celebrities live in our tonier neighborhoods and frequent local businesses. There are 841 museums and art galleries in the Los Angeles area, giving it the highest number of museums per capita in the world.

Economically the region is driven by numerous industries including international trade, video games, music, motion pictures, television, apparel, technology, aerospace, petroleum, finance, healthcare, telecommunications, law and tourism. The area is also the largest manufacturing center in the western United States with the fifth busiest port in the world. The area's GMP (gross metropolitan product) totaled $736 billion in 2010, ranking it as the third largest economic center globally after Tokyo and New York. The region also has the 15th largest economy in the world based on nominal GDP.

The LAUSD (Los Angeles Unified School District) has about 800,000 children in any given year and is the country's second largest. Major and minor universities abound, the most famous being UCLA, USC and CalTech.

Neighborhoods scatter like different worlds as you drive from the vast estates of Holmby Hills to the shantytown feel of Watts, with its flashing police lights a constant. And the experiences of the people housed in different parts of Los Angeles really don't bear much in common. A rich and poor place both, Los Angeles is a modern metropolis where you can find just about anything. Thus, since I'm writing in this grand city I'll continue adding some local children's stories, none of them representative yet each important. Indeed, with such diversity here, as in much of America, how can any one story really pertain to all?

JOBS OF THE FUTURE

Many of the jobs our children will be competing to get don't exist yet nor do the industries in which they'll fall. We can predict growth in biomedical engineering and the care professions but where else? When I was in college no one envisioned social networks or MRIs, let alone Internet radio or complex brain imaging. How do we train kids for unknown industries and undefined jobs?

We start with a great traditional education then encourage kids to develop their strengths, with judgment. And sometimes it's better to build up areas of talent at the expense of being well rounded. Later skills can be learned by those with good study habits, discipline and a desire to learn. Foster creativity, ongoing learning and entrepreneurship.

So what is the future expected to look like?

According to the federal government, the US economy will add over 20.5 million jobs between 2010 and 2020, or about 14.3 percent, and most will require education levels above a high school degree. Georgetown University Center on Education and the Workforce estimated that the US would add 46.8 million jobs by 2018 of which 63 percent will require a college education. Another report estimated over 6 million more (high school) dropouts in 2020 than there are jobs for them. Related, there will be a corresponding shortfall of college graduates to fill empty jobs in the same year of 1.5 million. The fastest growing fields are projected to be technology, math, engineering and science (based) yet most US students (as above) are ignoring these disciplines. Other reports estimate that in excess of 60 percent of US companies are having a hard time filling skilled positions already. Thus the jobs are there but the workers aren't qualified. Some of the basic skills identified as missing include effective written and oral communications, problem solving, computer literacy and basic math.

According to a report published by the Counsel of Foreign Relations entitled *US Education Reform and National Security*, "Despite sustained unemployment, employers are finding it difficult to hire Americans with necessary skills, and many expect this problem to intensify. For example, 63 percent of life science and aerospace firms report shortages of qualified workers". Additionally, the report states that of those Americans between ages seventeen and twenty-four a whopping 75 percent aren't qualified to join the military due to criminal records, lack of fitness and inadequate education. Both the 25 percent of high school dropouts and an additional 30 percent of high school graduates lack the educational level needed to serve. Intelligence agencies and the State Department are even more starved for qualified workers.

Quick conclusion: our workforce isn't changing to meet the evolving job realities of a globalized and increasingly technology driven world.

Indeed, between 1969 and 1999 the number of American workers holding blue collar and administrative support jobs dropped from 56 percent to 39 percent. Jobs requiring more specialized skills, including greater education, such as professional, technical or managerial jobs, jumped from 23 percent to 33 percent. Additionally, the actual number of skills necessary has expanded/grown, with rote or repetitive tasks, even skilled ones, being outsourced and those requiring complex analysis, technological or other prowess or communication skills being in greater demand. Workers with strong skills in math, reading, innovative problem solving and communications are also needed and that trend is both continuing and exacerbating.

The competitive landscape has shifted permanently.

Currently, four out of five jobs in the United States are in services. Technological, political and economic trends have increased the demand for skilled workers across a broad range of disciplines and the shift shows no sign of abating. Meanwhile, automation and outsourcing have caused a dramatic decrease in the number of quality manufacturing jobs in America and now even more rote "skilled" work is being outsourced to lower cost providers abroad.

Richard Freeman, a Harvard economist, writes about "the great doubling" of the global workforce as over a billion new workers from countries including Russian, Eastern Europe, India and China have been added to the pool of workers competing for jobs in developed countries. Initially, these workers took lower skilled, low paying jobs and could follow the rote scripted rules needed but are now taking on more complex tasks such as writing company reports or reading X-rays and MRIs.

Due to technological and communications innovations, many jobs can be filled from abroad, even increasingly those that call for the traditional American strength of innovation. According to the Governors report, innovation is being outsourced to India and China by such companies as Merck, Eli Lily and Johnson & Johnson, including advanced research and development not just clinical trials.

Many software programs can now replicate repetitive processes even in skilled jobs that had required a high level of education, such as writing articles and books, thus replacing those skilled workers who relied on those professions.

But opportunities still abound.

According to Daniel Pink in *A Whole New Mind*, due to overabundance creating a good is no longer enough but rather it must be better designed, more attractive or otherwise differentiated. Apple's iPad or Michael Graves' household goods for Target are such examples, and are able to win disproportionate market share and profits. Further expanding on his concept, he recalls Peter Drucker's "knowledge workers" defined as those workers with the "ability to acquire and to apply theoretical and analytical knowledge." Traditionally, they excelled at what Pink refers to as L-Directed thinking, or rather that sort driven by the left brain and including analysis, logic and the ability to zone in on a right answer. Yet these workers are now those who are more replaceable by rule based software, outsourcing to lower cost locales with an educated workforce and less distinguishable unless they have an especially complex area of specialty or skill with clients. Meanwhile, it is the workers with R-Directed thinking who have an edge creating or innovating in the products and services with a better design or unique capabilities.

Thus Pink concludes that to maintain a long term employment advantage workers now must either be offering a service or location specific offering (such as nursing), have better people skills or a wide network or offer a unique, innovative or creative advantage.

Pink dubs our new reality the "conceptual age" and provides a starting solution: "In a world tossed by Abundance, Asia and Automation, in which L-Directed Thinking remains necessary but no longer sufficient, we must become proficient in R-Directed Thinking and master aptitudes that are high concept and high touch." He identifies six specific high concept and high touch aptitudes he calls essential in today's world: design, story, symphony, empathy, play and meaning.

Education is not the filing of a pail, but the lighting of a fire
WILLIAM BUTLER YEATS

Of course, L-Directed workers are in great demand today just those having that added creativity are even more valuable. An aptitude for the left brain math and science expertise not only builds logic, discipline and knowledge it has long term pay implications: higher math performance at the end of high school leads to a twelve percent increase in future earnings. And the National Governors Association states, "If the United States raised students' math and science skills to globally competitive levels over the next two decades, its GDP would be an additional 36 percent higher 75 years from now."

But other regions are also training workers versed in math, science and technology. The National Academy of Engineering has stated that most of the top 20 US-based semiconductor companies now run design centers in India.

And higher education remains a differentiator in the job market. Income is growing much faster for those with a college degree or higher and creating the greater income disparity we're all reading about. In the years from 1973 to 2006, the income of households headed by a person with a college degree grew by almost 40 percent while those headed by someone with a high school diploma only grew about 6 percent. The hourly wage for a college graduate was about 1.5 times that of a high school graduate in 1979. By 2009 the ratio was 1.95

Not only is the income disparity growing but also college-educated workers were less impacted by our recent "great recession". The employment-to-population ratio fell by over 2 percent for adults without a bachelor's degree but only half a percentage point for those with such a degree from 2007 to 2009. According to the Brookings Institute, "Differences in employment levels by educational attainment are enormous. Roughly 30 percentage points separated the employment-to-population ratio for college-educated adults (82.5 percent) from that for adults without a high school diploma (52.9 percent)". And the Organization for Economic Co-Operation and Development (OECD) has estimated that each added year of schooling adds between 3 and 6 percent to a nation's economic output.

Unfortunately, our students as noted earlier aren't being educated, not only for life, but also for joining the workforce. Other countries, again, are doing better on a relative basis. Globally, children are learning English and about the United States while our students often aren't geopolitically or culturally educated let alone bi-lingual. An estimated 55 percent of Chinese students are learning English.

Currently, 57 percent of those receiving engineering doctorates in the US are foreign born, as are 54 percent of computer science doctorates and 51 percent of physics doctorates, most of who return to their home countries. At the undergraduate level, over half of American college graduates attain a social or behavioral science degree with under a third getting their first degree in any science or engineering discipline (only 4.5 percent graduate with an engineering degree). In China the numbers are vastly different, with over half of college graduates attaining a degree in science or engineering. Even United States vocational educational programs, more broadly popular in Europe, are getting cut here.

In 2011, at the Ideas Economy Harvard Business School Human potential event Nitia Nohria, dean of Harvard Business School noted the change of opportunities to which their students were responding.

According to Nohria, *Since the first class at Harvard, we've had students from all over the world. In the past, they were aiming to get a job in America. Not anymore. Today students are preparing to be leaders for the new global century.*

In *The Start-up of You*, Reid Hoffman and Ben Casnocha advice people to "adapt to the future, invest in yourself and transform yourself". They counsel that until recently and for about sixty years the career ladder worked like an escalator and as long as you didn't really mess up you could continue along a stable career path, hitting one milestone after the next until you retire. I remember growing up and knowing that certain companies, such as IBM, never had layoffs (guaranteed job for life). But I also grew up in and out of Silicon Valley (IBM headquarters wasn't local) which was a great training ground for our new world order as the Valley has long been subject to its booms and busts. Indeed, we had a joke about the Mercedes index which was that when times were good you saw a lot of new ones on the road, then the next year they were all for sale.

Hoffman and Casnocha advise people to treat their careers as a start-up company, not that everyone is suited to the risks of starting a company (the latter point I don't agree with; due to the lack of job security in most companies I now believe that the risks of starting a company are relatively small compared with more traditional jobs and the related lack of job security provided in the recent past). What do they mean? First, develop a competitive advantage, then plan to adapt, continually, as the environment changes. Resilience and adaptability are the new metrics going forward. They also counsel building networks and taking intelligent risks. I'll address some of these concepts in greater detail latter on.

When I originally reached out to Frank Baxter for insight into this book I was hoping to pick his brain regarding the schools of the future but he ended up making points similar to Hoffman and Casnocha but added new depth and sophistication. Frank headed the investment bank Jefferies and Company, taking over when the firm lost its founder in a crisis situation. Building the bank, a leader in many business areas, he later left his post to become US Ambassador to Uruguay. Numerous board posts now demand his time and he's also one of the leading drivers of school reform in the nation.

Frank pointed out that the job market has already started creating new dynamics which we can easily identify. *In the 21st century people will need to be their own CEO, CFO and marketing department, even at larger organizations.* Digital realities have made this model viable and increasingly required to stay competitive. The nature of work has also changed in that jobs or even parts of jobs can be posted online and sourced internationally or from other alert experts on a per project basis. More competitive, these opportunities also reward the proactive and create new opportunities for resume and expertise building. Technology has thus transformed the interaction between workers and those needing their services. Cost structures have likewise also evolved (with much getting vastly cheaper).

Online learning increasingly allows for certificates or other validation that someone had the discipline to build and complete courses in areas of expertise. While not replacing the credentials or networks formed in more traditional colleges they nonetheless are valuable to employers when evaluating potential hires: now people can be evaluated more easily on skills developed and not just diplomas.

Frank also pointed out what most smart employers are saying, that as many jobs will be created by employees as by traditional employers. That ability to create a needed skill set or product, innovating in services, allows individuals to better control their career but can also make them more valuable. And, different models are developing in that younger people can now easily team up with more experienced professionals to both learn and add more skills, including online ones at times, to established "masters", effectively apprenticing while also adding value. Starting businesses is also less expensive in either or other contexts, and students are following that path at younger ages.

In sum, you can help guide your children to learn what they'll need to be employable, even as our world evolves. Emphasizing science, math, technology or engineering should they have such an interest and aptitude is a good start. Creativity, communication skills and a broad education increase their options and build the ability to adapt as the world continues to change. Good study skills and a lifelong love of learning also help. More specific suggestions are detailed below.

A BRIEF HISTORY OF EDUCATION

Societies educate their children and always have. In a simple society the form of education can be as basic as demonstrating hunting or social behaviors, with the group example setting the precedent for what the child learns. As the influential John Dewey wrote in *Democracy and Education*, more complex societies must rely on schools to share the deeper breadth of knowledge that is expected of its members.

Thus the history of education is vast so I'll just hit some highlights below.

Plato founded his Academies in 385 BC at Akademia, the sanctuary of Athena, the goddess of wisdom and skill. The term is used to refer to an institute of learning or membership and initially was to develop the elite learners. Aristotle was among other of Plato's pupils to continue the tradition, which focused on developing a right purpose for the student, deeper than just memorizing facts. Indeed, the teacher was to counsel the chosen student in a range of disciplines that included the sciences, art, music, philosophy, poetry and morality. The emperor Justinian closed the Academies in 529 AD though they were rumored to survive underground. During the Renaissance the term became popular again as men strived to develop a broad education and deeper purpose.

Throughout history and cultures, epic or lyrical poems have told of myths and Gods since language existed. Songs and pictures, as in cave paintings, set social norms long before the printing press put words to paper. Music and language are two characteristics that distinguish man from apes. I myself recall memorizing the opening stanzas of Beowulf written early as Western man began scribing language and when cultural histories were mostly passed down verbally. Beowulf is an early epic poem dating to sometime between the 8th and 11th century AD and is an early example of written history being recorded in Europe after the dark ages hit.

In the Western world, of which I'm a part, the Catholic Church was the guiding light in beginning to educate the masses. Until the printing press was invented in 1440, libraries were mostly owned by the church and most scribes spent time copying mainly religious texts by hand. The Church began to connect with its flock through lectures of scripture. It then broadened its aims by enabling congregants to read to better understand the word of God. Many other religions likewise stressed the importance of learning to read their respective holy book or written traditions.

America was founded by settlers seeking an escape from religious persecution and thus homes and later communities stressed the value of literacy so that each individual could read the word of God for himself (women interestingly were more often taught to read than to write, thus they could read the bible but not sign their own name). Additionally, the three Rs were valued as they help create the *judicious republican citizens* (Wikipedia) later required for a democracy, in which people needed to be informed so they could help shape policy through voting.

Education is a better safeguard of liberty than a standing army
EDWARD EVERETT

The first American "public" schools opened in the 17th century when there were only thirteen colonies. Boston Latin School is the oldest and first school founded in America. Early schools focused on community, family, church and apprenticeship, and then later added socialization. Basic literacy and math were mostly taught in home, among the families that possessed such skills. "Common schools" were required by communities and were fee based, though girls and slaves were mostly excluded. By 1767 a few communities had established tax supported schools for girls though their acceptance took root slowly. Tutors for wealthier families were common, especially in the South. Rigor was added to the curriculum and the arts, philosophy, math and the sciences were expanded. Textbooks emphasized ethics and cultural norms, along with academics.

American colleges were initially founded to train the ministry, with Harvard College being the first. Future lawyers, politicians and leading planters also attended these institutions though often paid more. During the 18th century the American university system expanded rapidly. Curriculum focused on the liberal arts including: Latin, Greek, history, logic, geometry, rhetoric and ethics.

The United States pioneered universal free education in the mid-19th century – through grammar schools. Horace Mann became Secretary of Education of Massachusetts in 1837 and created a nationwide state based system of teachers, modeled on the Prussian model of "common schools" and meant to provide all kids with like curriculum. Age based grading was established in the United States. By 1870 all states had free elementary schools and the population had one of the world's highest literacy rates (which wasn't very high). As enrollment expanded beyond a few children in a room to larger classrooms and even multi-room schools what had been individualized instruction increasingly became impossible. Meanwhile, rural areas still had limited schooling.

Reconstruction after the Civil War increased funding and founding to expand the schooling for former slaves and the response from the community was enthusiastic. The Freedman's bureau opened around 1,000 schools across the South for black children and by 1865 over 90,000 such children were enrolled in school. The separate but equal doctrine dictated for a while longer.

By 1900 most states had compulsory schooling laws, less in the south. Thus by 1910 about 72 percent of American children attended school and by 1918 all states required that children complete elementary school. Instruction was generalized, repetitive and lecture-based for the masses, those headed for factory or farm work. According to Micheal Horn of the Innosight Institute, as quoted in a Lexington Institute study titled Building 21st Century Catholic Learning Communities:

The factory model was designed for standardized mass production of students and to prepare them for 20th Century industrial jobs. They required basic, undifferentiated skills churned out at regular intervals. The model assumes that highly regulated inputs of students, teachers, resources and time can produce uniform, high quality results at low cost. This is no longer true.

Meanwhile, higher education was only for the elite ruling class. Also by 1900, about 42 percent of the American population worked on farms.

High school access was increased from 1910 through 1940 with the surge of immigration, preparing the population for more highly skilled technical and managerial jobs. The GI bill after WWII increased dramatically the access of many to higher education. Most elite colleges still catered to the children of the wealthy however, even as these universities increased the social mobility of vast numbers of men on a broader scale. Still, much of our past fifty years of scientific innovation was built upon refuges from Europe during the WWII years.

In 1947, when the US government first measured educational attainment, about half of Americans graduated high school compared with 75 percent today. Over the years numerous reformers and theories gained favor and influenced how schools were run. John Dewey, a professor at the University of Chicago during the mid-twentieth century, had a big impact with his focus on education as the means for a student to realize their potential and use those skills for the greater good.

President Eisenhower supported the use of federal troops to segregate schools during the 1950s after the Supreme Court decided *Brown Versus the Board of Education*. Segregation ended up being a tricky process however and included a migration of blacks from the South, urban blight issues, a loss of manufacturing jobs, inner city poverty and ever shifting demographics, especially the rise of the Hispanic population.

In 1975 *The Education for All Handicapped Children Act* (Law 94-142) passed Congress granting appropriate education to be provided by public schools for all qualified handicapped children. In 1986 the law was amended to apply to younger children. In 1990 the moniker of handicapped was extended to include any disability. The application of the requirement has led to about 20 percent of American children qualifying for special accommodations from our already strapped public school system.

The report *A Nation At Risk* was released in 1983 by the National Commission on Excellence in Education and rocked America with its stinging assessment of the poor state of American education. Little has improved since its release (and some could justifiably argue that the state of education has only continued to deteriorate since). Later, E.D. Hirsch published an influential attack calling for an increase in "cultural literacy", or an increase in learning the influential texts that are essential for navigating and understanding our culture. His standards of what children should learn will be widely quoted and latter provide a much needed, aspirational guide for children's learning.

No Child Left Behind was passed during George W. Bush's tenure to better evaluate how schools were educating their students and to penalize schools that didn't make the grade. Mostly, critics complain that schools responded by "teaching to the test" and test subjects, ignoring practical learning, a true understanding of the subject and dropping electives. President Barack Obama has reportedly waived the legal requirements for about half the states.

As part of the *American Recovery and Reinvestment Act of 2009* as announced by President Obama and then Secretary of Education Arne Duncan, a $4.35 billion dollar fund was dedicated to increase reforms and innovation in local K to 12 education. States competed to win the funds but the criteria used for judging were often not verified or enforced. Thus states actively trying to reform and add innovative options and charter schools didn't win funds while those controlled by unions or others against reforms did.

Meanwhile, in higher education various professions have long exerted control over how their practitioners are trained, licensed and policed, thereby opting out of more generalized standards. The examples are extensive but include medicine, law, accounting and even management. By carefully controlling who is allowed to enter such professions these schools can ensure that at least a minimal level of expertise and knowledge is acquired by those so licensed (and can also aim to keep the cost of these services higher). Getting accepted into many of these programs is highly competitive thus student quality is kept within certain parameters.

Alternative school options have always existed mainly via private or religious schools while a subsector of our population home schools their children. Now we've added charter and magnet schools, which will be described in greater detail below, and which can vary widely in quality and mandate. All of these options lack one core element similar with the public schools, for the most part they are still teaching the same core curriculum and haven't fully evolved to address the differing skills needed for today's challenged workforce. Unlike Aristotle's Academies they don't typically seek to develop a child's "right purpose" as a balanced person, ignoring some key elements of that mandate and replacing it with standardized instruction.

Many of these schools are excellent institutions so I don't want to denigrate them unfairly. Yet they are evaluated on an institutional comparison and thus typically feel pressure to do as their peers/competitors do. The needed honest discourse on updating the curriculum is ignored, and children continue to be educated based on past requirements. Some schools might focus more on math and science or the arts, while others herald a developmental or more conservative curriculum, but rarely are they customized or designed to evolve as our world has and lack a focus on practical application in a globalized, modern economy. Technology is only slowly being introduced into the educational world while it's taken over the practical realities of our youth.

Institutions are known to change slowly, as do all companies and industries not forced to confront and address potentially destabilizing change. As Clay Christensen has noted in his influential book *Disrupting Class*, in which he discusses his concept of *disruptive innovation*, companies in a competitive marketplace tend to innovate oftentimes faster than their customers' needs require. One example is the complex features on new electronic devices which a vast number of people have a difficult time mastering and don't want to pay extra to get. This mismatch of company innovations and customer wants, even though the companies were theoretically evolving in the right way by anticipating the demand for better products, creates the opportunity for a company outside the industry. These newcomers are less driven by legacy products or reputation and can thus more easily introduce a *disruptive innovation* which might be a worse or more limited product than those made by the industry leaders but is cheaper and easier for consumers to use thus they prefer it.

One such example is the videos my kids watch on YouTube. They cost little to make yet are always available, even when their favored television shows aren't due to how restricted television schedules are from the industry distribution contracts and programming limitations. Also overcome are the rules on viewership placed by mom!

Schools aren't competing in a fair and open marketplace.

Christensen notes that while schools have been improving over time, evolving their curriculum, adding new and better technology and even modernizing, they are being forced to do so without the newer and more nimble outside companies having much leeway to create true disruptive change as happens in the private sectors. Due to the public nature of our school system, which makes change harder to effect, he claims that we in essence are asking our schools to re-design an airplane mid-flight. Institutional change comes much more slowly when outside innovators who can maximize lower cost structures, no legacy way of doing things and less risk in trying new things can't access a market. Many educators are desperately trying to change how children are educated even as I type these words but are limited by the rules, regulations and legacy way of doing things in our schools. They should be celebrated for their efforts and change is slowly happening. My concern as a parent is that it isn't coming fast enough to benefit my children.

A teacher friend of mine told me a story about a box of new iPod Touches he wasn't allowed to use until the school principal had time to "program" them. They sat unused in the classroom awaiting a process that they didn't need (they don't need to be programmed).

A note on teachers unions: I'm deliberately not discussing the pros and cons of their impact on the schools system herein. While I have strong opinions on this subject this book is focused not on policy but on ways to better prepare your child for the future.

Currently in the US there are over 15,000 school boards, all operating mostly independently. Do you know what your local school board is doing on behalf of your child and his or her education? The below quote is tongue in cheek but hopefully it encourages some to get involved with their local school board. They can't serve your student well without input.

> *In the first place, God made idiots. That was for practice.*
> *Then he made school boards.*
> **MARK TWAIN**

OUR CHILDREN'S WORLD

> *It is the mark of an educated mind to be able to entertain*
> *a thought without accepting it.*
> **ARISTOTLE**

I was born in Silicon Valley and moved around a lot, including living in Los Angeles, Boston and Dallas. Each place was unique but mostly my experience varied only in my choice of playmates. Each day when not in school I'd grab my bike and ride through the neighborhood or join with local friends to huddle over our Barbie dolls in my bedroom. Television was a limited pastime and indeed carried only a nominal amount of child focused programming limited to Sesame Street, Mr. Rogers and Bugs Bunny. Movies were something we saw occasionally in a theatre or during the series of Disney classics each summer.

My brother was an avid gamer, starting with Pac Man and Atari but his options were limited and visits to arcades sporadic. I didn't use a computer regularly until college though I did have a summer job at sixteen testing ICs (integrated circuits, a key component).

Responsibilities ranged from doing my homework to feeding our pets or helping with the dishes. The worlds I controlled were limited to my Barbie playhouse and various board or other games. We made up stories in our backyards and dressed up to act out the parts. An avid reader, I disappeared often into *Nancy Drew*, *Little House on the Prairie* or *Grimm's Fairy Tales*. I especially loved the latter and would write out my own rudimentary stories of princesses and evil witches. My childhood was perhaps less stable than some but for the most part it was fairly standard.

Our children's worlds are so very different. According to studies by the MacArthur Foundation 97 percent of teens 12 to 17 play video games, with half doing so daily. Since 2005, mobile device ownership for kids between 4 and 14 has had double-digit growth and almost all now have access to such devices. At ages 6 to 9, 93 percent live in a home with a cell phone. Meanwhile, 99 percent of undergraduates report owning their own computer; 76 percent have iPods or equivalent; 93 percent instant message with only 34 percent using daily cell phone messaging.

Children are also creating content, not just consuming it. Over fifty percent of teens using the Internet have created content (besides posting on a social networking site) be it through blogs, personal websites or sharing artwork, photos and videos. Sites such as GameSalad.com enable easier video game design. Curse.com provides an online forum for active users of massive multiplayer online games, many of which are teens. And obviously YouTube.com has spurred young stars such as Fred, Rebecca Black and Nigahiga (Ryan Higa).

No one has yet realized the wealth of sympathy, the kindness and
generosity hidden in the soul of a child. The effort of every true
education should be to unlock that treasure.
EMMA GOLDMAN

According to the MacArthur Foundation such creation and sharing starts well before the teen years. Of middle school and high school students combined: 38 percent share videos, photos and music; 23

percent repackage content to create a new work; 18 percent blog; and 11 percent use wikis. Of younger kids, those in grades 3 to 5, 32 percent share podcasts, video or photos and about 13 percent contribute to blogs, though often through established virtual reality sites.

Much of this new media is interactive, as opposed to being only passively consumed as with television. Instead, children interact with peers, influence outcomes, create worlds and get/provide feedback. Thus our children are learning to interact, collaborate and provide feedback outside of adult participation, input and often knowledge. The also learn from each other and proactively search for information and answers enabled by extensive Internet resources.

Content is suggested based on past interests and they are free to explore whatever topics intrigue them, often guided by other kids. The walkthrough culture fascinates me and my son is an active beneficiary. Essentially, for most to all video games other players have made "walkthroughs" which explain the tricks, cheats and hidden things in games. The latter can include weapons or information helpful in reaching the next level. My son uses them to improve his gaming skills, choosing videos from a complex list of very specific suggestions, and he'll spend hours running between the computer and television (which houses his game) learning. Someday such tutorials would be very helpful in a school context to "tutor" others as to how to learn or improve on a very specific skill or piece of knowledge. Certainly children are better able to speak at the same level as their peers and to explain things simply, in an age appropriate way, than are adults.

Many digital activities are also goal oriented, especially games in which a player is trying to achieve another level or win. What makes games intriguing for learning going forward is the specific dynamics of how they teach players to learn and improve willingly. A clear goal exists, rules are defined, a feedback system lets you learn through (almost risk free) trial and error and players participate voluntarily. This latter element is key in that people want to play games, and in vast numbers, and are thus learning because they want to not because they must.

In contrast, according the Jane McGonigal in her book *Reality is Broken*, school today is primarily a series of long obstacles producing

negative stress; the latter defined as stress due to real possible negative consequences. Schoolwork is required and standardized, leading to a permanent record of grades, a dynamic that creates stress.
Meanwhile, kid's online learning from games and other interactions is
more sophisticated, customized, interactive, high intensity, fast paced
and motivating (they understand and buy into their end objectives
while a concept like a grade is more of an intangible in that the impact
from a letter is more ambiguous and arbitrary). Online learning overall
is more engaging.

According to Laird Malamed, of Activision and USC's gaming school:

*Constance Steinkuhler, who is now special advisor to the president
in the Office of Science Technology and Policy, found that kids who play
World of Warcraft had better literacy in the game than in their studies. The implication is that kids who appear to be struggling can be
engaged with material that engages them. (http://www.allaboutthe-
games.co.uk/feature_story.php?article_id=8439) Plus, kids are also
learning to read complex interfaces, know their stats (like on Call of Duty
Elite webpages) and generally be familiar with numbers and data.*

Moreover, games are made by people who must sell copies to continue funding future game development, in contrast with most school
environments who stick with materials supplied by the large textbook companies that design based on state or national standards of
learning, not on creating compelling content. One fact which a teacher
friend told me I found shocking. He said that in his Los Angeles classroom many textbooks were designed for Texas state standards and
he had to personally tailor what he taught to meet California standards. The reason for this insanity is that Texas is a large buyer thus
the textbook company designed its content to appeal to that large
customer, forcing other state's teachers to interpret the textbooks
as needed.

Games on the other hand can be customized (try playing one...in
many the game you play is tailored by the choices you make during
the game and can be different every time). And the "learning" is how

you win or advance in the game. Thus if the game is either too complex (impossible to play) or easy (no ongoing challenge and rewards for advancing) it does not sell. Learning is a key element of the game and players choose these challenges. The now famous game Civilization has been used in many school systems as an engaging and active way for children to learn about history.

Another benefit of video games is that they create something called a psychosocial moratorium, termed by psychologist Eric Erickson, which is a place for learners to take risks with lowered consequences for mistakes. And these mistakes are even private, in contrast with much of the school experience. Other forms of online, computer-based learning can have this benefit. Technology doesn't judge.

Repetition and practice are also easier in a mechanized world where children can advance at their own pace and not get lost in a larger class schedule. Since much learning builds on past lessons, falling behind can disadvantage a child's classwork going forward, a concept I'll discuss later.

The implications of the above statistics and practical realities are staggering.

On average our children are spending as much time engaged in media as in school. They're also more likely to multitask, for example watching television as they text or play a video game. C. Shawn Green and Daphne Bavelier noted that video games expand what a person perceives in his field of vision while also speeding up the evaluation of visual information. Their assertion was backed up through extensive research with gamers and non-gamers alike. The latter notably and quickly improved their results after training in and practicing action based video games. Gamers respond faster and process more surrounding factors.

William D. Winn, the director of the Learning Center at the University of Washington's Human Interface Technology Lab stated that kids today "think differently from the rest of us. They develop hypertext minds. They leap around. It's as though their cognitive structures were parallel, not sequential."

While children may seem to be reading less, especially of classic books, overall they are reading more than we perhaps realize as they scan the Internet. In a 2007 study called *Reading at Risk* put out by the National Endowment for the Arts in the United States, only about a third of thirteen year olds read literature daily, down 14 percent from 20 years ago. Meanwhile, almost 20 percent of 17 year olds don't read literature ever; double the number from 20 years ago.

Yet, overall, the content available today is vastly greater than it was when today's adults were younger, and children can read on their own interests while interacting not just passively consuming. Problem solving, creative searches or even links from one related topic are norms online. Reading online always requires an ability to scan and process the quality or narrative of the content.

Marshall McLuhan stated in the 1950s that "the medium is the message", arguing that how people consume data impacts the absorption of it. Thus passive versus active consumption affects the brain and how it constructs the related message. Time and the development of brain scans have proven him right and scientists can now map and monitor the differences. Interacting teaches more than does passive listening or watching.

While increasingly researchers are focusing on defining the practical impacts of this change in how children are learning and processing data, and the impact of the structure of their brains as well, for parents the reality is that we don't really know yet. Most studies I've read consider the changes a "good" thing but the same data has been used to argue that kids today can't focus and that multitasking doesn't mean learning to juggle more better but rather leads to doing nothing well.

According to Don Tapscott in *Grown Up Digital*, multitasking numbers include a study in which a surveyed group of children fit 8.5 hours of digital media into 6 actual hours by multitasking. In another study he quotes three-quarters of students claim to instant message while doing their homework. What did they absorb?

Watching my children and their friends I'm in awe of how competent and fearless they are. That childish confidence and enterprising spirit can be a good thing as they will pick up any device and seemingly intuitively figure out how it works. My kids fall into that digital native category of children who never lived in a world without widespread digital technology; technically the cutoff between digital natives and the other - immigrants - is, according to Wikipedia, sometime in the 1960s but widespread usage seems to make the cutoff much later.

My children run restaurants and build communities. They save worlds, earn money and care for their pets online. On Club Penguin their avatar penguins own impressive wardrobes and can redecorate their igloos or pirate ships with a few keystrokes. My daughter has learned how to dress avatars well, do makeup and dictate hairstyles. My son is a better driver in games (by far) than I am and can seemingly handle a vehicle at a faster speed.

I can't imagine that the competencies and decision making they're doing outside, mostly, of an adult's guidance isn't shaping them as people. We build confidence through experience and taking responsibility. Kids today have more opportunities to do so than my generation did. While the real world consequences are mostly harmless (excluding some picture sharing, bullying and the like) children are getting to experiment and role-play, using their imaginations and directing activities by their own decisions.

We can't yet track the results of many of the above discussed factors because surveys of children play out over lifetimes and these innovations are relatively new but one thing we can track is that IQ scores have been going up roughly 3 points a decade since World War II, called the Flynn Effect. Actually however, results for vocabulary and reading comprehension are similar with today's children doing better at the sections which measure abstract reasoning. Is some of the more recent gain due to the changes in how content is being consumed, created and shared? In my opinion, watching the kids around me, it is.

The empires of the future are the empires of the mind.
WINSTON CHURCHILL

Alejandra

Driving to Alhambra I went to meet Alejandra. She lives a little way outside downtown and via generic freeway to the house her family shares with a Chinese family (the house is split so there is no crossover among units). Alhambra is a diverse town with numerous Asian businesses and a wide range of ethnicities. Like much of the inner coastal areas of Los Angeles, a hot sun beat down on wide streets and tidy houses, faded golden hillsides fading into the horizon.

Alejandra is of medium height and build and was wearing cutoff shorts and a t-shirt. She'd just had surgery a few weeks earlier to pull her jaw apart as it was so constricted she had a hard time breathing. As a result, her top front teeth had a wide gap between them. Her eyes are large, round and a calming brown. Her hair is long and she smiles hesitantly but genuinely. Her two younger brothers hid in the back bedroom and peaked out occasionally, friendly and curious. They live modestly but neatly.

Also a recent high school graduate, Alejandra was valedictorian of her class and will attend UC Irvine on scholarship. Mexican American, she was born in California and lived in the San Fernando Valley until she was 13 when her mother fled their physically abusive father and settled into a temporary shelter, tired of being beaten and her children berated. Alejandra and her two younger brothers were uprooted. Their father lost custody but still calls and visits regularly, mostly to deliver verbal abuse.

What followed their initial flight were numerous temporary moves from shelter, to shelter, to hotel to finally a home. The children meanwhile went from school to school. Alejandra managed to keep her grades up and eventually settled in at Semillas del Pueblo, a controversial charter school. During her sophomore year she won a trip to China based on her excellent grades. Such rewards helped keep her motivated.

Alejandra is a responsible girl who enjoys time with her family and is very close to her mother. Taking on the role of mother's helper she cares for her brother and helps out as needed, which has seemingly caused conflicts. Her mother is passive as a parent, yet warm and loving. Also coming from an abusive household and one of eleven siblings she has perhaps been overwhelmed with her life burdens. Alejandra's mother has been lucky professionally in that she works at the school so her hours allow her to be available to her children. And she is an elder care helper on the weekend. But Alejandra has taken on additional burdens helping her mother and sometimes takes out her frustrations verbally on her siblings. Grappling with her years of turmoil she still holds anger. Having said that, she is getting therapy to deal with the emotional damage that abuse and frequent moves have instilled. Last year she learned the ugly side that can attach to social support structures when she felt overwhelmed, complained to a counselor that she might as well end it all and ended up in a mental hospital overnight. Around her were numerous girls all more troubled than herself and she knew she didn't belong in that environment.

Coping well seems to be her personality, until she has a crisis. Alejandra works very hard at school, even skipping sleep repeatedly to complete an assignment perfectly. Disciplined and driven, she's very hard on herself and always aims to excel. Feeling that she's let her mother down in the past through bad boyfriend choices she views her good grades as a gift to her mother and an easing of the burdens her parent carries.

Alejandra is so mature, so reasoned as she speaks, that it's hard to imagine the demons with which she continues to wrestle. Having chosen a controlling boyfriend her senior year in high school and finally feeling the love of a man, her father not providing it, she alienated her friends. Other friends have fallen by the side as they chose drugs and promiscuity over studying and aiming for college.

In twenty years Alejandra wants to have a house, car and the luxury of travelling so she can share them all with her family. She'd like to be a lawyer and work with domestic abuse cases, a crisis she sees among the girls around her, from fathers and boyfriends both. Spending most of her time studying or with her family, she has little time for outside interests though enjoys reading classic novels and watching the Kardashians. She also likes reading the *Chicken Soup* series and considers them inspiring. Dancing is a passion and she likes to write. She's majoring in political science.

Mostly together but ever conflicted, Alejandra not only deals with keeping her own life on course she feels protective toward her two younger brothers. They are less academically focused and as she considers education an escape from bad circumstances she worries about them daily. Seemingly they were more outwardly impacted by the family turmoil and haven't put the past behind them.

Alejandra struggles still with anger and an over developed sense of obligation. She hasn't worked out her family dynamics with respect to unhealthy relationships. But she's inspiring in keeping her grades up and her life together. Never tempted by certain bad outside influences like drugs and alcohol she instead cherishes her family and her goals all include them. Underestimating her own intelligence she nonetheless always delivers solid results. Alejandra is only beginning to grow into the person she'll one day become.

BOOT CAMP: BASICS OF THE AMERICAN EDUCATIONAL SYSTEM TODAY

Overview

In this section are some basic educational concepts that will give parents an understanding of options and key efforts in education today. This issue is overflowing with term and theories thus I've taken editorial discretion to limit the discussion to the most relevant and potentially impactful areas. Skip freely as not all areas defined will be applicable to your family's situation.

State Versus Federal

Most control over education is directed at a state and local level. States set education standards that public schools are required to meet. Private schools mostly ignore them and look at the standards set by other private schools, which are typically higher. Or at least in those states with weak standards.

For parents the practical importance of this conflict is that very often what the federal government wants is in conflict with the political battles ongoing at a local level.

From what I've been told the more local the politics the more impact you can have. At a national level change is subject to very complex bartering and logjam. Meanwhile, at a local level you're dealing with individuals who face their community members on a daily basis. While they may still be subject to the influences of special interest groups, they also confront daily the consequences of their decisions. Of the $600 billion currently spent on K-12 public education in the United States about $550 billion is spent at the local or state level.

No Child Left Behind and Testing

No Child Left Behind was signed into law in January 2002. It imposed penalties for schools that didn't attain certain test scores for all students, essentially in math and English. The practical impact of the law and subsequent related revisions or efforts was to switch the focus for many schools and teachers from teaching a broad curriculum to teaching for the test. NCLB wasn't the only reason many schools dropped or diminished electives, sciences, history, arts and language but it was a factor (budget restraints being another).

Teaching to the test means that test scores rise if children are prepped on the type of questions and tests given and the steps required answering them. Repetition of these questions and methods of answering has shown to improve test scores in the short term (if the test is taken within a certain time after the exercises). For example, the steps required to calculate a percentage increase are consistent and children can be trained to recognize the type of problem and steps needed to solve it though they may not be able to do a percentage decrease (thus the test scores rise though the children haven't learned more).

The Common Core

Until recently, learning standards and curricula varied by state and sometimes school district. There existed federal standards and state ones, then further refinements and complications resulting in a mass of different learning standards throughout out country. Not only was this complexity confusing, it made teaching to a mobile student population virtually impossible. And the textbook companies would write for one large jurisdiction requiring teachers in other states to adapt the materials.

Now, all states but five have agreed to adopt *Common Core Standards*, which will greatly simplify and standardize learning throughout our country. The benchmarks are set to roll out in the 2014-2015 school year and cover shared math and literacy standards. They are also benchmarked to international standards, lacking in the past, and establish a "staircase" of increasing complexity. Not forming an expected curriculum they will be rather shared expectations and standards. For example, in the past reading assignments focused on fiction but will now include an increase in informational texts. Teachers are given more leeway in math and may deviate from the past focus on wide but shallow teaching.

Overall, algebra is algebra and complicating the subject with different standards and textbooks seemed a poor approach to educating students. With more universal expectations both students and teachers should find their path less confusing and success more attainable. All kids need to learn how to read.

Standards in General

The Federal government establishes learning standards of what all schools should teach children at any given grade level. These standards historically have been guidelines and states have flexibility as to how they interpret them. As above, most states have now agreed to adopt the Common Core Standards, which is a huge step toward universal uniformity of education across our country.

Why is this adoption such a big deal given that federal standards existed before (and any given state could choose to adopt them or not)? I'll use my state as an example. Here in California, our state standards are much more lax than those of the federal government. So my children's school reviewed them annually to ensure that they were aware of the local differences, such as including California history. Then they turned to the tougher private school standards, which is what most private schools likely do. The discretion allowed each school was often high!

So, not only are children learning varying amounts, and slightly different things, state by state, but the varying standards complicate life for everyone from the textbook companies (who have varying demands state by state and even school by school) to any innovator who needs a standardized curriculum to improve ways of delivering it. Even teachers are challenged by the ambiguity.

Children or teachers relocating to another state have also suffered.

Learning Styles

Many educators believe that different people learn differently, with some being more hearing-based, for example, and others better grasping concepts visually. Numerous experts have refined different models in an attempt to address the needs of all students. David A. Kolb explains his theories in his book *Experiential Learning: Experience as the source of learning and development*. Essentially, his model is based upon two approaches to understanding experiences, one is concrete experience and the other abstract conceptualization. Two related ways transform these experiences and are termed reflective observation and active experimentation. Ideally, learning uses all four modes, and to be effective indeed must. Practically speaking people develop these modes differently and in varying balances resulting in four types of learners: convergers; divergers; assimilators; and accommodator. Convergers actively experiment and conceptualize abstractly. Thus they can implement practical solutions based on deductive reasoning. Divergers observe reflectively and note practical experience. They're able to view things from different or unusual perspectives and are creative in formulating new ideas. Assimilators conceptualize abstractly and observe thoughtfully. Using inductive reasoning they can create models based on theory, drawn from observation and reasoning. Accommodators experiment actively and draw from actual experience. They are engaged with outside environments and are doers, not just academics.

The Kolb model was refined by Honey and Mumford such that the styles were labeled: activist; reflector; theorist; and pragmatist.

Another widely used categorization of learning styles is Fleming's VARK model: visual; auditory; and kinesthetic or tactile learners. Essentially, people learn better visually, through hearing or through touch. Learners can not only prefer the delivery form of learning but may think in terms of pictures, words, sounds or physical sensations, including doing.

Most people blend a mix of learning such that they can learn from all methods but not equally balanced among them. Others are more extreme. According to David Brooks, Einstein claimed that he thought in signs and images that he could manipulate in his mind, and called such thinking his "intuitions".

Charter Schools

Charter schools have gone from zero in 1991 when the first charter law passed in Minnesota to now spanning 41 states and the District of Columbia. Charter schools basically get public and sometimes private funding but have more accountability for achieving results and more flexibility in how they do so. They aren't allowed to charge for admission and very often must resort to a lottery system for admission, as more students want to attend them than spots are available, especially for established schools. About 5,600 charter schools were operating nationwide at the end of 2011, in which over 2 million students were enrolled. Growth of charter school students is estimated at 13 percent annually with over 500 opening in the 2011-2012 school year alone and educating about 200,000 students. Many are non-union.

Indeed, according to Wikipedia and quoting a 2008 study, 59 percent of charter schools had a waiting list of on average 198 students. The schools operate based on a "charter" which typically lasts between 3 to 5 years and they must show positive results for the school to renew its charter. The parent body is often more engaged as the application process self selects those parents willing to make an effort to better their children's education (leading some critics to charge that their positive academic results are due to a skimming of the local population).

Visiting a charter school in Watts, a not very nice part of my local Los Angeles, I must comment that those kids really want to learn and whether they're skimmed or not shouldn't detract from the utter ambition of such inner city kids who are willing to take a dangerous bus daily to improve their own education. The school had gates and bars, like a prison, but it also had a population of bright and dedicated children. I saw firsthand how much some children want to learn, despite the forces that make doing so difficult.

Charter schools get much less money per child, on average according to a study quoted on Wikipedia, of about 22 percent per child per year. In some districts such as San Diego or Atlanta the funding gap is estimated at 40 percent. They also typically need to find and fund a school building. Twenty-six states and the District of Columbia cap the number of charter schools allowed, even though many such schools have long waiting lists for students (an estimated 365,000 nationwide). Overall, these children are ethnically diverse, about 54 percent qualify for school lunch programs (meaning they come from poor families) and are often newer and smaller. While small classrooms seemingly don't much impact student performance positively small school size does. Those schools that don't perform are shut down after or before their charter expires and Wikipedia estimates that number at about 12.5 percent.

Highly controversial and much attacked, charter schools provide a more accountable option to other public schools. Principals are given more discretion and the programs vary. Each school should be evaluated based upon their leadership which puts parents in a difficult position. A new school will likely have room for your child as the program is untested; older and better schools will subject your child to a lottery for acceptance.

My hometown of Los Angeles has one of the best infrastructures of charter schools, from the Alliance, to Green Dot, ICEF and others. Parents ultimately need to research the school they're considering and then make a decision. The bottom line is that unlike other publicly funded schools charter schools are more accountable for their results, which is wonderful for their students.

Magnet Schools

Magnet schools are public schools that have more specialized curriculum or programs, very often being math, science, arts or vocationally oriented. Originating during the 1960s to decrease the impacts of segregation, they now operate on a decentralized and sporadic basis. Originally part of the busing and forced desegregation movement they've moved away from that legacy and now often require admittance by a tough exam, interview and/or audition. Others rely on a lottery. Their adoption varies by locale but can be a good option for parents who want to get their child established on a certain track. Local research is the best way to explore this option.

Catholic Schools

Catholic schools have such a tradition and continue to provide a lower cost alternative to private schools as the church funds part of the costs, as do donations. They get no state funding and generally spend less per pupil than do public schools. Numerous studies show that Catholic and religious schools have a low drop out rate, including relative to schools with similar demographics. Indeed, the national drop out rate at Catholic or religious schools was half that of local public schools (in the 2011-2012 school year 99.4% of children in Catholic schools graduated high school; in Los Angeles the number is 98%

graduating with a high school degree in four years). A higher percentage of these children go to and graduate college. Their test scores are also higher than those in our public schools.

Why are Catholic schools able to perform so well relative to public schools, especially as they often serve a high-risk population? Kathy Anderson, who runs the Catholic Education Foundation, shed some light on the proposition offered by faith-based schools. One relevant factor is the social structure which forms an inherent part of these schools. Catholic schools follow traditional curriculums, including a focus on values, respect and character. They are often smaller, and such schools tend to increase social capital as parents find getting involved easier and more effective. Religious schools have the allure of their religious services and a related community, both of which provide ongoing support for students and their families. At risk children are more likely to be protected and nurtured by the larger community than those at schools without such an extensive social structure. The principals and teachers are encouraged to note when students are struggling and step in to help. The most cited reason for choosing Catholic schools in Los Angeles is safety, followed by the curriculum then faith.

Catholic schools offer more school days, locally it's 200 compared with about 175 in public schools, and extensive after school programs. These extra days help counteract the summer brain drain discussed later. Children are tested diagnostically, at the beginning of the school year to tailor the curriculum, not just at year-end.

Racial minorities constitute about 30 percent of the student body and in 2012 at least 15 percent of the students weren't Catholic.

Yes, the Catholic Church in the United States has lately been rocked by scandals with respect to the mistreatment of children but largely these schools have done an excellent job of educating children for centuries. And other religious schools have likewise done the same in their respective communities. They should be considered a viable option for all families.

Home Schools

Over one million children are home schooled and the curriculum options continue to grow rapidly, with K12 being the best known. This option can range from one child, one parent to a mini-school handling a range of children at different levels. A friend told me about a high school child he interviewed for a possible place in an ivy league college who supplemented his home schooling with community college classes, putting him much farther ahead of his more traditionally schooled peers. Thus, this option exists but is very taxing on parents.

Vouchers

Voucher or tuition tax credits have also been growing and as of 2007 twenty-one such programs existed. A voucher is a certificate issued by the government, which can be applied to pay tuition at a private school or used by parents to reimburse the cost of home schooling. Education tax credits offset taxes and can be used to donate toward other children's education or to fund that of your own kids. If you can put your child in a better school, and have the government fund the process, you should at least try to do so.

Private Schools

Private schools can be run as either a non-profit or for-profit entity. Is one better than the other? My children have attended both and the only issue has been that since they typically require donations beyond your initial tuition payments, the not-for profit related donations are better on a tax-affected basis.

Practically speaking the application process is generally very competitive with many more students wanting the limited number of spots available, creating an odd dynamic of wealthy parents paying a lot of money to keep their schools happy.

But most private schools really deliver and the education they offer can range from good to exceptional (and sometimes almost exist in a different category from the public schools). Private schools vary greatly in theory, ranging from developmental to traditional. The former addresses more how children relate to each other and their environment while the latter focuses on competency in the basic literacy skills, discipline and values.

Private schools today are also very expensive and scholarships are hard to get (though they do happen, especially to increase the diversity within the school). Try.

After School Programs

Afterschool programs are a big deal in many communities. Some are glorified childcare but done right can have a major impact on children's learning, especially in poorer communities. Children are often spending over 30 hours a week in these supplemental programs thus the substance and quality of that time has a major impact on what they learn on any given day. Parents in public schools should ask their faculty about options in their school or area. Generally, most are free or carry a nominal cost.

Private schools often have after school programs as well. These options are very different, are defined by an elective orientation and cost money.

Southern California is rich in options.

LA's Best is the oldest locally and serves 28,000 kids in 186 elementary schools throughout Los Angeles. Children range from age 5 to 12 and typically live in the most gang and drug ridden areas of the city. The program gives children a place to go, to study and to play.

More academically oriented is Think Together which started in Orange Country, California and has now expanded as far as San Diego to the south and Sacramento to the north. The organization serves about 100,000 children across 400 locations and 30 school districts. Think Together is actively expanding.

Hathaway-Sycamores in the Los Angeles area offers a very broad range of child and family services, from transitional living, to gang resources, to an afterschool program. Open later than many afterschool programs, it also works with families and not just their children. The organization is discussed elsewhere in the book but is a good example of a program that can help with more than homework or group activities and also shelter a family in crisis.

J.K. Livin Foundation was founded by actor Matthew McConaughey and Camila Alves in 2008. Executive Director Shannon Mabrey Rotenberg is a friend and provided insight into the program that targets underprivileged youth during the crucial high school years. J.K. Livin stands for "just keep living", a personal motto inspired by McConaughey's father's death, which occurred just as the actor's career took off. The actor credits his father for instilling in him good values such as giving back, working hard and heading outdoors when possible.

Meeting for two hours twice a week after school on a public school campus, the fitness and wellness program also stresses gratitude, giving back and making good decisions. As the actor phrased it in a WebMD article by Lauren Paige Kennedy, teens are *in that transition age, where the consequences aren't just another demerit if you screw up again*. The most vulnerable part of the day is right after school so the program provides an alternative to the streets, seeking to bring in a diverse group of kids who can learn from each other and add differing skills and interests, from football to dance to tuba. The program acts as an exercise and healthy eating program, community outreach, safe haven and support group.

Rotenberg shared the curriculum, which they make available upon request to others schools or educators. Each month McConaughey provides a quote on an important topic such as leadership or risking failure. For example:

Don't fear failure. Don't try to fail, but don't be afraid to fail.
Missing the shot you take is better than not taking the shot at all.
Each failed attempt brings you one step closer to success.
In line, you gotta shoot to score. Don't fear failure.
MATTHEW MCCONAUGHEY

The kids have a lesson plan centering around the topic and are given related group and individual activities to complete. For ten minutes they share thoughts and later work on their journal. In keeping with the mind/body focus the balance of the time is used for exercise. Each 4-week session adds a physical challenge, nutritional tip and even a recipe. Physical goals are encouraged, in large part to instill self-esteem. An added bonus is that McConaughey often shows up for a jog with the participants.

A related speaker visits with the group, the latter of whom are all expected to prepare questions in advance. Supporting worksheets are provided. At the end of the program the kids have an outing at a Dodgers game, the zoo or even at the San Francisco 49s Academy School (with the team in attendance!). Trying something new and risk taking are encouraged, but within the safe confines of the supportive program. A gratitude circle is often the starting point for kids to open up begin allowing themselves to be vulnerable before the group.

Community service is required, whether packing care packages for our troops or feeding the homeless.

Now with 14 active programs in California, Texas and Louisiana, J.K. Livin helps on average 200 kids per school and has teamed up with numerous corporate partners such as Samsung and Target, along with curriculum provider Scholastic. Nutritionist Rachel Beller, MS, Rd, from NBC's *The Biggest Loser*, and fitness director Missy Shepherd round out the actual program expertise. Since 75 percent of the programs' kids come from families below the poverty line these resources often provide access to something the youth won't otherwise experience. Over 2,000 children have benefited from the program to date.

Search for like opportunities for your children if they need an activity to keep them busy, extra tutoring or help with academics, a support structure or group activities. Many gang prevention programs leverage this at risk time to pull kids off the streets by providing an alternative and support structure.

Blended Learning

No definitive definition for blended learning yet exists, as the concept is fairly new and still subject to revision. Essentially, blended learning brings technology into the classroom to a greater extent than it has been used in the past as a means of customizing instruction to a child. Thus, blended learning isn't just adding computers or whiteboards to support the existing curriculum but rather blends in new learning techniques.

The Innosight Institute defines blended learning, in an already mentioned study by the Lexington Institute, as:

A formal education program in which a student learns at least in part through online delivery of content and instruction with some element of student control over time, place, path and/or pace; and at least in part at a supervised brick and mortar location way from home.

One example is a program at the Alliance Charter Schools in Los Angeles. They call their program BLAST. Classroom time per subject is divided into three student sections of 16 students in 3 stations. The first station is traditional instruction with a teacher, the second is independent study and the third is a group project, with the students rotating among the three. In the last group grading is based both on individual participation and the group result, incenting students to find ways of working together.

Blended learning is currently a huge topic within education. One advantage of technology based instruction is that it can be customized, allowing students to work at their own pace, useful for gifted kids but even more so for those who need to catch up (and are motivated to do so). At one Alliance campus, in their first year, many children advanced about four grade levels, with 68 percent of the kids needing some remediation.

However, the Alliance program has a dedicated information technology firm consulting on how to best organize their programs. This firm set up an online platform that ties together all that the children touch, from textbooks, to modules for completion, to grades updated daily, to interactions among peers. Thus far such an advanced program hasn't been implemented nationally (but there is hope).

More common is the gradual introduction of various technological innovations into the regular school program. My children's school has a web site, the children interact on Wikis for homework or posting stories and use various learning software. Their teachers are wonderful, and thus the technology is a small compliment to what happens daily in the classroom.

Innovative Schooling

Should you try a new school or unproven program? The answer to that question is very complex for the simple reason that some of these programs perform spectacularly and others fail. Then there is the question of fit for your child.

NOCCA (New Orleans Center for Performing Arts) builds creative outlets for their students, with hours devoted to perfecting whatever discipline they've chosen, ranging from drama to music to dance. These children have applied for acceptance; they typically feel passion for their discipline and tend to do well with respect to college applications and attendance. Do they learn more? If nothing else they're learning discipline, creativity and control over their decisions. But are the sorts of children or parents who seek out such programs more dedicated and perhaps even more capable? We don't know.

So practically, any answer depends on your child and your other options. If your child is passionate about or skilled in a discipline be it arts or science, and a local school is targeted at this discipline, then applying and attending make sense. A quick web search or conversation with your current school should provide the information you need. If your local public school is terrible (one source for information is www.greatschools.org; locally, the Los Angeles Times has made rankings of local schools public) than taking a risk on a specialized school also makes sense.

Many charter school organizations run a number of schools. Just because one school in their group has done well does not mean that others will but there is a long-term correlation. The school group in incented to maintain a high level of performance as each school's reputation is somewhat dependent on the group itself. However, each is captive to the principal at their school and the resulting program. Still, overall, a good charter school maintains a high level of consistency across campuses and when a new one opens getting accepted is much easier than after the school has proven itself.

Proactive parents can evaluate these options with some degree of certainty but when human beings are involved no outcome is ever set. For example, some children will object to leaving their friends behind at a new school while others will enjoy starting fresh with a blank slate.

Parental Impact

Isn't this the billion-dollar issue? Numerous studies have reiterated that parental impact starts to decline somewhere around age six, being replaced increasingly by peers. But by age six much of our future is set, luckily not all.

Later, I'll discuss early childhood education on a personal level but for a minute let's focus on the larger picture. We're all born into a time and place. The most important indicator of your eventual income is where and when you are born: Zimbabwe or Beverly Hills. After that, it's your parents. But neither of those factors is absolute. One only needs to look at the very varying backgrounds of our recent Presidents to see that neither privilege nor poverty made the difference but parental support did. America is still a society that allows and accepts success based on hard work and ambition, not the case globally.

I wouldn't write this book if I didn't think parents could make a substantial difference in their child's future to the point that, while there will always be those who due to personal grit and strength overcome a bad childhood, parental support has continued to increase in importance.

One morning I was walking on the beach in Santa Monica, near the pier with a bike path winding through vast expanses of sand. Lifeguard stands, deserted in the mornings when I'm walking or running, dot the landscape. While the bike path can get crowded mostly the beach is peaceful and a great place to ponder my day or the ideas that are troubling me. Santa Monica is also homeless heaven and I've gotten more wary after jogging by one with a kitchen knife in the midst of an argument and having another try to grab me.

Thus this day, when a man with a backpack (long story) ahead of me kept turning around to look back, I accosted a nice couple and asked them to walk with me for a minute. The husband joked that perhaps they were the ones to fear but, honestly, looking at the two options you would have chosen this couple over about anyone on the beach.

Within minutes the husband had to take a call and so I started grilling his poor, unsuspecting wife about education. I do that. She told me they'd moved from a public school in Santa Monica to a charter school in Pacific Palisades called Marquez Elementary when they realized their oldest son wasn't learning much (and the school didn't provide resources to help resolve that issue). Marquez not only had the advantage of many non-working dedicated moms and a proactive school administration and teachers, they were also actively seeking educational options, for example being among the first to get iPads from Apple. Amazingly, she and many other mothers volunteered twice a week to tutor kids in need of extra help. Her son excelled.

Teachers are strapped. They cannot provide all that your children need in school. Parents must supplement that instruction.

In *Freakonomics,* the first book in Steven Levitt and Stephen Dubner's related series, the authors address parental impact. One less obvious tying point they make is to contrast white and black children's achievement. Black children perform worse yet not when adjusted for socioeconomic factors and the education level of their parents. But that factor only holds true for the first few years of schooling then black children overall begin to perform worse regardless. Writing from the viewpoint of economists, the authors dug through the data to find that black children are more often in heavily minority schools where the white children at those schools likewise underperform. Meanwhile, the balance of white children are in schools where the number of black children is about 6 percent (and other minorities are likewise a small percentage). The demographics of where we send our children to school matters, and more on a socio-economic level than on a racial one (minorities are more concentrated in poorer school districts).

Thus performance can matter more based on parental choices than race or even aptitude (to a limited degree). Oh, and, minority students in predominantly white schools perform on par with their in school peers.

The authors also quote eight parental related factors that have a big impact on student performance and eight that don't. Overall they found that what parents are has a bigger impact than what parents do. Thus the parents who were better educated and had many books in the house tended to raise children with better grades than parents who moved to a better neighborhood and had a non-working mother. Those parents who live an educated person lifestyle model the related behaviors thus their children pick it up. These behaviors, and not affluence itself, have the most important impact on how children do in school.

Notably, children whose parents seek out better options like charter schools do better even if they don't get admitted to the charter school. Parents can make a difference, at any age, again by valuing education and getting involved.

To address the influence that peers have on our children from a shockingly (to me) young age I have a few comments to make. First, we control the environment in which our children grow up thus the "peers" they meet. We pick a neighborhood, which leads to a school and neighbors. We let them have play dates and go places or we don't. We set an example as to behavior and social conventions, be it saying please and thank you or drinking in moderation or excess.

Parents decide where children vacation and whether or not they do. We treat their peers well or make them ashamed to bring them home. Our children pick up our ethics, values and behaviors early, as all parents learn, watching themselves being played back by the next generation.

REDEFINE LITERACY

A human being is not attaining his full heights until he is educated.
HORACE MANN

When a subject becomes totally obsolete we make it a required course.
PETER DRUCKER

Why has the concept of literacy and the 3 Rs progressed so little in the over 100 years when it was first accepted? Then, we needed only aspire to educated voters and worshippers.

In the interim we've learned to fly, sent a man to the moon, wired our globe via the Internet, invented electricity and vaccines...well, I could go on but I think I've made my point. I've read that Aristotle was the first person to know all the information that was available at his time. The last person stated varies from William Shakespeare to Francis Bacon and beyond but seemingly that distinction falls in the Renaissance time period (hundreds and hundreds of years ago).

As a parent I object to the concept that literacy today comes down to math and English. For what? Voting? Going to church? Coding a new software program, starting a company and then expanding it internationally? Designing a rocket or decoding DNA?

According to the PISA study overview : "PISA's conception of reading literacy encompasses the range of situations in which people read, the different ways written texts are presented, and the variety of ways that readers approach and use texts, from the functional and finite, such as finding a particular piece of practical information, to the deep and far-reaching, such as understanding other ways of doing, thinking and being. Research shows that these kinds of reading literacy skills are more reliable predictors of economic and social well-being than the number of years spent in school or in post-formal education." Note: that definition of literacy extends well beyond reading and writing (to understanding, conceptualizing, applying and using what is read).

Literacy is not an absolute term but rather a relative one, based on the society and time in which a person lives. No constant definition will ever be enough, as knowledge available varies among populations but also continues to grow. One reason we tapped out the list of those capable of learning everything hundreds of years ago is that knowledge accumulates like a snowball rolling down a hill. I read that YouTube adds 72 hours of video a minute - up from 48 a year ago! We watch 4 billion hours of YouTube a month and growing.

Science 100 years ago ignored pasteurization, vaccines, medical devices, space travel and all electronics...because they weren't known. Does that mean they don't matter or that our relative literacy definition doesn't matter? Maybe and just a guess but it seems that our literacy definition is hopelessly outdated.

Turns out, on an international basis, American "literacy" is about 19th in the world at around 99 percent. Functional illiteracy, in contrast, is over 20 percent. Why the discrepancy? Well, the old test used to be signing your name versus just an X but that definition isn't counting much practically these days.

We need to do better and redefine literacy in the context of the modern world and the skills needed for the jobs of the future. As these jobs keep evolving (no social media marketers ten years ago) our new definition needs to expand beyond minimal basic information to include the ability to adapt to market changes, keep learning and perhaps even invent new jobs, roles or markets.

Recently I heard an analogy about getting hired in today's increasingly competitive job market that I found especially relevant. Chris Lewis runs a private equity fund: Riordan, Lewis & Haden. A competitive and ranked tennis player while younger, he's channeled that drive into getting returns on the fund that average over 30 percent a year for well over 20 years. Lewis is a smart guy and usually has a spark of wisdom to generously share. Tall and lean, with alert eyes, he speaks clearly and confidently, but with warmth. He noted that in *The Hunger Games*, where Katniss is meeting with the judges alone for the first time. they ignore her, talking, laughing, as she performs her skills for them. Annoyed, she shoots the roasted pig on their table, creating bedlam. She gets a very high score. Lewis stated that *in today's world you need to shoot the pig to stand out*. Reading, writing and 'rithmatic don't even get you in the door.

According to Thomas Friedman and Michael Mandelbaum in *That Used To Be Us*: "Not only does everyone today need *more* education to build the critical thinking and problem-solving skills that are now necessary for any good job; students also need *better* education. We define 'better education' as an education that nurtures young people to be creative creators and creative servers. That is, we need our education system not only to strengthen everyone's basics - reading, writing, and arithmetic - but to teach and inspire all Americans to start something new, to add something extra, or to adapt something old in whatever job they are doing."

Tony Wagner in his book The *Global Achievement Gap* brings up the concept of the Seven Survival Skills. These are: critical thinking and problem solving; collaboration across networks and leading by influence; agility and adaptability; initiative and entrepreneurialism; effective oral and written communication; accessing and analyzing information; curiosity and imagination. Also widely respected are the popular similar 21st Century Skills, as defined by the Partnership for 21st Century Skills. Their skills set starts with the three Rs then adds critical thinking, collaboration, creativity and communication. Importantly, life and career skills are also considered, as are media and technology proficiency.

Obviously, I'm not the only one dissatisfied with our old definition of literacy.

As a parent, I appreciate these concepts in practice but question whether most schools can teach them, already juggling their mandate of knowledge force-feeding and the quest for demonstrated results (in the form of test results not innovation or employment). Yes, all things being equal they're great to have but only after basic literacy is mastered. Unfortunately, these skills are also hard to measure. The practical impact of these theories, to me, is that literacy should be broadened to include building and guiding an integrated whole person not just stuffing children with facts. It's partially the difference between a child knowing an answer and knowing the why behind the answer. Literacy is no longer just memorization in our now complex world. True mastery requires a wide and deep skill set and knowledge base.

Our definition of literacy also isn't working with respect to increasing the social mobility of our citizens. While today it's still reasonably possible to achieve an upper income level starting from the middle class, the United States ranks 50th worldwide in one study in going from a poor household to a middle class one.

My definition is simple: start with the 3 Rs and add: technology skills; social networking mastery; an understanding of globalization and the different world regions (including how they interact); analysis and clarity of language; economics; creativity; leadership; risk and entrepreneurship; context; ethics; a grasp of art and music; and a broad sense of the world. This rounded definition will create not Renaissance boys and girls but enlightened one.

Honestly, I'd like to add spirituality to the mix but believe that doing so is too ambitious.

Our children are online and deciding their own parameters. Shouldn't we provide more guidelines beyond the outdated 3 R's and a vague sense of the future?

EVALUATING YOUR CHILD

As a parent I'd never advocate a 1984 or big brother approach to coldly appraising your child and making decisions based on those expectations, ignoring the reality that tests can be wrong or your child might be having a bad day. Having done a lot of research I'm a true believer in high expectations and some efforts have a huge impact on children's long-term success.

Can you accurately evaluate your child to better develop a customized education plan? Yes!

For example, let's start with an I.Q. test which has a genetic component thus is a good starting metric though not a prognosis. An estimated 20 to 50 percent of the variances shown in twins are due to other factors including social, school or family.

According to David Brooks in *The Social Animal*, a mother's IQ is the highest predictor of a child's. Studies by Dean Hamer and Peter

Copeland show "in study after study, IQ is the single best predictor of school performance." And an IQ threshold of about 120 does seemingly differentiate work success, but marginal differences above that level have little impact according to a multitude of studies. Indeed, IQ points seem to help most in logical or computation based tasks, yet don't account for the personality or character traits that can be more important in overall success.

Thus I'd advocate getting the test taken as the results are a predictor of certain academic abilities and it's better to know what raw material your child is starting with. As Charles Murray says in his book *Real Education* half of all children are below average and might not be candidates for becoming a physicist. He also points out that pushing all children on an idealized path only sets them up for disappointment and failure. The example he gives is that a top electrician out earns a bottom manager and is probably happier. Life lesson: coolly assess your child's assets, interests and options and guide from the reality not what the societal expectations dictate. But don't assume that a number on a test is a deciding factor; it's but one of many that forms a child.

What an I.Q means from the above mentioned New York Times article?

116+ 17 percent of the population; superior I.Q.; approximate average for individuals in professional occupations	
121+ 10 percent; potentially gifted; average for college graduates	
132+ 2 percent; borderline genius; average I.Q. of most Ph.D. recipients	
143+ 1 percent; genius level; about average for Ph.Ds. in physics	
158+ 1 in 10,000; Nobel Prize winners	
164+ 1 in 30,000; Wolfgang Amadeus Mozart and the chess champion Bobby Fischer	

Murray also quotes Howard Gardner's multiple intelligences which were originally detailed in 1983. The original list of seven is: bodily-kinesthetic, musical, interpersonal, intrapersonal, spatial, linguistic and logical-mathematical. Gardner has since added naturalistic intelligence. I'll explain them below but the point of mentioning them here is that your child will not be equally good at all of these qualities and should be guided based on his or her individual strengths as each intelligence is of differing value in academics and specific careers. They all impact what jobs your child will likely love and master.

Bodily-kinesthetic intelligence is physical, be it gross motor skills, fine motor skills or physical control over movements. Professional athletes, some performers and other physically based jobs require excellence in this area. According to Murray quoting the Labor Department, in 2005 about 12,230 Americans worked as professional athletes and 16,240 dancers, or one of every 4,600 workers.

Musical intelligence **includes** a skill at sensing pitch, tones, rhythm and other related elements of music and how they combine. According to Murray again drawing from Labor Department statistics, in 2005 50,410 people earned a living as musicians and singers with 8,610 earning a living as music directors and composers, or one in 2,200 workers.

Interpersonal intelligence includes interactions with others. Empathy, sensitivity to others' emotions and motivations, ability to work within a group and manipulate others' responses are key. Useful in most careers, this skill is important for politicians, teachers, nurses, managers, salespeople and clergy.

Intrapersonal intelligence focuses on knowing yourself and being able to apply that knowledge. Discipline, staying calm and being analytical under pressure, controlling and understanding your emotions, and courage are integral aspects. Being able to evaluate and understand yourself are others. Within paralyzing limits of over-analysis this intelligence is useful in most professions.

Spatial intelligence encompasses the ability to visualize and manipulate objects intellectually as in a board game or designer. Hand-eye coordination is another aspect. This intelligence is important for any visually based or design job, math, engineering, some sciences and architecture.

Logical-mathematical intelligence includes the obvious of grasping numbers, formulas, logics and abstractions but also goes deeper. Complex arguments, chains of reasoning, pattern recognition and noticing small distinctions are all inherently part of this intelligence. Thus this ability, while clearly needed for many sciences and even law, is valuable in all professions.

Linguistic intelligence includes both the ability to read and grasp complex texts but also the ability to express oneself clearly. The ability to learn languages easily is also a characteristic, as is memory. This intelligence is an obvious advantage in professions which require writing or speaking but cuts across most.

Getting back to our discussion of I.Q., spatial ability, logical-mathematical ability and linguistic ability all correlate to I.Q. scoring and each other. Very often, someone who is good at one (or not good) will be good at another. These three intelligences also have an impact on someone's success in many if not all professions. And, not surprisingly, some personal characteristics including leadership, conscientiousness, extroversion, achievement orientation and persistence have also been correlated with both I.Q. and eventual success in life (discussed later in the book).

But all is not lost regardless of where your child falls on an IQ test or how hard you find such understanding to be. Studies vary with respect to how much change we can effect but a lot of good news exists. First, many charter schools show numbers which blow out of the water any predictions that poverty, race or demographics have an insolvable negative impact on children's performance. This book isn't about charter schools alone, but examples include raising scores two grade levels in a year and taking kids from otherwise failing schools and getting 100 percent of them accepted into college – in only a few years time. Children's progress can be guided and developed.

Heard of neuroplasticity? No, neither had I until I buried myself in books the Dalai Lama has helped sponsor. I'm a yoga and positive thinking nut. As long as I can make it to yoga and continue breathing all will be well. Indeed, I've even added a yoga and spirituality section to this education-based book. What good do smart successful kids do us if they aren't grounded and happy?

The Dalai Lama, it turns out, is not only a spiritual leader and freedom fighter he's also a science buff who used to take radios and the like apart growing up in the monastery. This interest led him to a number of institutes in which he brought together top scientists and spiritual leaders. Studying neuroplasticity, his group was able to corroborate that the brain, once thought to stop developing at a certain point, can continue to develop throughout a person's lifetime. Other neuroscientists have found the same results.

Essentially, in the brain certain pathways close at a "critical period" in development. Scientists used to think that people's brains (neural/sensory pathways, brain cells, etc.) were set at a certain point and could not grow or be added. We now know that environmental or developmental changes can alter behavior and learning by modifying connections between existing neurons and perhaps otherwise. In simple terms, brains can change.

And brains can be educated to change. In the New York Times, Dan Hurley wrote about a working memory game that showed a substantial increase in raising I.Q. points. The N-back tests "require players to remember the location of a symbol or the sound of a particular letter represented just before 1-back, 2-back and the like". Other studies have shown that active video games change children's brains to respond faster to circumstance and with a broader response. What isn't known is how long these impacts on intelligence scores last or what their practical impact is in the real world, either in school or post academics.

Exercise also has a positive impact on intelligence and immediately after physical exertion on academic results. Another New York Times article, *Jogging Your Brain* by Gretchen Reynolds, discussed an experiment in which researchers led by Justin S. Rhodes, a psychology professor at the Beckman Institute for Advanced Science and Technology at the University of Illinois, took four sets of mice and gave them different living arrangements. The first had it all: great food, lots of toys, colors and sensations mixed into the environment and a treadmill. Variations on that ideal took away the rich and tasteful food, the toys and the treadmill. While the mice loved the toys and rich diets, fancy beds and stimulation, only the presence of the treadmill ended up with trackable changes in their brain structure, signaling improved brains.

Exercise also seems to slow or reverse the brain's physical decay, as it does with muscles. Exercise causes neurogenesis, or the creation of new brain cells. And exercise also changes the functioning of newly formed neurons. Brain cells only increase intellect if they can join the existing neural network. One way to do so is to learn something. One example used by Reynolds in the article is that of a maze, but the mice could only use the new neurons when navigating the same maze, a cognitively but not physically taxing task. But exercise made the new neurons more nimble and the new neurons were able to wire themselves into the existing neural network. Other stimulus, including food and comfortable bedding, didn't have the same motivating impact.

In *Spark*, by John Ratey and Eric Hagerman, the authors address the transformative effects on the brain itself and how exercise before a test or difficult lesson has a measurable and positive impact on children's academic performance.

The net message? Evaluate your child then maximize their distinctive opportunities.

A SIMPLE ASSESSMENT TEST

The below children's assessment quiz is written with common sense in mind. In high school I remember taking a test that was supposed to identify my vocation and I hated the idea of all jobs suggested, as did most of my friends. Psychological tests have their place and one of my points below is to get an IQ test for your child (other possible tests include the Woodcock-Johnson, Wechsler and Stanford-Binet tests). But at the end of the day they can't substitute for a parent's day-to-day knowledge of their child over time, and not just a point in time.

The schools and teachers don't have time to realistically assess your children in the context of their ideal place in our ever-evolving world so you need to. Our children when young lack the maturity and perspective to begin making the choices that will determine their future. Step one? Start below.

Continuous effort – not strength or intelligence –
is the key to unlocking our potential.

WINSTON CHURCHILL

Quiz: Where Do I Belong in Life?

1. Rate your child from one to ten on each of Gardner's types of intelligence: bodily-kinesthetic; musical; interpersonal; intrapersonal; spatial; logical-mathematical; linguistic.
2. Get an IQ or comparable test. How does the result change the options you thought your child has in life? What can you do to raise the results (read below!)?
3. Evaluate your child's personality on some of the traits that will have an impact beyond IQ and even grades.
   a. Resilience
   b. Creativity
   c. Sociability and empathy
   d. Perseverance
   e. Discipline
   f. Leadership
   g. Courage
   h. Ambition
   i. Goal orientation and achievement

Learning is not attained by chance, it must be sought for
with ardor and diligence.

AMBROSE BIERCE

4. What are your child's passions? Dislikes? Mark Cuban said something which struck me. He basically said to follow not your passion, as we all have passions, but rather follow your effort – where do

you spend your time? Where does your child spend his or her time and why (what is the draw and how will that apply to effort when the child is older)?

5. Ask your child about the life they'd like. Then, apply a practical gloss to what they say. For example, Jason likes to perform and I'm not thrilled about the idea of him being an actor. But he does live in Los Angeles where, if you want to be an actor, is ground zero. However, performing is more than acting. It is a skill useful in politics, business, sales, teaching, preaching and even writing (what with the marketing demands). A child who wants a family may end up building the next Zappos while a child who likes Legos might be an urban planner. All skills transfer somewhere.

6. Get practical and honest. Some kids want to run the world and others don't. Our children don't exist to validate our lives but rather to master their own right purpose. Listen, guide then step back.

7. Engage in a community. According to Robert Putnam in his groundbreaking book *Bowling Alone*, "Child development is powerfully shaped by social capital. A considerable body of research dating back at least fifty years has demonstrated that trust, networks, and norms of reciprocity within a child's family, school, peer group, and larger community have wide ranging effects on a child's opportunities and choices and, hence, on his behavior and development." If you read on education you will eventually encounter the name Geoffrey Canada, President of the Harlem Children's Zone in New York. In my opinion he has grasped this concept expertly – children exist in a community and not alone thus all need to work together. He improves children's options by working on raising the entire community surrounding the child along with the child itself.

8. How much work are you willing to do and how much is your child willing to contribute? Lauren is disciplined and tough, naturally, and more so than I am. Sometimes I'm in awe of her focus. I meander and always have. Still, I did a lot of research for this book and apply it in the context of my children – to a degree, as I also need to support them. What works for your family? A single, divorced parent myself I understand the challenges. Hence I'll close the book

with some easy steps to start somewhere for those parents like me that confront a multitude of obligations each day.

9. Where do you live, what resources are available and what can you afford? Later, I'll discuss ways to pay for college but practically the debt levels kids are taking on today to fund their educations is unsustainable and will hopefully be changed before your child makes it there. That old adage that it takes money to make money has never been truer than it is today.

Write out your answers and think about them for a day or two.

What did you learn or evaluate based on the above questions? Remember please that you have only established a starting point for your efforts and leave open the growth of your child and changes to any related goals.

I want to mention one touching story I read researching this book which was titled *A Drug for Down Syndrome* and was written by Dan Hurley for the New York Times. Dr. Alberto Costa, a physician and neuroscientist, was told upon the birth of his first and only daughter that she likely had Down Syndrome. Asking her doctor the chance of the condition before they got the actual test results he was told about 100 percent. He named her Tyche, after the Greek goddess of fortune or chance. Most genetic diseases are the result of one mutation on one gene of one amino acid. In Down Syndrome there is an extra copy of all 500 or so genes on Chromosome 21, which makes finding a solution much harder (as a mutation in 500 genes, not one or two, must be corrected). Costa devoted his life to finding a fix for Down Syndrome, a task complicated by the fact that many others are working on a better and safer pre-natal test which would eventually decrease the need for Costa's drug as there would likely be fewer Down Syndrome children born needing the drug (which also dilutes funding for Costa's research).

In Down Syndrome the child typically has an IQ around 50 points below the average for other children, all falling obviously within a range. The affected children also have a susceptibility to other physical ailments. Costa refused to accept those realities and worked extensively with Tyche.

And Tyche, now 16, is one of only two Down Syndrome children who can do algebra. She is also well on her way to learning Portuguese (Costa was born in Brazil) through Rosetta Stone courses. Costa is in the process of conducting the first randomized clinical test on Down Syndrome patients that has been proven to work on Down Syndrome mice. Physically, life expectancy for Down Syndrome children has risen from 25 to 49 in only the 14 years between 1983 and 1997. Great things are possible for parents who try. While I will never achieve the dedication of someone like Costa, who has made his life's work helping improve his child's ability to live life, we can all add something.

What I found disheartening in the story is that it quotes a recent Canadian study which found that of parents with Down Syndrome parents if a cure was found 27 percent wouldn't use it and 32 percent weren't sure. They didn't want to change who their child was. Yet. Wouldn't it be better to let your child soar than to keep them boxed in a cage of low expectations?

Our children's options are endless but not forever. In Europe, and historically here, many children were designated for professions that required dedicated studies outside of college. Vocational schools are now known as CTE (career and technical education). Currently, they can be stand alone specialized schools, classes within a regular high school, collaborating programs with community colleges or apprenticeships with local employers. Keep them in mind.

Then there are those children who seemed set on their own path to greatness independent of college. We all know their names: Mark Zuckerberg, Bill Gates, Michael Dell, Ron Meyers, Steve Jobs and a number of others. These are the kids who don't need college and seem to stumble into success as if driven by a higher power. These are not mostly the kids (or young adults) who drop out of high school because they can't keep up, though sometimes they do drop out from boredom. More often, they are busy dedicating and building their lives elsewhere. These are the kids Malcolm Gladwell profiles in *Outliers*. The basic point of that book is that repetition makes for expertise that makes for success.

According to Gladwell, those that succeed in a field have at least 10,000 hours practicing before they perfect their craft. Many of the computer and software geniuses (Jobs and Gates) had access to early mainframe computers and used them. The Beatles played at every gig they could get until they became an integrated unit, working harder. None of them needed school because they were too busy learning their craft. Added to that hard work was the luck element.

Also noted in the book is the birth cycle, with certain professional sports being dominated by players born at the early end of the cutoff date for playing in leagues who were thus larger and more coordinated than those born later. These older kids seemed better relative to those born later thus got the positive reinforcement and extra opportunities their "talent" deserved. The killer point is that more important than birth date regarding whether or not a boy became a professional athlete in a given sport was whether his father had professionally played that sport or not (which trumped all else). But was that factor the killer app because it connoted genetic skills or just the focus and knowledge to train a professional athlete? We don't know.

I'm not willing to bet on luck and being the one in a million exception to the rule where my children are concerned. I'm sending mine to school.

MOTIVATION 101

We all hate being criticized and judged. I always tell my children that in the long run they will win...kids leave us and not the other way around. Embrace, love and let some things go.

At yoga today a friend was telling me about having her oldest son back in the house for Mother's Day. She was recounting when he first moved out and how the expected, that groundhog day feeling of our children always being there, changed overnight. He was moving out on January 1 and by 10:00 pm December 31 when she went to bed he hadn't started packing. She assumed he'd be there when she woke up.

At 4:00 am he nudged her in bed to say good-bye and then she fell back asleep. When she woke up he was gone. I cried when she told me that story.

So I put together a checklist of points to remember as you push your child to excel and succeed.

1. Focus on their efforts as much as their results. We all start in different places. Those who learn to keep working to a goal irrespective of where they are have a better chance of achieving it.
2. Failure is part of learning. In Silicon Valley failure shows you're pushing the envelope and aiming at innovation. The key is learning from the failure and doing better next time.

The only real failure in life is the one not learned from.

ANTHONY J D'ANGELO

3. Hard work pays off more often than not. It doesn't always pay off but not working always leads you nowhere. So focus on the positive that no effort is guaranteed but a lack of effort is. I read a great quote from Barry Diller to Oprah Winfrey which was essentially, "don't complain, do the work and it will be okay."
4. Make sure your child has the foundational knowledge to master what they are currently working on otherwise they will not succeed. Catching up is the goal if they aren't yet at that level.
5. Teach study skills. They set those students who are a success apart from those who aren't. Begin with repetition, which reinforces memory. You cannot apply or interpret without building foundational knowledge. Then build writing skills. Quiz your child and discuss concepts they don't understand. Teach them to apply what they're learning with real examples.
6. Believe in your child. They may never achieve your goals for them but support them in reaching their own. No one can replace a parent's faith in their own child nor let them down so harshly. Teachers and administrators do make mistakes.

7. Don't judge. Try not to criticize or yell. Hug often and remember to smile. They'll be gone before you know it.
8. Don't talk down to your child. You can motivate using fear or sheer power but in doing so you miss an opportunity to understand your unique child and engage them. Later, when they get older your efforts now will pay off and you'll be able to continue relating and influencing once your control position has evaporated.

Jack

Jack is a mellow, almost eighteen year old heading into his last year of high school. Under 6 feet tall, with conservatively short brown hair and glistening dusky brown eyes, Jack looks like most teenagers, neither rebellious nor overly conservative, but with perhaps too knowing smile. A liberal democrat with a strong social conscience Jack had wanted to be a journalist until a few months ago, even getting his blog posted on the Huffington Post. Then he began to question whether he'd perhaps rather aspire to a career more focused on actually doing good not just writing about it. Jack also came out of the closet at the same time, telling his friends and family that he is gay.

I was always attracted to men but never thought about it until one day.

We met for "slim" ice tea drinks at a Starbucks under my yoga studio, this being Southern California. Jack beat me there and was reading when I arrived, dressed in a plain t-shirt and jeans. He smiles readily and talks quickly, interested and thoughtful. Jack has taken time to reflect on numerous issues and thus is well spoken across a broad spectrum.

His interests include politics, swimming, good music, running, travel, journalism and going to the beach. Adventurous, he also likes to take a wrong turn occasionally while driving to explore a new neighborhood. The travel bug has also bitten hard and Jack looks at planes and airports now as gateways to new experiences and exciting places. Personable, Jack is also a swimmer who's in the pool about two hours daily.

He attends Palisades High School, better known as Pali. Pali is a charter school located in the heart of Pacific Palisades and perched on a hill above a vast beach. The Palisades is or has been home to such celebrities as Tom Cruise, Tom Hanks and the Schwarzeneggers. Adam's home is nestled in a quiet modest neighborhood and anything but a mansion, as is so typical of our Southern California enclaves. The area is north of Los Angeles proper and thus less congested, with a small town feel. It even has a quant downtown with upscale shops and a few local restaurants.

Pali is about 42 percent white children, most from the immediately surrounding neighborhood. Hispanics compose about 26 percent, with African Americans at just over 20 percent, Asians at around 8 percent and the balance a mix. Kids from the local community are automatically accepted into the school while the remaining spots are filled from outside the community (and are mostly minority).

A couple years ago LAUSD stopped funding buses to transport students to this affluent community north and west of the vaster expanse that forms broader Los Angeles. The cost is now $100 per month per student, which is out of the budget of most "travelling" students, who now take perhaps three local buses daily, waking at 4:00 to 5:00 am to get to school on time.

His father is a serial entrepreneur while his mother is a specialized nurse. The oldest of three boys, he stands as a roll model for his younger brothers, 16 and 12. Jack graduated from the same private lower school my children attend which is how we met. After graduating private school upon completing 6th grade he started at another private middle school only to eventually transfer to public school. His middle brother made a like transition while his youngest brother will go directly into public school as he's just graduated 6th grade.

Why the switch to public schools? Non-religious private schools in Los Angeles cost $20,000 to $30,000 per year. Meanwhile, Pali is free and is ranked 73 of the top 100 schools in California. It's ranked 49th in the nations best charter schools and sends 95 percent of graduating seniors to college. The curriculum has expansive Advanced Placement classes and the faculty mostly does a good job. According to *Newsweek*, Pali ranks in the top 1 percent of high schools nationwide.

Jack struggles with the normal high school issues all kids face. With only one more year of high school he now has to start making tough decisions about his future. Among his friends it's accepted that they'll go to college and many are charting out stable career paths as investment bankers, lawyers and doctors like their parents. However, conversations about college, jobs or the future are almost non-existent among Jack's peers as they're so sick of the topics from listening to their parents who don't stop raising them.

Yet Jack is in a strange microcosm of society in Pali. The ethnic groups mix little and are composed of children whose parents struggle to provide food, to solidly middle class kids, to those who live in the vast local mansions which can cost in excess of $15 million. Not surprisingly, the groups interact little and each falls into its own stereotype, a fate that has befallen much of our greater society.

Recently, Jack read F. Scott Fitzgerald's *The Great Gatsby* for school, and the book and its symbolism really spoke to him. *What I loved about Gatsby was how each word, sentence, character and setting could be read into further and how they each held their own meanings that required the reader to read between the lines.* And perhaps being part of his oddly constructed mixed society has taught him to see some of the artifice behind affluent images.

Teenagers dealing with their sexual identity only get so much support, especially if they're gay and have fewer role models. With accepting and liberal parents and living in a diverse, heavily Democratic city Jack has felt mostly support as he began to open up about his sexual orientation. But he also felt somewhat alone as most of the people with whom his family socialized fell into a narrow demographic and included almost no gay people. Doing online search he was able to find three blogs written by gay teenage swimmers, which provided some context for the challenges he's facing. He also began to see an excellent therapist. How does one develop with no directly relevant role models?

Jack is a proactive kid, but not all people are similarly blessed. For the summer, he actively sought out an internship with a local assembly member and another with a non-profit political organization that focuses on gay rights. These jobs enabled him to both pursue his interests of politics and social activism while also immersing himself in new worlds, outside of the traditional Palisades. His blog, jackd.co, as already mentioned, has been reprinted on the Huffington Post, unusual for a 17 year old. Evolving from wanting to be a journalist he's now actively searching for his optimal path, questioning but also deciding that he'd be happy living on beach somewhere exotic if need entails.

Last year Jack won a Cathay Pacific trip to China, along with 40 other kids of about the same age, from a diverse range of counties including South Africa, Japan and Belgium. In our era of mass media they became emotionally close quickly, sharing the same musical tastes and movie preferences. The world for sixteen year olds truly is flat. And it's ever available as the group today stays in touch through Facebook, no farther apart than a mouse click and new photo posted.

What most struck me about Jack is his thoughtfulness and willingness to question the norms of his regimented community. Perhaps having to acknowledge his sexual orientation and finding himself alone in navigating the implications, he turned inside and began to deeply question what his peers accept as truths. Jack is globally and politically aware. He also values his impact on the world above financial success. The naiveté of youth, greater maturity among our more challenged young or a passing phase? Only time will tell. I have high hopes for Jack.

Asked about the future Jack said:

In the past few years, I've had quite a few different visions of myself in the future, from being a journalist, to a wealthy, globe trotting investment banker, to a journalist, and now everything I'm doing now. As I've said and as I'll keep saying, I love working with Equality California and I will continue to as much as I can during the school year. My hopes for the future right now are a lot: the past few months I've sort of adopted the mottos, 'make a difference/change the world & to get shit done.' a little cocky, yes, but they are really two things that I'd like to do. Perhaps make a dent on the universe as Steve Jobs hoped to do? When I grow up, I want to do something tangible. I would not like to be a businessman where I'm working to make money. (I'd want to be a businessman if that was my passion.. you know.. ?) I want to work for things I want to do (which may at some point be making money) and for things that will have an impact on society. I also want to find an awesome husband, have some kids, and just be happy. I'm not sure if I'll be in politics, a non-profit or some sort or a journalist. Recently, I have begun to find what really makes me happy and what I really want to do.. and I love it. So when I'm older I'd like to do just that. I would think that other kids my age might have a more descriptive path that they hope to see themselves follow in the next five, ten, twenty years, but as of now, I am alright doing what I want to do and being happy.

PART TWO

SUBJECTS TO BE STUDIED

Be aware of wonder. Live a balanced life – learn some and think some and draw and paint and sing.
ROBERT FULGHUM

The more ugly, older, more cantankerous, more ill and poorer I become, the more I try to make amends by making my colors more vibrant, more balanced and beaming.
VINCENT VAN GOGH

SCHOOL SHOULD EDUCATE CHILDREN YET AS MANY FACTORS SUCH as test scores and employment projections show they aren't always succeeding. I've argued for a broader definition of literacy yet still maintain that a solid grounding in the fundamentals is the only foundation which works. Much as many well-meaning innovators might argue for less easily defined and softer skills, competencies and test scores are still what your child, any child, will be judged on first. As a Director of Admissions at a prestigious local school explained, they show that someone you respect has already pre-vetted a child and done the hard work.

Armed with a Harvard degree or a killer amount of empathy and resilience the former will usually win. To get those test scores and a college degree children need to learn a broad range of topics and master them all. Context and foundational knowledge matter in any environment.

In my enclave there is no discussion of cutting science, art, history, physical education or even music programs. I'm not even in the 1 percent yet I can verify that not only do the children in my local school not have to deal with rampant crime and violence in their neighborhood they're also getting a good basic education (though I've argued already that this basic literacy prepares them for the world 100 years ago and not the realities of today where many of their competitors in Asia attend school for longer school days and Saturday too).

Thus it still isn't enough. What do our children really need to learn and how do we get there from here?

The music masters familiarizes children's minds with rhythms and melodies, thus making them more civilized, more balanced, better adjusted in themselves, and more capable in whatever they say or do, for rhythm and harmony are essential to the whole.

PLATO

Under Horace Mann, the "father of our common school system" and over a hundred years ago, our universal school system was designed based on a factory model. Mann believed that teaching character was as important as teaching basic literacy (the three r's of reading, writing and 'rithmatic) but he also emulated the structured Prussian educational system. Thus each grade was specified by age, spanning a full 365 days, regardless of where children fell on that spectrum. Children were and are taught a mostly uniform curriculum and on a schedule. They're tested and graded. Learning is based on the only tools available long ago: lectures and reading. How many people reading this learned from forced lectures? How much do you remember from those you sat through? And only about 20 percent of the population learns best from reading (textbooks).

Horace Mann never used a computer, didn't know iPads and wasn't competing with a better-educated engineer and MBA in India for his job.

Arguably more modern than the factory based learning structure of the American based school system, with its added bureaucracy (support staff are now 50 percent versus 25 percent 20 years ago; the balance is made up of teachers), were Aristotle's academies, the one he founded being named the Lyceum. Key to his thoughts was the idea of shaping a person, through education and guidance, such that they could achieve their right purpose. Education for theory alone created philosophers; application of concepts in the real world was more important, as was a balanced person. A teacher was found and instruction customized.

Most parents don't aim to create philosophers. While during our children's teens we may wonder how we only created philosophers, I'd venture that we aspire to children who've found their right purpose, and their passions, and are living them. We may even question why we weren't guided to find the same.

Currently, in the United States, and as already noted, many schools systems are being accused of "teaching to the test" in which they focus more on preparing children for the types of questions asked on the standardized tests upon which the schools are judged. Lost in the process is a dizzying array of subjects: art, music, history, science and languages, to start. Check out your child's curriculum to see it has been thus negatively impacted. Creativity and developing a global perspective both require a broad spectrum of disciplines from which to draw, and are of increasing importance. More urgent is that those children limited in their learning can never become the next Albert Einstein or Benjamin Franklin because they've never been exposed to necessary subject matter thus haven't started developing an interest or a competency.

Peter Thiel, founder of PayPal, prominent Silicon Valley investor and intellectual offered to fund twenty college students if they dropped out of college and started a company instead. He ended up increasing his number to 22 in year one and then created a second year class. What struck me reading the company ideas and biographies of those funded were the depth of mostly scientific knowledge the founders had and the sophistication – science wise – of most related companies. Robotics, neuroscience, coding, biology, alternative energy and the like make up the Thiel Fellow descriptions. And the founders dropped out of college (ages 18 to early 20s) to start those companies. They learned the background knowledge in an American high school? Not believable. Indeed, I doubt very many children today are graduating from our high schools, and definitely not inner city high schools, with the knowledge and skills to drop out of high school to start a science heavy company. With guidance your child can.

We argue about the earning gap between the top one percent of our country, or even just that of the top demographic. How about the education divergence? And the ethnic one. In my hometown of Los Angeles, with well over 50 percent of children in our schools being minority, the actual public school numbers are more divergent: only about 8 percent are white. Separate but equal? No, the children in some schools are learning more and in wealthier neighborhoods typically get more funding (based on property tax and varies by state). And those wealthier, often better-educated parents are still supplementing their higher-ranking schools with tutors, camps, classes and other resources.

This breakdown ensures that those children in the top percentage of schools generally have an ongoing advantage and will likely be disproportionately (to the general population) represented among future top earners.

While they may not found a neuroscience company one absolute I heard from numerous sources while researching this book is that today's generation of youths will need to create as many jobs as the large companies do, perhaps even their own. Small and faster growing companies already create most of the new jobs in our country, with BusinessWeek recently estimating the number at 65 percent. That trend is only growing as larger corporations continue shifting jobs overseas. Thus we need to re-invigorate the entrepreneurial spirit that made our country great and teach children to start and build something new (which they love doing while young and before we scare risk out of them).

Inherent in that concept is the drive to keep learning throughout a lifetime, a willingness to take risk and an ability to adapt to evolving environments and seize opportunities. Creating becomes a focus, not mimicking or responding.

E.D. Hirsch, Jr. came up with something called the Core Knowledge Sequence (www.coreknowledge.org). Much cited in William Bennett's *The Educated Child*, this resource is among the best offered to parents. Essentially, it defines an ideal curriculum that students should study and master to be well-educated members of our society. It's much more rigorous than the recently adopted national standards but a great additional resource for parents who want to supplement what their children are learning. Hirsch's are available free to all. One qualification on the contents of the standards is that schools don't necessarily teach subjects in the same order, or chronology. Thus they're only a rough suggestion and it's the balance of knowledge taught over the years that matter. He even suggests age appropriate reading list. I will draw from his content below, along with Bennett's book *The Educated Child*, and urge you to go directly to these resources for more details.

EARLY INFLUENCES: TO PRESCHOOL AND BEYOND

What you're holding in your hands isn't a baby book. Plenty of other books address the pre-natal and first few years, and on a detailed basis. But I do want to make a few points as to what you do (or have done) in the months before or first few years after your child is born can have a huge impact.

First, early influences starting perhaps even before a baby is in the womb, matter a lot. Any quick search will get you a multitude of resources, some of which sound good only to be discredited and others which are sound. Nonetheless, the time to start planning for a baby is before you're pregnant (if possible). Many of our local preschools require an application within a baby's first year or months.

Next, what you do might matter less than the environment you create. Children are differentiated early on by watching the influences their parents. Eric Turkheimer of the University of Virginia published a landmark study in 2003 showing that growing up in poverty leads to a lower IQ. Asked about what factors exactly led to this outcome the answers weren't simple. Rather, being born into poverty is falling into what's known as an emergent system, or a system in which a number of factors come together and feed off one and other to create a greater whole. Emergent systems are very effective in passing down customs, mindsets and behaviors. Basically, people pick up on the complex interactions among group members and the interrelated dynamics. Families, marriages, and even ants follow this pattern. No one tells a member to behave a certain way but by long observance they know what to do, but not instinctively. This behavior is taught. Pulling the behaviors apart is mind-numbingly difficult, thus changing them is even harder.

Therefore, in lower income households children are raised differently from those in higher income homes. In our immediate neighborhood we see this difference in practice. Middle and upper income children are driven around to numerous activities from sports to art lessons to piano to nice restaurants where they learn grown-up behavior. Parents are constantly explaining, questioning, teaching and quizzing. They stay engaged, even when busy on a work call or otherwise multi-tasking.

Turkheimer studied lower income families and found that they believed that the busier more affluent kids must be stressed with all that was expected of them (yet which actually trains them for the complex demands of the modern world). Kids played and interacted more, yet parents were less likely to engage on the child's level, thinking it was only for kids. Thus lower income children were more likely to be left to organize their own playtime. These children weren't asked their opinion as much as were children in more affluent households, and discussions on complex topics with parents were rare. Authority was more absolute. Overall, these subtle or not so subtle differences of interacting created what Turkheimer termed the *Gloomy Prospect*, in which clarifying the specific behaviors that doomed an outcome was lost in a morass of loosely correlated factors.

Other variables also matter.

Attached children, whose parents actively engage and respond to a baby's cues also do better. This early lesson in how to bond and create relationships develops different children, being 77 percent accurate in predicting which children drop out of high school. Thus if you hire regular childcare while working those that you hire can make a big impact.

According to a much quoted study by Betty Hart and Todd Risley of the University of Kansas, children raised in poor families had heard 32 million less words than children raised in professional, though not designated as affluent, families by age 4. Broken down hourly, children raised in welfare homes heard 178 while those in professional homes heard 487. And the quality of interactions is different, with more interactive dialogue, questioning and other interaction in professional families. Jason at seven used a word (in context) that seemed well out of his knowledge level. Questioned about his usage he remarked that mom had used the word ten minutes earlier but he had no idea what it meant. But he used it correctly and had the confidence to make the attempt. That's how children begin learning relative to their peers.

Thus parents must be cognizant of all aspects of the environment in which they're raising children. Having books around is a good start but if you aren't reading then likely your child won't pick them up either. Spend time explaining and drawing your child into the broader world. Don't passively sit them in front of puppets on a dvd (unless it's so you can make dinner but not to enrich their brains). And limit television.

Thus the most important resource you can give your child is the right environment, which is harder than buying books or videos. I'm highly influenced in this arena by Rita Cornyn who has run my children's pre-school, The Sunshine School, for over 30 years. She was often criticized by the more developmental schools for teaching both phonics and Spanish to young children (who universally loved the classes). Rita also had a waiting list like you wouldn't believe, and was in high demand among local celebrity parents who had their choice of schools. She is an advocate for making learning fun and challenging young brains but not for pushing or overloading them. Eschewing tutoring or outside academic classes ("they're just little kids") she nonetheless ensured they knew their alphabet orally and could write it. They could also write their name.

Thus, her advice will always be my constant. Make learning fun early on but recognize that they are young children and learn the most by playing.

Resources

Two books cover early influences on children in a great narrative way. *The Social Animal* by David Brooks *and Whatever It Takes: Geoffrey Canada's Quest to Change Harlem and America* by Paul Tough.

Engage young children. Show them art books and discuss what you see. What pictures do they like? Listen to music and ask similar questions. Classical is wonderful but so is other music. Talk to your child. Teach and explain your day.

Brain Rules for Baby: How to Raise a Smart and Happy Child from Zero to Five by John Medina. While a skeptic about overdoing it with young children I think a good book or two won't hurt. This one has a well-respected author and constructive information.

Go for walks together and discuss what you see. Read books aloud. Draw together.

THE THREE R'S DEFINED TODAY

Math

Robert P. Moses and Charles E. Cobb, Jr. in *Radical Equations* assert that algebra is a gatekeeper course that determines whether children grow up to be the sharecroppers of the future or have better knowledge-based jobs. They also state that while literacy used to be defined by reading and writing it is now math, leading to the likewise logic based technological skills, that defines literacy today.

Oh for the days when math competency was just basic calculations; yet one doesn't live by equations alone. Below I'll argue that financial literacy is important as well, and for some children perhaps more so. But! Everyone should know the basic addition, subtraction, multiplication, division and fractions charts. You cannot deal with the practical realities of our world without a quick facility with these numbers. Rote memorization has its uses and memorizing basic calculations is one of them. All people will have a tough time in life without knowing addition, subtraction, multiplication and division. Playing nice about their importance and the ubiquitous of calculators is a non-starter in my household. Simple transactions like going to a store or managing a checking account mandate basic math.

Professionally, as an investment banker, I was expected to do rough million dollar calculations in meetings with CEO clients and if I didn't do it the guy who worked for me did (and would have had my job quickly). A working knowledge of math is required in much of the business world.

Math also teaches logic and building the solution to a problem through mastering disciplined steps to find an ultimate answer. Each step is crucial to reaching the right answer, and each successive one builds on the last concept. All sciences are likewise built on the same idea of creating a foundational theory or answer, then using what you've learned from that initial step to progress to the next, often harder one, and on until you reach a conclusion. This sort of disciplined thinking is the opposite of rote task performance, where each step is mimicked over and over to produce the same predictable response. Indeed, Moses and Cobb revisit the founding of our school system and draw an even more important distinction:

Industrial technology created schools that educated an elite to run society, while the rest were prepared for factory work by performing repetitive tasks that mimicked factories. New technology demands a new literacy – higher math skills for everyone, urban and rural

The authors then go on to point out that this gap in math skills, while worse in poorer or minority neighborhoods, extends throughout our country with even the educated sometimes joking at their lack of math skills. They decry this attitude and call for more discipline in teaching children core thinking skills. Calling upon the teachings of W.V.O. Quine and his philosophy of math they point out that part of math's complexity is its use of symbols instead of "people talk", the latter of which is more understandable to all and not just children. Essentially, Quine claimed that math (and much of learning) is just trying out a problem, thinking about the results of your effort, figuring out what you did wrong and then trying again. By replacing symbols with understandable words in context a child can begin to grasp what the problem is asking and how they can chart an answer. Later, once they grasp the concepts, a symbol can replace the "people talk". The first step in math literacy sometimes can be demystifying it.

Math builds discipline and being meticulous with your work.

Math also requires a good memory. Unfortunately for many students, and as above, it also requires a strong mastery of earlier principles or the child will fail in subsequent levels. Arithmetic builds on arithmetic, and practice embeds the principles on a child's mind. Hence when a student begins to fall behind in math, catching up can be difficult, especially if not flagged by an observant teacher, most of whom are already overburdened and can't always identify those students acting up versus those lost in a standardized lesson plan.

Today, math mastery is too often quantified not by learning and logic but by strict test preparation schedules and results. With its clear yes and no answers math brings out the worst in tests and teachers. It's also subject to endless repetitive problems even if children don't understand the concept behind the problem. One evening, when I was especially busy, my daughter came to me with her long division problems. She clearly hadn't heard whatever lecture her teacher had given earlier that day and was beyond frustrated, being a perfectionist, and had reached distraught. She wasn't listening to what I was explaining and I'm not patient. So I took a deep breath and recognized that she was panicked because she had no grasp of her lesson or where to begin. We pulled out a calculator to simplify the division so we could focus on the actual process (of carrying values forward). Calm now, she grasped the concept in less than five minutes but still wanted to rely on the calculator to check the answers after she completed the problem. After the first one she got them all right.

Math is simple yet too many of us likewise panic when confronted with a concept we can't remember or don't recognize. A simple Google search only leads to a more complicated exercise requiring our attention and can surely increase our confusion.

Yet math is a pre-courser skill not only to higher math but also to most of the sciences. The classification of STEM in education lumps the concepts together under this acronym that stands for science, technology, engineering and math. Any science-based discipline requires that step-by-step logic of building upon our first proven concepts and testing our hypothesis. I'll discuss these concepts in more detail later but the STEM grouping is much more complex than they were when any parent reading this page was in school. The growth in the related innovations, including using computers to crunch and process data, is unparalleled in history. Computer programs require mastering rules then following them in a prescribed manner and order (as in math). We're moving at light speed to build upon core math knowledge and that progress is only continuing. As discussed above, the bulk of future great jobs fall into this complex bucket. And this grouping is especially reliant on the core foundations in the area that a child has built – thus leading to Moses and Cobb's assertion that without Algebra, the beginnings of advanced math, a child will not advance economically. Moreover, that related logical thinking and ability to discipline an argument when dealing with complexity defines or at least lays the path to future academic achievement.

Mathematics is the door and key to the sciences.
ROGER BACON

Math also teaches the concepts of abstraction. In the realm of math a perfection can exist that doesn't necessarily exist in the real world (though science has proven that certain proportions exist consistently throughout nature...meaning mathematically defined ratios). Circles can be perfect and numbers manipulated. Abstract principles, out of which uncertainty is withdrawn, underlie theory and are crucial in fields like economics or, again, science. Any experiment requires some constants to remain such so other factors in response to the experiment can be measured. We need to think in broad theory to discern such concepts as democracy or God to be then argued with the messier realities of application. Most people aren't born thinking of the abstract and learn only after years of trial and error.

Symmetry in the universe is likewise defined by math. Snowflakes, a star's brightness, an ocean wave and the pattern of a snail's shell are defined by mathematical formulas, and hold constant. DNA, the mapping of the atom, the sun's course, the movement of planets and the speed of light are all defined by mathematical formulas. Who can ignore Einstein's famous physics formula, E= MC2 math and science blending?

Math is clear, precise and can be mastered. Unlike more subjective subjects students can learn to be right and to explain the steps that got them an answer. Thus math is an inspiring way to build a child's self esteem. I even feel accomplishment when I get my children's homework right.

One can always reason with reason.
HERI BERGSON

Why is math so often poorly taught? First of all, many schools have a hard time finding qualified math and science teachers. Next, as with phonics and reading, missing mastering the early concepts of math prohibits later problem solving. As a child can't progress academically without reading well they likewise can't progress without foundational math.

Resources

Numerous websites have online math and other educational games for kids. The best way to see if your children like them is to try them out – most are free. My kids didn't gravitate to these sites but others enjoy them more. Some good ones are: www.funbrain.com, www.coolmath4kids.com, www.coolmath.com (which is the same as the previous site but for ages 13 and up) and www.mathplayground.com.

What some prefer are old-fashioned workbooks available at any bookstore, online or off.

www.khanacademy.org offers great instructive math tutorials, along with those addressing other fact-based subjects, such as an array of sciences.

English

Perhaps it is only in childhood that books have any deep influence on our lives. In later life we admire, we are entertained, we may modify some views we already hold, but we are more likely to find in books merely a confirmation of what is in our minds already: as in a love affair it is our own features that we see reflected flatteringly back. But in childhood all books are books of divination, telling us about the future, and like the fortune teller we sees a long journey in the cards or death by water they influence the future.
GRAHAM GREENE IN *THE LOST CHILDHOOD*

Children begin picking up language skills very early, possibly before birth. According David Brooks in *The Social Animal*, French babies cry differently than German babies due to the fetus having heard the lilt in their mother's voice before birth. Indeed, much of our mental processing is taking the vast range of stimuli we get each moment and integrating it into sophisticated models that mirror our understanding of patterns. Children begin grasping patterns in sounds and before their first year are already picking up the underlying rhyme scheme from which they'll begin discerning words over time.

Centuries ago, before the discovery of the printing press and increased literacy, learning was passed down through story telling and song, and the Catholic Church held great masses to teach the holy book to its believers. Language is the essence of learning.

By the time children have entered preschool they've heard an amazing number of words daily, with an unfortunate divergence typically occurring between middle class and poorer families, and even within a social class. This difference sets the children apart before they've even begun learning their ABCs, with those children who've heard more words from their parents greatly outperforming those who haven't. Reading to your children also gives them a vast academic advantage later.

Thus for all of us grasping language for the first time, we pick up words by learning and speaking. Only later do we grab pencil, paper and books. Hence the early instruction of English covers the very basic skills of speaking, writing, listening and reading. Deeper comprehension and nuanced expression develops over time. But language also opens concepts to children and takes them to worlds and subjects beyond their daily experience. It should arouse their natural curiosity even further and teach that learning can be fun. Proper language skills are essential for later studies as without them one cannot master, let alone grasp, instruction. So what should your child be getting out of their English classes?

Reading

All children should be taught to read and to read well. This skill is a foundational one for our schools and some of them are failing and horribly. But even good schools can't promise that all children are reading at grade level. Some children won't put their books down while others are loath to pick them up, and it makes a difference! Thus as a parent you should encourage your child to read beyond what is required by their teachers. Our school mandates that each child read at least 15 minutes each night on top of their homework and including on weekends.

Basic phonics, or sounding out letters, is typically thought to be the best way to teach reading. Once the basic letters, compound letters and exceptions are understood any word can be phonetically figured out, with definitions being supplied thereafter.

All reading helps improve a child's skills, and a wide range builds the ability to develop context. Books, magazines, websites (especially those written for or by children!), newspapers, poems and even menus help. I bought a book of prayers, which included those from numerous denominations and cultures, for my children to read aloud each night before dinner. Read together and explain concepts too complex for your child, it's a wonderful way to bond. And ask their opinion on what you read together. My children and their friends love to share their thoughts and feelings.

Great literature also instructs well beyond language. Myths and fairy tales are morality tales, full of the challenges that each of us confront in life. These great stories follow the classic storylines such as a coming of age challenges, a quest to prove oneself in society, breaking away into independence from a parent or the conflict of love versus duty. In *Cinderella* we see that with the right attitude and hard work we'll eventually escape a bad situation. In *Alice in Wonderland* the scary world sometimes isn't as it seems but we can escape. And in the quest of *Odysseus* we learn how hard returning home can be, though it's worth the effort.

And children also learn the ways of the world and how to live a good, moral life. *The Ant and the Grasshopper* is a classic example of the virtues of work versus play. *Pinocchio* is a vivid vision of why not to lie. Children are able to learn by example and see a thought in practice. They learn complex cultural expectations in an interesting format, that of a story line with often-multifaceted characters. The theory applied makes more sense than does a boring lecture. Would Harry Potter have been as interesting had he not lived for years with an aunt and uncle who didn't appreciate him or treat him as an equal? How did Harry cope first as an underdog and then in a superior role (with grace).

In his book, *The Uses of Enchantment*, Bruno Bettelheim brilliantly explains to adult minds how frightening the world around children can be. Children are powerless. Fairy tales allow them to explore their overwhelming emotions and worries in a less direct thus less challenging way. Perhaps that's why so many children's shows poke fun at adults: by allowing children to laugh at them it takes away the fearsomeness of their authority. Children can get mad at adults, even parents, and play out those fantasies in a harmless way, through a narrative. They can test limits, ask questions, get angry and defy authority. Children's imaginations can soar with no worry of judgment or being punished. Stories create worlds of possibility and let us dream. As Bettelheim states,

For a story truly to hold the child's attention, it must entertain him and arouse his curiosity. But to enrich his life, it must stimulate his imagination; help him to develop his intellect and to clarify his emotions; be attuned to his anxieties and aspirations; give full recognition to his difficulties, while at the same time suggesting solutions to the problems which perturb him. In short, it must at one and the same time relate to all aspects of his personality – and this without ever belittling it but, on the contrary, giving full credence to the seriousness of the child's predicaments, while simultaneously promoting confidence in himself and in his future.

Reading also teaches children about their society and how to relate within it. One of the traditional reasons behind schools was to socialize children and make them a part of the community. Stories provide a context. My son and his friends love *Diary of a Wimpy Kid* (as do so many other children) because it provides social guidance dealing with the practical insanities of sibling manipulation, school machinations and irrational parents. Many fairy tales document the coming of age story, as a child goes off in search of a golden fleece or encounters college.

Biographies and histories provide the actual stories that make up our country's or world's past. They provide a context and common identity. Along with myths they provide insight into common terms like a Trojan horse (via Homer) and Valley Forge (Washington's important battle). To be a well-informed citizen, and future voter, such cultural heritage is vital knowledge and so often picked up through reading along with history class. These cultural allusions are very much present in the conversations of more educated Americans and not having them in memory can be a professional or personal liability – you can't carry the same conversations. I myself am sports illiterate and can attest to the importance of literacy in a topic before you can engage others and add meaningful commentary.

My daughter had to write about a patriot while studying American history and ended up with Thomas Paine, a writer. While much of his work was too difficult for her to grasp at 11 she nonetheless attempted passages and understood enough. In reading about him she learned about the early documents upon which our nation was built and now can discuss the Bill of Rights with some grounding (unfortunately). She also grasps the importance of our Constitution and why each individual is considered important in the United States (not a universal concept). Reading got her there.

Yet classics are no longer widely taught in many schools, having been replaced with more diverse perspectives or even little required reading at all. Each year my children get a summer reading list with only a few required books but many suggested ones. Too often they pick the newer ones that discuss topics they find more relevant, including fantasy. I don't disapprove of these books! Many of them address the issues children are facing on a daily basis, carefully crafted into a narrative. Katniss, in *The Hunger Games*, is the main character and the heroine in the series. She lives in a futuristic wasteland of 12 districts with the mysterious 13 having been extinguished by the capital for disobedience. Her peers and neighbors are barely surviving and risk punishment any time they break a rule. The story is harsh but perhaps fitting in the context of America's ongoing recession and school system crisis (based more on obedience and rote mimicry than actual teaching to some). All citizens are subject to the edicts of the capital, not again dissimilar to how the adult world can appear to children (who likewise have little ability to control their environment or question authority). Katniss confronts multiple complex issues: a widowed and non-functioning mother; her own future along with that of those she loves; a boy who adores her yet she doesn't likewise love; betrayal; survival; and an oppressive institution that both grooms and threatens her. The story very much parallels some of the great conflicts present in classic literature.

Indeed, there is a whole genre of young adult fiction called dystopia which deals with society that is the opposite of a utopia.

I live in a diverse state and grew up surrounded by what I thought was diversity. Also the child of immigrants who visited her foreign grandparents I loved exposure to different cultures and worlds. While

I support the broadening of the curriculum to expand the groups and experiences it covers, reading also needs to draw from the works that formed the foundation of Western society as they shaped who Americans are today. Don't neglect the classics even if your schools do. They got that designation for a reason.

My father paid me a dollar per book read when I was a child. It worked, but doesn't work for my son and didn't for my brother. Find books your child will like, whether at a library, online or bookstore. My son currently only likes non-fiction and biographies. He never reads fantasy or scary books, which makes him harder to please than you'd expect. He discovered an out of print series called "Great Minds of Science" so we got him access to a number of them. All children love to learn about something. But still sometimes I find him lost in fiction. Reading is an easy path for children to quench that curiosity, even if you have to start together online, reading, until you find an appropriate book or website.

And read to and with your child. Readers score better on tests and those children whose parents read and read to them not surprisingly read more. Keep books around.

The decline of literature indicates the decline of a nation.
JOHANN WOLFGANG VON GOETHE

Writing

There is nothing to writing. All you do is sit down
at a typewriter and bleed.
ERNEST HEMINGWAY

I have such a fondness for the quote above because it sums up exactly how hard good writing is (note I didn't say "can be"). Anyone with children has seen toddlers mimic writing, sprawling out crooked letters and mismatching the order. How hard can it be to populate a blank page with the limited number of options, 26 letters but ever so many words?

We live in the communication age and as noted earlier many want to consider communication an essential skill or part of functional literacy, and really, it already is. Listening, reading, talking and writing are the components. At my first real job out of college, at Merrill Lynch, my boss counseled us all to write out what we planned to say on a call before we made it, even though the conversation would never go as planned and we'd end up winging it. But we'd start knowing our key points and what at a bare minimum we must say thus would get there quickly. It works, disciplining thoughts and solidifying arguments. If we can't explain what we're trying to say it likely doesn't make sense.

But it can! Speaking is immediate but writing can be shaped and developed. It can get better. To make sense on paper we must first organize our thoughts and ideas. Then we structure them in sentences and paragraphs, tying like ideas with like ideas and allowing for a flow in our reasoning. Word choices can easily become repetitive, which we don't hear as we speak but which glare on a single page. Precision requires revision and clarification, both instilling discipline but also confidence as we can craft our position with depth, insight, wisdom and even humor.

Email, business letters, resumes, presentations and company memos can now be shared by the disgruntled in a second, spreading widely and entailing potential legal liability. They're also very often how people judge you, as the written word is there to be re-visited as desired.

Either write something worth reading or do something worth writing.
BENJAMIN FRANKLIN

Writing is also a key part of school. Children are required to write reports, essays and essay test answers. They are graded on spelling tests and grammar quizzes. I can write and write and write – painfully at times – because I like to talk so always have something to add. Google and dictionary.com are my best friends when it comes to helping my children with their grammar homework – precise writing skills are hard to learn! But without them no child can learn to craft a proper sentence.

Penmanship doesn't come easily to my family yet one of my son's best friends loves the subject (which goes to show that doing so is possible). Others being able to read what you scribe matters, even in the day and age of computers. None of us walks around lugging large hardware so we need to write well with a pencil or pen.

Give your children extra writing assignments? That depends on how much homework they have already. Even if you don't get them actually writing ask them about their opinions and make them follow a coherent structured explanation – the first step to writing an essay. Sketch out an argument. Ask questions, provide suggestions and help them craft a narrative. If you aren't confident in doing so all the better – you can learn together.

A classic structure for a simple essay is as follows: think of five paragraphs. The first is the introduction in which you introduce key concepts and make your main defining point of the essay. The next three paragraphs shore up your central argument or point. In these paragraphs you start with a sentence that defines your point in support of the thesis. Then three or so examples follow. Your closing sentence sums up why your three points prove your opening one. The last paragraph sums up your opening point, your supporting arguments and then adds a distinctive conclusion.

Some will skewer you for this structure, and argue that on standardized tests the answers all predictably follow it and thus are unoriginal. They are wrong and have yet to come up with a better alternative. Children are using this structure on standardized tests because the test prep tutors and classes tell them to do so because the examiners expect it. Yes, if you're Hemingway you can do better. I'll bet at 16 even he couldn't. By teaching kids to clarify their thoughts they'll do better on essays. Initially, they likely can't spread their wings and get creative with their points but as they become more comfortable with writing essays and with your active encouragement, I'll bet your children will.

By the way, I didn't learn the above structure until law school and I started college as an English major in honors English (so take no instruction for granted).

Speaking

I'll make a quick point about speaking, as it's a wonderful art that most of us struggle to master. Touring my children's school everyone is struck with how articulate and well spoken the student tour guides are. These students, all fifth graders, stand out against those from other schools and their poise is a huge selling point. How do they develop such polish and poise? Starting in third grade they are required to stand up in front of their class and speak for a minute on a topic. The stress and preparation that goes into this minute is intense initially. The children scour their parent's newspapers looking for interesting stories then rip them apart for the key points. They then practice repeatedly for their family. The risk in not doing so is embarrassment in front of their peers – who do ask piercing questions. They do one presentation a week for two years!

By the end of that two years they coolly prepare themselves for yet another presentation and their words flow, their arguments are more easily prepared and their responses to heckling unflappable. It' among the most amazing things I've seen studying education. Good speaking can be taught.

And there are other elements beyond a well-prepared argument and time practicing that play well to an audience. Manners sell well. Polite people tend to get better responses from others. Vocabulary sounds impressive and enables the correct descriptive word choice that makes an impact (cool is altogether overused and lacks clarity of meaning). Good grammar makes any point sound more important. Those who speak well sound educated.

Teaching children how to ask concise questions is also a skill. Listen and you'll soon notice how rambling many people's questions can be, such that their actual query is hard to recognize. Short and sweet is a classic term for a reason. Twitter might be the best thing to happen to the English language in centuries, as it requires people to focus their thought.

And a note on creativity.

True ease in writing comes from art, not chance, as those who move easiest have learned to dance.
ALEXANDER POPE

I'll discuss creativity in greater detail below but all that writing and reading can make a difference. Creativity is essentially taking known concepts and applying them in new ways or coming up with an entirely new concept. To be creative, you need multiple sources from which to draw and perhaps even examples of how to apply concepts in novel new ways. Writers are one group that does this well. Moreover, they provide a roadmap for adding new competencies from which a child can draw disparate straws to form a new whole. A great way to learn them is through reading. Authors very often take risks or write about those who do.

Poetry is finer and more philosophical than history; for poetry expresses the universal, and history only the particular.
ARISTOTLE

Resources

The reading list at the end of the book will provide a beginning list of options. Reading and practicing writing are truly the best ways to learn English.

www.dictionary.com and its partner www.thesaurus.com are great go tos when looking for a word.

The Grammar girl website is a less intimidating option than some other sites. www.grammar.quickanddirtytips.com

HISTORY

History will be kind to me for I intend to write it.
WINSTON CHURCHILL

History = social studies? Yes, but perhaps it shouldn't. In *The Educated Child* authors William Bennett, Chester Finn, Jr. and T.E. Cribb unapologetically state: *we believe that history and geography, along with the beginnings of civics and economics, should comprise the core of what is widely referred to as "social studies".* I agree. History provides context, experience, explanations and insight. History defines a society and thus is a solid predictor of how different peoples and places will react to seemingly new events. As our family defines us to a point as a person, our shared cultural history defines us as a people. For example, those of us in the United States view events through a prism of expecting the given of basic human rights. Much of the world views events differently.

History does nothing; it does not possess immense riches, it does not fight battles. It is men, real, living, who do all this.
KARL MARX

History explains how people have related to each other and it's closely linked to geography, which addresses how men have interacted with the spaces across our earth. Both tie together how customs and institutions have grown and influenced others. Man is interdependent and lives within the confines of a natural universe. History and geography provide context and insight as to how these factors have intersected practically over time.

History and geography are both especially subject to being taught according to a regional/geographic bias, and falling into the trap of not just perhaps favoring the victor but also the prevailing ideology. Thus Americans are learning a vastly different version of communism than are the Chinese and a different Vietnam War experience than the people attending school in Hanoi.

Much of the world has evolved in a mostly uncontested way. Man began to emerge from an animal like existence, eventually cultivating music, art and language. Forming into communities, labors were split such that some farmed, others hunted, and the rest took on domestic tasks. Then came religion and writing, churches and governments. Man got the vote, lights and modern medicine. We went to the moon and signed in online. Cell phones now best landline telephones and we both drive and fly. Yet this brief summary completely ignores the passions of men striving against each other and nature to found great civilizations that persist in influencing us today or the impact of decade long wars, and the price paid for certain beliefs.

Too much history is taught as a recitation of facts and events, not as a more riveting story of men. Biographies can be more compelling than mere events because we can better identify with the conflicts of a particular man or woman, coping in a time of peril or confusion, then with a list of facts. History happens to and because of people, it doesn't merely exist independent of them. And history can too often be seen as something that occurred long in the past, without being directly relevant to current conflicts and lives. We each of us need the context of geography and society to fully grasp the immediacy of the past, and why certain alliances or animosities still exert such passions.

Learning from others' actions also personalizes the past and makes it real; we can see ourselves facing similar challenges (indeed history famously repeats) and can learn from their responses. Reliving antiquity is among the most potentially exciting forms of engaging narrative in which we can immerse ourselves. The people and places already exist thus we must only slip into imagination to join them.

There are many histories, and not just defined by geography. Biographical, cultural and societal deal with people, including how they interact and effect or are affected by others, events and their environment. Economic addresses the growth of practical liberties through the command of nature, or how commerce works in a given society. Industrial history covers production and work. It demonstrates how people harness others and the environment (and resources in the environment) to create. Political history ranges across the vast machinations of man dealing with those within his own society and using diplomacy or strength to master, or not master, others abroad. Intellectual history encompasses the thoughts of visionaries or tastemakers as they address the complexities of a society over the vast reaches of time. Cultural history holds that intangible of the literature, music and art defining a people in their place and time. Together all of these disperse arenas form what we consider history. So different, and of differing fascinations, for any modern population standing distanced from their ongoing impact they easily fade into the past, irrelevant and intangible.

History also tells us what is and why. It's a quick lesson in cause and effect and the intractable conflicts that define many lives, countries or regions. I might not like a balance of power or particular fight but it has arisen out of a confluence of past and ever changing events and can only be fixed by sensitivity to the events that led us to the present.

Worse, history as an educational subject has been watered down in numerous American classrooms. History is not an immediately testable subject, like math and English, thus its instruction has been cut in too many classrooms. A subject that provides context for many others, it must be highlighted if children are to understand in context the importance of life's evolution.

And history can be subjective, as while some facts are certainties many more are clouded by multiple written narratives and perspectives allowing for interpretation by those who wish to sell a particular story line.

History also has many perspectives within a society itself. In our own country a child of African American background will view the past history of slavery differently than that of a child with European ancestors. While both can agree the institution was wrong, only the former looks back and sees family members holding chains. Each experience is different as it relates to a personal or familial history. Separating the distinct from the broader history is important and sometimes our education system pushes for an inclusion of experience that borders on the absurd and ignores our shared past (in favor of the personal or equal time for varied, though of differing impact, events).

The personal is insightful; the universal is profound.

Civics or government is only one small part of history, as defined above. It's often taught independently of the broader historical picture. While breaking apart historical components does have its place, ultimately the pieces need to eventually be tied back together again. Our current curriculum doesn't always re-attach these pieces, rather focusing on a module instead of a whole. For example, children may study American Indians in fourth grade then the founding in our country in the fifth, with no tying lesson between the two. Thus, they've memorized a time and place but not a continuum.

If history repeats itself, and the unexpected always happens, how incapable must Man be of learning from experience.
GEORGE BERNARD SHAW

Our country has certain deeply held beliefs, all of which are routed in history. Education was an early focus, here in contrast to other societies, to create reasoned citizens and read the word of God. Yet one can't be a reasoned citizen without being well versed in our country's past.

We hold these truths to be self-evident, that all men are created equal, that they are endowed by their Creator with certain unalienable Rights, that among these are Life, Liberty and the pursuit of Happiness.
US DECLARATION OF INDEPENDENCE

The above words don't exist without the history of brave colonists who risked their life to found a new land and the soldiers who fought to protect them. Our country has a proud narrative and without being taught of its struggles, including a mix of successes and painful losses, our children can't learn to be proud Americans and to understand all that stands with them, as they fight their own individual battles. Life doesn't always come easily but there is solidarity in knowing your values. For most of us our family also has a past that originated beyond these shores yet some brave ancestor brought us here, risking everything they owned for a new start. History gives those sacrifices a context and a proud justification.

We can't reasonably vote without understanding democracy, we can't give context to fiscal challenges without understanding the Great Depression or the Industrial Revolution and we can't understand the fight for equality without the women's movement, the Civil Rights movement or recent immigration battles. People have had to fight to be heard across history and some succeeded. How?

Economics is broken apart in this book, and discussed separately from history but it's still a related concept. We live in a market economy that impacts much in our country. Relatively free market based and capitalistic, our government regulates economic activities to a limited extent. Thus much of our economy is based on an open exchange of services and goods. The implications of such a system play out over business cycles, and the years, booming in the times of high growth or innovation and contracting when they dry up. To prosper in the resulting environment children should be given a good grounding in economics and especially how it relates to historical realities (war tends to lead to inflation from shortages; a contraction of capital, or lending and investment from uncertainty hinders growth).

But most of all, history is a vast collection of stories which in the worst case are upsetting but in the ultimate form show mankind at its best and inspiring. It also provides perspective, clarifying that while times can be harsh they don't last forever and a new dawn breaks, ushering in a newer and better phase.

The republican is the only form of government which is not eternally at open or secret war with the rights of mankind.
THOMAS JEFFERSON

Resources

Get a map or globe. Weekly pick a place to research and discuss.

Talk about your family heritage and get on the computer to research locales, family dishes, historical events and how family members responded or look at pictures.

Read American historical documents or foundational books. These can include: The Declaration of Independence, The Federalist Papers, Common Sense by Thomas Paine, Lincoln's Second Inaugural Address, The Wealth of Nations by Adam Smith or a biography of a founding father or recent president.

Adopt a time period. Learn about it as a family. Discuss. And read some more. We absorb more by this iterative method of learning.

Play the game Civilization, which has been broadly used in schools to help teach history.

Susan Wise Barer wrote a history series, *The Story of the World*, that is better read alone and as a family as, while a fun narrative, it can get overwhelming.

SCIENCE

The whole history of science has been the gradual realization that events do not happen in an arbitrary manner, but that they reflect a certain underlying order, which may or may not be divinely inspired.
STEPHEN HAWKING

Looking at education's development and going back to the Greeks we see a difference in how purely intellectual, meaning of the mind, and material, meaning of the practical world, were judged. Essentially, a small elite group of people had the luxury to study those disciplines such as literature or history, which did not directly impact their ability to use that knowledge to produce concrete work. Material disciplines such as science were used in the furtherance of producing a form of work and were held in less esteem.

This ideology came into play in our own educational system when the masses were educated for basic literacy and to work at unskilled job. Science was considered practical thus of lower value.

Those distinctions no longer apply with respect to science and how it has evolved over recent years, most especially over the past hundred. What had been a limited field somewhat separate from much of our daily intellectual life, being more about how we interact with objects, has vastly expanded. Science now touches us all in both practical and intellectual ways; from the use of computers to the aspirin we take. No field has experienced greater intellectual evolution in the recent past than has science.

And science is the discipline in which many of the high skilled jobs of the future reside. History and literature remain relevant to distinguish the better educated but less so. Science is a vast field now, encompassing medicine, space, engineering, drilling, all devices from phones to cars, cosmetics and on. Almost 220,000 patents were granted in the United States in 2011. This number has been called inflated since the patent office stepped up its pace that year (with the previous high granted in 2006 and totaling about 170,000 patents, still a lot). Science truly is the new frontier.

Science is what you know. Philosophy is what you don't know.
BERTRAND RUSSELL

Yet despite the advances in science and its increased importance in our daily lives, science mastery today is not widely considered a key part of literacy and the curriculum has evolved only minimally. Indeed, numerous experts have advocated for switching the order of science classes, starting with physics before proceeding to chemistry and then biology, instead of the reverse. The latter was originally taught first when science was mostly memorization, many students were farmers who could get practical knowledge from biology teachings and dropped out of school before physics was taught and because biology didn't require math (and many students lacked the necessary math for the other classes thus got at least a little science training while in school). Yet an updated evaluation shows that biology now requires more math proficiency as well as prerequisites taught in both chemistry and physics. More students learn math, and more make it through higher-level science classes when on a college track (and more educated jobs require the related knowledge and skills).

Science has often been taught based on memorization: we memorize the planets, the elements and periodic table and the composition of objects. Yet the most important part of science is not absolute information. We ourselves have directly seen how knowledge can change and evolve as discoveries about the natural world continue. Rather, science is a process, based on making a reasoned hypothesis about something then methodically changing different related elements to test the accuracy of that hypothesis. Facts change, especially as technology allows us to better control and monitor the elements, accelerating new discoveries. Not long ago we all learned that our solar system had nine planets but now with new advances scientists have declared the number to be eight, with Pluto being classified as a dwarf planet. Polio used to wipe out a certain number of children with regular frequency; a vaccine has virtually eradicated the disease in the developed world.

Thus the most important concept a child should learn from science is the ability to formulate a theory and take methodical and reasoned steps to test its accuracy. This logical thought process prepares children for higher-level learning, which typically relies on applying past knowledge in new, novel or more sophisticated ways. Additionally, it trains the mind to formulate a conclusion based on observation and drawing points from those criteria.

Science today is a vast conglomeration of individual disciplines.

The word science comes from the Latin scientia, which simply means knowledge. This quest for learning has driven the experiments of countless scientists and reordered how we all relate to our environment. Children should be encouraged to develop the ability to discern the truth, as science best teaches. How to do so? First observe. A truth can only be judged based upon its ability to replicate itself repeatedly and over time. By observing we can see that the sun does rise every 24 hours only to set later in the day, with the exact times depending on the season and geographical location. The tide comes in on a likewise predictable pattern the world over. What we observe that replicates proves truth.

Science is the systematic classification of experience.
GEORGE HENRY LEWES

Scientists also classify based on predefined criteria. Classifying makes knowledge more manageable and findable. Thus we have species and categories, all of which correspond to specific rules or qualities. There are approximately 20,000 species of butterflies around the world with 750 found in the United States.

Relying more than most subjects on instruments, devices or other forms of technology science also develops the practical ability to evaluate which resources can help discern the answer to a hypothesis or problem. Specificity in their use can have large implications on results thus children must use care with their efforts to follow directions and a reasoned set of steps. Imaging adding eggs to a cake after you've baked it!

While conducting experiments students also need to keep detailed and ordered notes. A small difference or variable can be hugely important in discovery. In 1928 Alexander Fleming, a Scottish doctor, picked up a bacteria culture that he'd left by an open window. Searching for years trying to find a substance to kill bacterial diseases he'd been cleaning up after a like experiment, wanting to wash out his ruined specimen. On this dish he saw something new, likely impacted by the outside substances that had contaminated the dish. In the area around the bacteria the mold had seemingly stopped its normal growth, forming a perimeter beyond which it didn't grow. Fleming had just discovered penicillin, and he did so by carefully observing and noting his meticulous experiments, pausing to question why something new had occurred and what the implications were. The detailed record, in this case internalized in his mind, of how the bacteria tended to grow, meant an anomaly was an immediate standout.

[Science is] the knowledge of consequences, and dependence
of one fact upon another.
THOMAS HOBBES

Persistence is also learned in science as it is in math. Getting to a right answer takes time and careful, often repetitive steps. How different from the immediacy expected in our society today, where we only need "drive through" a line to get food delivered to our car. Fleming wasn't able to mass-produce his discovery of penicillin for about fifteen years after his initial results, as he had to test and retest his mold cultures. To pass the FDA (Food and Drug Administration) approval process for a new drug today an innovator must likewise go through multiple tests and levels of review which can take over ten years and millions of dollars to satisfy. Science doesn't come easily thus it teaches fortitude. The impact of those efforts can change the world immeasurably and thus can be rewarding beyond progress in other fields.

In many public schools science isn't taught until fifth grade or later. Imagine the wonder and mystery those children have lost by beginning this topic so late. Children are natural inquisitors about their physical environment and many of their endless why questions relate to what they observe around them. How many parents take time to explain in the detail of a science class why grass is green or how to measure the distance to the sun?

And to many parents chagrin children are also natural experimenters, willing to destroy kitchen or yard unhesitantly in their quest for an answer. They are seeking the truth about the world around them, utilizing their curiosity and persistence.

As mentioned earlier, science is no longer just something to learn, it's now also one of the best foundations for a solid long-term career. Our world has many ongoing physical challenges and problems to solve and many of the practical solutions will come from science disciplines. And while philosophy continues to find resolutions in its realm challenging, for example what value does a life have, science is now rapidly adding further clarifying information to define and expand on such issues. We can now perform open-heart surgery to save a life and can thus estimate the cost of one life (or hundreds of thousands). Challenges in energy, healthcare, aging, food production and processing, transportation and information technology are continuously being addressed by those savvy in science and that reality will only continue.

These scientists are founding companies and creating jobs; they're even creating industries. Such disciplines are crafting the new roles that didn't exist but a few years ago, from social media marketer to web based software developer or MRI technician. Ongoing learning in science will differentiate employees even among those who aren't starting something new. Being web proficient is no longer a differentiator among college age students but is rather a given. Our children have raised the bar on self-learning and will continue to do so. How many kids above 8 need to be taught to use Instagram or iTunes? With so many industries being science based or dependent the ability to keep learning in this realm creates relevance.

Science based literacy is also now the sign of an educated person. We're all impacted daily by the vagaries of science and people discuss such issues. Be they natural disasters or a friend's recent cancer diagnosis, related terms are part of our everyday vocabulary. Steve Jobs, a scientist, is the main character in a best selling biography and will be in a big budget film. Transformers is a franchise based on science run amuck with an advanced civilization battling to the death (potentially) on earth. Even raising money for a president of the US can be accomplished using social networks and online site, based on advances in software and networking (sciences).

More than just academic, science is also fun. Teach your children not just to memorize facts but to also apply what they learn to the world around them. All things can be questioned and sometimes disproven, from whether the world is flat to how the earth came to be. Inquisitive and often very patient and observant with details, children are natural born scientists.

Resources

Great Minds of Science series of books. These books are available in many libraries or on Amazon.com. Great biographies of pivotal scientists (philosophers and artists), they are targeted at children.

Khan Academy videos: www.khanacademy.org . Salman Khan provides thousands of science instructional videos, growing seemingly by the week, along with a guide as to suggested order. The videos are also available on www.youtube.com.

NASA/Jet Propulsion Lab website: http://www.jpl.nasa.gov/ . This website offers stunning and extensive videos of space and all that NASA uses to touch it, from building spaceships to insights into new discoveries.

Adopt a species, a planet, a plant or any other object you can study with your child.

Make a cake and discuss the chemistry of mixing the ingredients and cooking it at a specific temperature. Try changing the amounts of ingredients.

Watch free courses online from MIT, Stanford and Harvard. Watch a movie about a scientist.

Physicist Stephen Hawking co-wrote two children's stories about space with Lucy Hawking and Garry Parsins: *George's Secret Key to the Universe* and *George's Cosmic Treasure Hunt*.

FINANCIAL LITERACY

Financial literacy is an issue that should command our attention because many Americans are not adequately organizing finances for their education, healthcare and retirement.
RON LEWIS

Many children won't use algebra or geometry in their professional careers. Indeed, as this book has noted before, not enough children will excel at math to the degree that they can major in the related technology or science based college programs needed to develop skills for many future job openings.

I worked as an investment banker, valuing companies and doing simple calculations in my head when asked for insight from clients, often without having access to their company numbers beforehand. Much of what I told clients was based on my core knowledge base of valuation, public stock market conditions and similar companies' trading value. Even though I did math on a daily basis for years I still can't remember how to do certain things on my daughter's fifth grade homework assignments. We forget what we don't use. But math mastery also builds on past application of earlier classes and thus once a child has fallen behind, catching up can prove difficult. And not all children are good at math.

Thus some experts have urged a shift from theoretical math to financial literacy, the latter being a skill all children will need when they grow up and can learn. Financial literacy is essentially the practical math that we all should understand to better manage our life and finances as adults. To master the related skills children will still need to have a thorough understanding of addition, subtraction, multiplication, division, fractions, percentages and money. Moreover, they will also learn about financial markets, investing, economics and budgeting.

The topics included in financial literacy are easy discussions with your children as they often readily grasp the core concepts discussed daily in most newspapers. And the PISA test results show that children whose parents discuss current affairs with them on a regular basis score higher on tests. I suspect that the better test results are due to those conversations teaching how to apply concepts children have learned in school, thus they become doers and solution providers, not just listeners. What does it mean when unemployment trends higher? And what are the practical implications for your family? What is a trade imbalance and how does it impact the price of shoes at Target? Such discussions are a great way to encourage creativity in your child and teach him something practical about how the world works in application not just theory.

Economics is a good starting point to discuss financial literacy. A social science, it addresses the production, distribution and consumption of services and goods. Essentially it covers all transactions across a market in which some form of currency is exchanged. Currency can be defined as money or any other substitute, including a service or product.

Macroeconomics addresses the whole economy and its issues, such as unemployment, growth, monetary and financial policy, inflation and a balance of payments. Microeconomics analyzes the more basic or local elements including individuals, companies, buyers and sellers.

Economics can be defined in many ways, and indeed, is easily expanded to address issues in politics, education, history, public policy and even science as it touches so many disciplines. Adam Smith over 200 years ago termed it as "an inquiry into the nature and causes of the wealth of nations". Children easily grasp the concepts of limited goods and unlimited wants yet don't always understand that a simple credit card swipe won't solve those shortages. An allowance is a good practical introduction to the realities and paying for performance like grades or chores is another.

Economics is a subject that does not greatly respect one's wishes.
NIKITA KHRUSHCHEV

Gary Becker, who has helped expand economics into new areas, provided a great clarification as "combin[ing the] assumptions of maximizing behavior, stable preferences, and market equilibrium, used relentlessly and unflinchingly".

Macroeconomics can sometimes seem conceptual though its implications affect us all. How quickly an economy grows has a direct relationship on the jobs available as higher growth traditionally has signaled an expansion of building and hiring. Inflation is another concept that people see impact their daily existence as costs fluctuate. Predicting inflation can seem difficult though often it's tied to an increase in demand for workers and goods, which drives the prices of both up. Yet global conditions can skew this dynamic, complicating the core issues, and lead to stagflation, with low growth and a rapid increase in prices.

Money is merely a means of value and monetary policy has to do with how much liquidity, or volume of money, a government wants to flow through an economy. Expansionary policies are meant to trigger growth, thus credit is easier and cheaper to get and businesses are encouraged to grow through this ease of borrowing to fund expansion. Alan Greenspan's famous reference to the Federal Reserve's job being "to take away the punch bowl just as the party gets going is somewhat true. The Fed directs monetary (essentially having to do with the supply of money in our economy) policy and common wisdom holds that too much easy money eventually leads to inflation (or market crashes).

Business cycles are thought to follow that logic, in that there is a period of rapid growth with increasing employment. Then, the market reaches a top and further expansion becomes too expensive to justify the decreased demands of a saturated market of employed people working and spending. The contraction in the business activity, to meet the reduced demand of those already consuming at maximum capacity leads to layoffs and a resulting further decrease in spending. Labor becomes cheaper and as people are hired their pent up demand leads to yet the next upswing in the business cycle.

Individual markets are guided by the law of limited supply. Production costs money. In a perfect market no firm dominates and all can compete on mostly equal terms. A monopoly means one company dominates a market and others can't enter or compete within it. Duopoly connotes a similar situation to a monopoly with two companies dominating, while an oligopoly means a small cluster of controlling firms.

Supply and demand realities mean that absent outside influences, such as the government mandating a certain price, the price of a good will be determined by how much is available at various prices and how much consumers want to buy across that range. At a higher price more people want to sell and fewer want to buy, thus an ultimate balance is found matching buyers to sellers.

Inelastic goods are those for which demand is less influenced by price, for example an Andy Warhol original picture. If someone wants the iconic Coke bottles or Marilyn they will pay whatever they can afford to buy it. Elastic goods are the opposite end of the spectrum meaning if I can't get the item at a reasonable price I'll just buy another brand or item. For example, I may prefer Granny Smith apples for a pie but if they're too expensive relative to Fuji apples I'll likely buy the latter (unless I'm a real foodie purist!).

Firms specialize and add other efficiencies to stay price competitive with others.

Markets also refers to the public and private securities exchanges upon which stocks, bonds and other securities are traded daily. These investments are ubiquitous in most retirement plans today. Those who do the related research can hope to make money long term through investing in growing, high quality companies.

Common stocks are an ownership stake in a company. These are traded either on a public exchange, which provides liquidity, or privately, which typically doesn't. Anyone who starts a small company or goes to work for one that allows for stock ownership will eventually deal with the laborious realities of owning a stake in a company with no ready value or easy means of selling shares.

Bonds are debt and are meant to pay back the principal, or face value of the bond, plus a predetermined interest rate (most typically every three to six months). Bonds are often bought or sold at a value different to their face, or payback, value and that price is based on whether interest rates have gone up or down since the bond was issued. If interest rates have gone up the bond is worth less and is typically discounted to make the interest rate competitive with newer bond issuances with higher rates. The opposite happens when rates go down.

Other securities include preferred stock, which has different restrictions than does common stock and often has a dividend. Should a company declare bankruptcy preferred stock holders get paid any leftover funds after bondholders but before common stock holders. Numerous other types of securities exist, from warrants, to options, to complicated hybrids or stripped and remarketed securities. I'll recommend a few books below for those whose children want to explore this complex area further. For now, the importance of these financial instruments is that they raise money for companies to grow. Debt such as bond must be paid back and interest is a constant expense, which limits the cash a company has on hand to fund growth. But the company also gives up no ownership to raise this money.

Stock means ownership and, while the money raised doesn't need to be paid back, the company has sacrificed some of its own upside in giving up this stake.

All securities are legal instruments thus subject to some sort of disclosure and selling document, along with a contract that sets the actual terms. Your child might enjoy paging through a common stock prospectus of a familiar company and these can be found on the Security and Exchange Commission's (SEC) Edgar website. If nothing else, picking a stock to track from Googlefinance.com or Yahoo's stock pages can be fun.

A money market fund is not government insured like a bank account, though security accounts have their own insurance. It's meant to hold a basket of low risk, short-term investments that enable to the fund to maintain a $1.00 value every day and pay a low interest rate. During the financial crisis of 2008 this reality proved impossible for some funds to maintain.

CDs, or certificates of deposit, are held for a fixed time, with penalty for early withdrawal, with a higher interest rate typically paid than on a money market fund. Annuities are an insurance product that pays out a certain pre-set amount, under certain conditions, and for a predetermined time period (which can be until death, or even survive for a beneficiary after death). Annuities can be based on a fixed or variable return, the later payouts being based on the investment returns of the funding pool designated for the contract. Mutual funds are a pool of securities that are chosen based on the fund's objective, which can range from mirroring an index or market, to a set allocation among types of securities. Many investors like mutual funds because they allocate risk among a broad range of stocks and are invested by experts. Fees to buy range from nothing to over 6 percent though all funds charge something for managing the assets.

Children need to be taught more than evaluating the economy and investing their money – children need to budget. They need to save. And they need to decide if someday they want to buy a house. Should they run a business, and that reality seems increasingly likely in our evolving economy, they will need to understand the basics of accounting, payrolls and the realities of payable and receivables. Whether they hire an accountant or not, understanding the flow of money is a necessity for us all.

Insurance covers people from the risk of an unexpected financial loss. Medical insurance will cover our medical bills up to a certain amount. People also typically buy car insurance (to protect us should we get in an accident or our car get stolen), house or rental insurance (to protect our house and the goods inside it) and often life insurance (to protect those dependents who outlive us).

Typical loans taken out today are for houses, cars, a college education and on credit cards. Not only do we need to pay back what we borrow but we also need to pay the lender an interest rate (amount of money) for loaning us funds.

And let's not forget the importance of saving. Numerous studies have shown that young children who delay gratification are more successful as adults. In a much quoted studies young children were left alone with a marshmallow and told they could have that piece and more if they didn't eat it while left unsupervised. The adult then left the room and monitored how long it took before the child ate the marshmallow. Those same children were then tracked as young adults and not surprisingly those who waited the longest were more likely to attend and graduate from college.

Unless our children understand the above basic concepts their financial future is at risk (or at least harder to optimize). Discuss these concepts with them, use the resources suggested below and read related news articles together.

If we don't change, millions of American families are just one medical emergency, or one layoff, away from financial disaster and bankruptcy.
JIM COOPER

Resources

Pick a stock or portfolio of a few stocks to watch. Decide how much to theoretically invest then track your results. Discuss the results and why you think your family lost or made money. Get the company's annual report and 10-K (the former is more of a business overview while the latter focuses more on financial results) from the SEC's Edgar database. Go to the company's website and do further research.

The SEC website with all public company filings is at: <u>www.sec.gov/edgar.shtml</u>

Read *Securing Your Financial Future* by Chris Smith as a family.

Budget for something. Have your children set a financial goal and attach a reward. So, for example, have them pick an achievable item they'd like to buy. Then give them "jobs" to help them earn the money to reach their financial goal.

CREATIVITY

And by the way, everything in life is writable about if you have the outgoing guts to do it, and the imagination to improvise. The worst enemy to creativity is self-doubt.
SYLVIA PLATH

Marty Albertson, Chairman and former CEO of Guitar Center, the largest retailer of instruments in the United States, is a very likeable guy. I met him at UCLA where he was speaking in front of a group of MBA students in a class taught by our mutual friend ex-mayor Richard Riordan. Marty was consistently among the students' favorite speakers over a few year period. He was able to connect broadly because he brought application into theory, providing context and a new perspective on clichéd ideas. He engaged openly, self deprecating and always insightful.

Initially wanting to produce records, his love of music led him to a sales job at Guitar Center, who wisely promoted him (eventually) to the top office. He expanded the stores internationally and achieved true cult appreciation with the acquisitions of some legendary guitars (available not just for bragging rights but for customers to purchase).

At a certain level everyone with whom you'll be competing will be smart and hard working. Creativity is the only thing that will set you apart, he told the students. For me the statement was a monumental shift in perspective. We are often trained to be better or work harder but those around us are often proceeding to do exactly the same thing. In a field like investment banking or corporate law this extreme can lead to the insane, with work hours that trend up over 80 or more per week. But is more better when everyone is delivering more? I think Marty put his finger on the pulse of success. Do something different to stand out, and that requires creativity.

An example he gave was buying Eric Clapton's Blackie guitar for $2 million dollars. Then, after discussing it with Clapton and getting his buy in, Guitar Center created 25 copies which they sold for $50,000 each, selling out within ten minutes (covering most costs and getting a cool, valuable guitar as well). That's creative!

But the person who scored well on an SAT will not necessarily be the best doctor or the best lawyer or the best businessman. These tests do not measure character, leadership, creativity, perseverance.
WILLIAM JULIUS WILSON

Albertson made one other point that has haunted me. He urged people to find something at which they can be number two or three. He asserted that aiming for the number one spot is too tough, and can sometime be more dependent on luck than any other factor (note, Guitar Center has 40 percent market share!). But if you are number two or three in any career you will still do very well indeed, without having to focus most of your efforts on retaining your top billing.

And if we think about the top people or companies in any profession they really do bring something special into their efforts. Whether it's a unique perspective or glass that comes to the edge of a smart phone like the iPhone these people or companies are just different from their competitors, and beyond simply better. Even the big box stores when they first introduced their warehouses, inventory software, scale and rock bottom prices were bringing something new to the market. Each great artist or innovator is likewise unique. Distinctive adds value across all disciplines, not just the ones typically considered creative.

All religions, arts and sciences are branches of the same tree.
ALBERT EINSTEIN

Creativity can be tough to define, and attempts easily fall into cliché. Researching various sources I kept bumping into a few truisms. First, to be truly creative you need to develop a broad knowledge base from which to build your ideas. Creative visions most often come from someone who draws across disciplines and discerns a new solution. Thus creativity isn't pulling from a void but rather drawing order from disorder. The truly creative see the world where it's going and not where it has already been. I remember reading advice years ago about how if you meet someone like that follow them very closely.

But does creativity have to be widely accepted or recognized, or to succeed at its end game to be truly creative? I think that this question is important for our quick fix society with its expectation of overnight success or easy answers. Most success stories take place over time, encompassing iteration after iteration, or at least letting the market catch up before they become mainstream. But long-term successful creativity at the very least is eventually more than an idea. Indeed, people place too much importance oftentimes on ideas, not acknowledging that it's the application or execution of that core concept which ultimately determines success (or, to rephrase, talk is cheap).

As with a lot of disciplines, one can only develop a new skill set with ongoing practice and by risking failure. Those who are too careful don't push the limits in trying to define new solutions or seeing outside the accepted realms. When I write I find the words simpler to type when I know that they're safe and don't risk embarrassing me. Yet the writers I love explore tough issues and display vulnerability, bordering on the uncomfortable. How to learn that abandon when so many, including our own critical minds, will judge?

I had a conversation along these lines with a friend of mine, Kate Register. We both lived near the beach in Santa Monica and went for walks along the nearby bike path, among the surfers, bicyclists and homeless. Seagulls fluttered overhead as we walked and that random cloud broke our blue sky. I got to know her over time as we ran into each other repeatedly on that concrete path, each lost in our own reflection.

Kate has a wide, ready smile with the blonde hair that so characterizes this city (a cliché). A mom and an artist, she's managed to juggle these two diverse realities and has started getting gallery showings for her work (which is lovely). Interestingly, Kate grew up as the daughter of a very successful artist, John Register, and all her siblings likewise found their way into artistic professions.

John started out in advertising with a background in design but then got ill and couldn't work the regular hours of his job. He began to paint, stark modernist images that in my mind are very reflective of a certain American sensibility.

One morning Kate and I were talking about clichés and how quickly a writer, artist or creator can bump into the expected because it's easier and safer. Kate's work is softer than her father's, and draws more from nature and the surroundings of our sheltered canyon. We discussed how hard it was not to just paint a beach, because anyone could paint a beach or even take a photo. Kate and John's work both draw from the everyday so avoiding the standard version of something is key to making the result iconic or moving. We agreed that to do so one needed to draw or express the essence without overwhelming an image in clutter.

That's creativity: discerning the essence be it in a shape or a distinguishing feature. A wonderful F. Scott Fitzgerald characterization stated that a character liked new friends better than old because they hadn't yet heard her stories. Iconic and memorable.

Kate also explained that the children in her family were never pushed to do art. However, numerous supplies were always scattered around the house and available for those who wanted them. And her father would frequently pull the kids from what they were doing, even halting their car to paint something that caught his eye. He'd point out to the children what he saw and why it struck his fancy. They learned to see and discern the essence, those distinctive elements that identify an object.

So Kate picked up a paintbrush and began to paint, but not what the rest of us see but rather what her father taught her to pull from an object, that which struck her alone.

There is also a collaborative aspect to creativity. People often feed off one another. Grouping together is the best way to pool a diverse set of perspectives and knowledge. I'm amazed at the theater program at my children's school, which the kids love. The teacher, Brent Vernon, writes the plays based on common fairy tales but changes them to bring in the school itself. The children brainstorm with him and the result is magical, if a bit silly sometimes. But the parents and children are enthralled by the result. Parodying a talk show interviewing fairy tale characters the children wrote the ads. They had one for a twenty-four hour energy drink guaranteed to work that had the audience (of parents) in tears of laughter.

Creativity is fun, funny and the ultimate form of play. And remember that play is serious work for children as it is one of the key ways they test concepts and learn. Moreover, creativity is all about taking risks. It's about learning and puttering around with options. There will always be people that are smarter, work harder, know more important people or who are more talented. No one can think exactly like your child. Help them develop that voice, as it's the only competitive advantage no one can take away.

Creativity can be taught and children have an advantage in this realm so you only need encourage and not stifle it. Spend time reading, drawing or even just going for a walk and observing. Discuss what you see and brainstorm with respect to the qualities. Teach your children to trust their own impressions of things. Learn to discern the essence of an object, person or place in time.

Resources

Stage plays at home. Draw. Read fairy tales or science fiction together.

Smash (a brand) scrapbooks and an instant camera, then perhaps stickers, markers and crayons. Create!

Sign your children up for a class in a creative discipline. Don't criticize.

Read *Where Good Ideas Come From* by Steve Johnson, a look at creativity. A lighter option is *Steal Like an Artist: 10 Things Nobody Told You About Being Creative* by Austin Kleon.

Create a family story. Craft a book...even if you don't feel confident putting the words to paper. Define chapters and what they will cover. Then write down what happened with a twist of make believe and nonsense. If someone draws then add pictures to story. Get the book published. Kinkos or www.createspace.com are two places that are relatively inexpensive.

ENTREPRENEURSHIP, INNOVATION AND RISK TAKING

Life in Silicon Valley is different. The area is possessed by the magic of new industries continually blooming and greatly impacting lives around the world. With an infrastructure in place of smart people, funding and support the region is a great example of what our country is capable of creating. We can't even touch on the products and industries that have been built with either the expertise or funds of those in the area.

Composed of rolling green hills and towering buildings that have taken over the orchards of past times, traffic moves until it hits hilly San Francisco, otherwise known as *The City*. People work hard and the bordering support systems never seem to grow fast enough for the growth of creative people.

Silicon Valley is also the land of opportunity for educated immigrants. It's estimated that 24 percent of firms in Silicon Valley are run by Chinese or Indian immigrants. 14 percent are foreign owned and over 60 percent of immigrants in the area plan to start their own business. The American born prosper on a relative basis as well when compared to slower growth and less innovative regions. The area typically ranks as having the top highest per capita income in the United States or just directly below that number, depending on the year. Per capita income is $66,000 with the median being about $86,000 (the latter number is skewed by high incomes among top earners).

By background I advised growing companies, including in the technology and Internet based industries, but not solely. I also worked with media, healthcare and consumer retail. Sometimes people have a misconception that they don't have what it takes to start something, if only because the media highlights the billion dollar companies like Facebook and not the corner store that provides fresh produce in the inner city.

Anyone can start a company. Many will fail, but some will succeed.
Anyone who starts one will have an interesting life.
TIM DRAPER

Starting a company is hard but it can also be somewhat formulaic, which is why serial entrepreneurs and venture capitalists can repeat their successes (but only those who master the steps...which most people don't).

When beginning to write this chapter I decided to reach out to someone who funds new companies thus recognizes those qualities in the founders that early on predict success. My premise was that those who can innovate and think creatively, then pair that with hard work, can create their own jobs and don't need to worry about finding one (a parent's dream?).

I met Tim Draper, of Draper Fisher Jurvetson right after he spoke at a Milken Institute State of the State Conference discussing California. He'd given a focused talk on innovation and entrepreneurship in front of an audience of about 1,000 people. Tim was direct and practical, with solutions not just sound bites. His venture capital firm is among the most successful in Silicon Valley, having invested in companies ranging from Skype to Baidu, and across a broad range of groundbreaking industries. He is also a third generation venture capitalist; with a grandfather who founded one of the first venture firms in Silicon Valley. And Tim is passionate about education, creating BizWorld which provides K-12 schools with a curriculum in entrepreneurship and business creation, and having served on the California board of education. Recently, Draper launched Draper University, a program in entrepreneurship for those in the 18 to 24 age range to foster a strong set of values along with practical curriculum. I'd urge any parent to encourage their child to apply.

Tim is also well over six feet tall (or seems to be) with a direct gaze and seeming sense of utter fearlessness. With a BS in electrical engineering from Stanford and Harvard MBA Draper is also brilliant and on Wikipedia is credited with arguably being the creator of "viral marketing". Having funded countless innovative companies he's also an expert in guiding those starting something great and building lasting value.

Asked about entrepreneurship and what qualities set apart those whom are able to create and develop innovative solutions his response was equally direct. With respect to entrepreneurs he stated, "we look for enthusiasm, flexibility, open-mindedness and determination." He also stated, surprising me, that experience is overrated, asserting that his firm had a lot of success with first time entrepreneurs. The quality most lacking in those with whom he meets is the willingness to try new things.

Career paths have changed over the past ten years, with those stable trajectories falling by the wayside of mass personnel cuts and dissolving industries. Asking Draper about whether it's now relatively less risky to start a business he agreed but pointed out that success in doing so is just as difficult as ever. He asserted that people now need to think of multiple careers going forward and added that companies are also challenged, with employees being less "lifelong" and more "as long as there isn't something better."

Thinking differently and willing to explore, children are creative until we tell them to stop and become more practical. Speaking with one, Jack, he mentioned the pressure that adults put on their charges, making a dialogue too tense to continue. Your children may be more open to the qualities asserted as most important for innovation by a top investor than their parents are. Let your child explore his passions.

Indeed, when I asked Draper his advice for his own children it didn't deviate from his advice for other people's kids: *I advise them to pursue their interests and figure out how to create a profitable company around them.* His daughter, Jesse Draper, did just that, using an estimated $50,000 to launch her show, "The Valley Girl Show" four years ago. Syndicated and partnered, it's expanding rapidly and features unconventional interviews with entrepreneurs. Initially wanting to be an actress she combined her love for being on camera with a novel show concept, got funding and began shooting video.

So how does one launch a company, whether of the sort to get venture funding or not? How do you guide your child to begin thinking along these lines, and to create jobs not just search for one? First, understand the related steps.

The first step is to innovate. Draper claims that true innovation is: *something that people want. More convenient, more fun, cheaper, faster, better performing. Something that can help us all get more done with less effort.* What can you do that is different, better or more convenient? Even cheaper? Innovative isn't just inventing the Internet. Simply delivering cars or dry cleaning in a new neighborhood is enough. Creating better ice cream or cupcakes. Delivering last minute babysitting is enough. So is inventing social networking. Kids are great at innovating.

What is your child doing that is different, distinctive, new or better?

Next ask how defensible is the related product or service? What protects it from another company just copying then executing better? Is there something proprietary or patented? Unique content. Innovative technology. Relationships. A different and more efficient form of energy. All add value.

Then one must look at the people surrounding them. Years ago it seemed that having a bigger mission was less important. A clear path to revenues and profitability was enough to incent people to pour their heart and soul into a new venture. Increasingly, and with the younger generation, a deeper mission is valued. I won't argue that it's the most important thing but Google picked "do no evil" as their mission statement (versus something more traditionally corporate) for a reason.

And add the best people to a venture, whether based on a mission statement or core product/service. Gaining the support of a solid team validates the company, showing that quality people believe in it and the company's mission. If a company can't get a following it either isn't selling itself well enough or isn't founded on a strong idea. A good friend of mine only invests in new ideas after showing them to competitors or co-investors and gauging their reaction. There always exists a new idea. Who believes in yours?

Children should begin developing a reputation for accomplishment and small ones are perfect; let them master a piano piece or take a tough class. That risk of failure and resulting success at mastering a challenge will begin teaching them to take risks and aim high.

David Karp, the young founder of Tumblr, is a great example of the above principals. After his freshman year at Bronx Science, one of New York's most prestigious high schools, he leveraged his love of technology into an internship at Frederator Studios. The company is an animation production company with a web element and a seasoned founder, Fred Seibert who'd worked at MTV and Hanna-Barbera.

Never much enthused with school he thrived at Frederator. At the end of the summer Karp's mother sensed his reluctance to leave the internship and offered to home school him so he could continue. The 15-year-old Karp jumped at the option. At 16 he became head of product at a new start-up, UrbanBaby.com, and was given equity after he completed an engineering project in 4 hours that was expected in a few days. As success built on success and Karp's reputation (and one can guess confidence) built he founded Tumblr, a blogging tool and social network, raising $750,000 from a prestigious group of investors. He never earned his high school diploma. Not advocating dropping out of school, the story illustrates what a child/teenager can accomplish when allowed to explore their imagination. Karp is perhaps exceptional but he isn't alone. Kids create, and modern technology gives them the tools to do so at increasingly younger ages.

We're all judged on what we've done before. As mentioned above, Draper noted that experience isn't the key to success but rather other personal characters are. And past actions, no matter how young, highlight whether you possess those qualities.

What is the market and can it support the vision? For someone starting a company that will seek outside funding, including from the venture community, a large market of hopefully a billion or more in market size is ideal. If you take outside investment you risk losing control of your company and your idea; smaller visions can often lead to greater control. For some people, thinking smaller, at least additionally, and keeping control is more important than the quick growth outside funding can add. Scale and aspire to the company you want to create not to what the media or society pushes. A doctor's office, specialized retailor or tutoring service can be a perfect business for the person who runs it with passion.

Teach your child to impact true change; those with good ideas will find opportunities. Remember to think about not just what you're doing but also why. Great visions usually tie with big change and a glaring need. Solving the energy shortage. Fixing education. Connecting people globally. Funders also like these types of opportunity in that, while they offer the biggest risk, they also offer the biggest potential reward. A ten times return is hoped for in any venture investment, but lower if the risk is likewise less. The ballpark returns come from those rare investments that change how we all interact on a daily basis. Not everyone needs to hit a homerun but at least decide beforehand what you're aiming to hit.

Begin introducing the concept of a business plan, for your child's own life if he isn't the type to start a company. People need to develop such a focus on where they want to go if they want to arrive at a specific destination. And add a financial plan, be it for college or for starting a company. We won't always estimate right and over time our goals may evolve but at least at any given time we know what we're doing and how we plan on paying for it. Financial plans often end up being wrong but ultimately what mattered in projecting the future was that someone understood and accounted for all potential contingencies. Homework and common sense matter more for an early stage company, or in life, than does accuracy. Life surprises often but outcomes favor those who have planned.

What if your child really does start a company and it begins to scale? At a certain size taking either equity capital or debt financing makes sense as growth costs money. But the pressure to be right and perform also grows, as they should. A company now scaling has built a hopefully more sustainable and predictable path. Their obligations have grown and they need to financially meet them but they're also more able to estimate the demands.

Inherent in the financial plan is having a clear path to profitability and a breakdown of reasonable, or unreasonable, expenses (for a person or a company).

Have a context and a grasp of where your venture fits in the bigger scheme of things. In advising a child on future career opportunities we all make a judgment call as to the future, be it from a start-up or more established industry. Find a mentor to advise them on their thoughts or business. When Lauren had an idea for a necklace I had her speak to a friend of mine who designs and manufactures jewelry. Lauren ultimately took a pass but she first explored the idea and learned what it would take to design and where it would fit into a larger industry.

And be optimistic.

The press might have you believe that this is the best
we can get, and that things are getting worse. But
the reality is that the world continues to get better.
TIM DRAPER

I agree that the world is getting better, regardless of what we read in the papers. There was a time before TiVo, Starbucks, the Internet, electricity, running water and cars. We should savor the advances and not complain that sometimes life isn't perfect. Our children faces monumental challenges but also opportunities.

The nuts and bolts of innovation are simple but the implementation is difficult. Like Icarus, who sought to fly up to the sky but bound his feather wings with wax only to fall to the earth once it melted closer to the sun, we all must aspire to a height that suits our skill and ambitions. But everyone can start a company, and thus create a job dependent upon their own work and passions not the mood of their employer. The worst job I had was one where I watched my boss make bad decision after bad decision, impervious to input, until our office could no longer afford to stay open. In creating your own business you rise and fall on your own decisions and judgments, not relying on those to whom you report. Do well and you create a job not only for yourself but also for many others?

I think it is all about human imagination. Jobs will go where
imaginations go. Whether curing disease, inventing new vehicles,
finding new sources of energy, or finding new sources of entertainment,
opportunities follow those who drive them.
TIM DRAPER

Not content to speak with a funder, no matter how well respected, I also called a serial entrepreneur, Kris Duggan. Duggan sold his first company for seven figures in his twenties then went on to take a sales job at WebEx for around $50,000 a year because he felt he needed to learn the key skills a larger more organized company could teach. He's worked for seven start-ups.

> *Learn on other people's dimes not your own.*
> **KRIS DUGGAN**

Those lessons learned were what propelled his most recent company growth trajectory.

> *You must decide if you're investing in yourself or cashing out of yourself.*
> **KRIS DUGGAN**

Duggan started Badgeville, in 2010 with a total of four employees. According to Duggan, the company *makes it possible for any web or mobile publisher to reward users for behaviors that align with business metrics — site visits, pages read, photos uploaded, comments posted, links shared, and more.*

Badgeville has grown to a projected $10 to $20 million of revenues for 2012, 70 employees and adding one or two on average a week and around 165 corporate customers. He noted that looking back it *was hard to see how the dots connect.* But they do. His advice to parents guiding young future entrepreneurs was first not to rush but rather learn. An early company start, followed by a more formal company training ground, partnered with his extensive domain expertise to create Badgeville, recently called by Forbes one of America's most promising companies. They also concurrently closed a $25 million funding round.

He notes that ambition, drive, relentlessness, creativity and passion are important for founders in the early stages of starting a company. Hard qualities to define, he mentioned the ability to see the world in a new way and emotional intelligence. At a latter stage operational, leadership and organizational skills take over, perhaps why some who start aren't great at running a later version of their own company. To apply this distinction, Duggan's past experience in founding a company helped get Badgeville off the ground; his time at WebEx enabled him to scale the company to large corporate customers.

Much as stories like his are romanticized, he pointed out that in business to business software companies, such as his own, knowledge of your business creates something the corporate customers will buy, which leads to funding. *Sell or die,* he stated, essentially meaning that without customers you're dead. Once his client base started rolling in he didn't need to work at funding but rather investors found him.

Note that many companies are advised to focus on fundraising early on; Duggan reversed that process, building up a solid customer base first to tempt investors and succeeded.

> *Pitch your customers before you pitch investors.*
> **KRIS DUGGAN**

To further prove the point of entrepreneurs seeing the world differently he believes that there are too many companies being founded, due to the excess of capital, lower expense to start, changed risk parameters with more traditional careers having gotten riskier and the well publicized success stories.

He also pointed out that while not a consumer products expert, those related success stories were more often hit driven and tapped a well networked demographic or even luck unlike most businesses, such as his own in corporate software, which made a start-ups seem easier than it often is. While anyone can win at gambling, long-term success depends on discipline and experience. Thus he urged younger start-up hopefuls not to hurry but rather to learn.

And know your domain.

Duggan is also an approachable founder who frequently mentors others. A father of two boys he encourages them to find whatever career will make them happy (not rich, please note) but expects that at least one will follow him into entrepreneurship. First, as befits his counsel to get experience before starting a company, as that foundation is important to long-term success, he also wants his boys to get a solid traditional education before they embark on professional endeavors.

In sum, know what you're doing before you start a company.

Below I have two checklists as guidance to simplify some of the concepts discussed above. The first is the characteristics your child should be born with or develop if they want to succeed as an entrepreneur. The second is a brief overview of the steps required to start most businesses.

The initial list is pulled from the website of Mark Suster whose blog is www.bothsidesofthetable. The comments after the traits I wrote. Mark founded two successful companies then went to work for his venture funders, GRP Partners, in Los Angeles. He frequently tops surveys of most respected or trusted venture capitalists and his blog has built a regular and extensive following both because he gives honest feedback and is a likeable person. The second I wrote based on years of experience guiding companies.

Mark Suster's list of the qualities of an entrepreneur:

1. **Tenacity**: an inborn quality, tenacity can also be taught. Let your child learn how to hear no so that they can learn to find way to transform it into yes. Stated another way, letting your child always get what they want without working for it won't build a tenacious adult.
2. **Street smarts**: as a parent learning street smarts means letting your child get beaten up a bit. Too sheltered children can't learn to coolly assess a situation or person accurately.
3. **Ability to pivot**: tenacity is good but too much stubbornness doesn't allow for accepting that one approach isn't working and trying another. Pivoting is the Silicon Valley term for turning failure into success by trying a new way.
4. **Resiliency**: this characteristic is both inborn and developed. Don't be too tough on your kids when they make early mistakes; let them learn from the decision and bounce back. Giving up is easier when you're allowed to fail; resiliency develops when you know that you can fight another day.

5. **Inspiration**: passion and creativity develop inspiration. Your child should be encouraged to run free with early interests so he can learn and should be allowed to develop and grow constructively.

6. **Perspiration**: nothing beats hard work in life. Just make sure you're working at something that can help you achieve your goals. Teach your children to recognize the difference.

7. **Willingness to accept risk**: Duggan had a great point about risk. All careers now entail risk, even those that used to be safer. Let your child fail at small things so they can learn to try bigger endeavors.

8. **Attention to detail**: Investment banking is a profession that requires rigorous detail orientation. Everything matters; teach your child that.

9. **Competitiveness**: not all children are competitive; not all children need to be entrepreneurs. Don't force this quality if it isn't there.

10. **Decisiveness/gets stuff done**: many people don't like to make decisions or take action. In part, doing either is an inborn predilection. But you can develop this quality by expecting it in your children. Make them decide and make them follow up.

11. **Domain experience**: ultimately, we do better at things we know well. In allowing your child to develop their passions and interest they will be pre-disposed to learn about it.

12. **Integrity**: this quality is addressed elsewhere in the book. Once your reputation is gone it's almost impossible to regain. Good people choose to work with those who possess integrity. Children are born with it; don't waste that natural talent in your child.
    From: http://www.bothsidesofthetable.com/entrepreneur-dna/

Checklist For Starting a Business

I included the below not expecting that we should put our children to work and set them up running a business. But note, I don't object to children doing so and many are. Rather, the list is a fun exercise in brainstorming. Develop a business sense and entrepreneurial thinking in your children. Who knows, one of the ideas may turn into a viable business.

1. Can you afford to not have guaranteed income for a time period as the business gets off the ground? What sort of parental support can you expect and what age is the kid!
2. What is your idea? How does it improve over your competitor's offerings? Why do people need it? Come up with a one or two line-inspiring summary of your business.
3. How well do you know the business area? The competitors? The market? Learn it all better than anyone else. How does your experience boost your ideas?
4. What resources do you need to produce your product or provide your services? What do you need to do to get them?
5. Research your competition and market.
6. Develop a business plan. A business plan is more than a time sink. When we are forced to write down our ideas we hone in on our strategy and notice where our arguments for going forward are weak or non-existent. Having a plan makes discipline and ongoing evaluation more realistic. Reviewing the plan helps you monitor whether or not you are succeeding at reaching milestones.
7. Who can help you build the business? Contact them.
8. Will you eventually need to raise money? Suster characterizing venture funding as being for rocket ship companies only. He means that such funding is only for those companies who can and are scaling very quickly.
9. Do you need to hire help or services?
10. What is your marketing plan?
11. Partner if possible. Who makes sense from that standpoint?
12. Get working.

In the real world, someone who starts a company would be constantly evaluating the results of their efforts and adapting (or pivoting) as new data or results dictate. Children do start businesses (a few locally are one that sells homemade lollypops and another distributing stationary online).

Risky, yes? But Draper claimed that most people can learn to take risks, perhaps starting with small ones then build up to larger ones as their initial efforts pay off or at least teach them enough to try again, but in a slightly different manner. Starting a business doesn't always lead to success or riches but today it is still one of the few ways anyone can still get rich or at least have more control over their destiny.

Colleges are increasingly offering courses in start-ups and entrepreneurship. According to the National Business Incubators Association about one third of the estimated 1,250 American business incubators are located within a university; not all are useful. Some notable examples include: TechArb at the University of Michigan, Duke, Syracuse, Northern Kentucky University and the University of Pennsylvania. MIT, Stanford and others have competitive classes or seminars that require a student to actually launch a business during the semester or applicable time period.

Resources:

Bizworld.org – free child focused curriculum for developing business creation or financial expertise. The resources are meant for teachers and pupils but are easily used by parents.

Draper University – a hands on and group oriented effort to train entrepreneurs. The curriculum is both values oriented and proactive. Devoted to four sessions of ten weeks each the student body is internationally diverse and includes students mostly between 21 and 24. The curriculum includes guest speakers, group activities/ and even physical efforts. Initially aiming to pilot with around 25 students the ultimate goal is to host about 150.

Thiel Fellows – each year entrepreneur, investor and billionaire Peter Thiel accepts roughly 20 kids (www.thielfellowship.org/connect), giving them $100,000 each and support to start a company. The first set of fellows was funded in 2011, with one already cashing out in a company sale by 2012. Past fellows have demonstrated very technology or science heavy ideas for new businesses.

The Art of the Start by Guy Kawasaki. This book is really only for older kids (it's targeted at adults) but is the classic, simple primer on starting a business. Kawasaki was an early employee at Apple and has since gone on to advise on innovation and business building.

TECHNOLOGY

Any sufficiently advanced technology is indistinguishable from magic.
ARTHUR C. CLARKE

I'm a techno-geek. Having said that, I do everything wrong that has a technological aspect at least the first time. My children are better at many forms of technology than I am though I set up my home network (with a lot of time on the Cisco and Verizon help lines...perhaps the longest calls in their history).

Having grown up in and out of Silicon Valley with a dad who spent his career in the high-tech industry, I grew up getting calculators each year for my birthday but my children get iPads. Numerous friends and acquaintances started companies using their geek backgrounds and did phenomenally well. Thus, I feel strongly about the importance of bringing technology into your child's life. They will not do as well professionally without that easy and early grasp of technology, which quickly turns into an instinctive feel and confidence. There is a solid reason why children are called digital natives versus those older generations who only immigrated into the related world.

But what do I mean about technology? Certainly not unlimited YouTube, Spotify during homework and video games? Well, not exactly but let me tell you one story before I reveal where I'm headed.

One day my seven year old wanted to learn about Adolf Hitler. I don't know why, did consider it odd but he's persistent and I don't know a lot about Hitler, or at least not in terms I wanted to share with a seven year old. I decided to look for videos on YouTube not wanting to just quote death statistics and battles. The top video for Hitler turned out not to be a dry black and white speech but rather a color one made by

Nice Peter, with millions of views. If you've never seen *Epic Rap Battles of History* and have an issue with bad language don't. If you're curious anyway watch Adolf Hitler versus Darth Vader, Season One. Then perhaps watch the cameo appearance by "Stephen Hawking" in Season Two. My son became obsessed with the next video in the series he saw, as suggested by YouTube in the side bar. What parent can object to Albert Einstein versus Stephen Hawking (a lot, by the way)?

Jason now wants to be a physicist on the weekend (his weekday schedule will be filled with video game design). He's already been to his school library to ask for books on famous physicists and read those. They didn't have many so he's added Benjamin Franklin, Galileo, Marie Curie and a slew of other biographies. Stephen Hawking he considers the most interesting physicist and he's taken an interest in genetics, but Albert Einstein is his favorite.

All from a gag video on YouTube. It made physics fun.

So, obviously I'm a fan of technology.

Earlier I'd discussed the prevalence and importance of technology in our children's lives today. Additionally, they are collaborating and sharing on social networks and via texts. Many companies require video resumes (which are simple and easy to make using Flip cameras and even I can grasp iMovie from Apple). Pictures are customized and shared, blogs are increasingly easy to set up and use and the kids love devices.

Asking one boy in the above mentioned Alliance Schools why he transferred to a charter school when he lived only two blocks from his old school he said, "the laptops" and held out his MacBook.

So, again, what do I mean about technology? Your kids should be learning deep literacy. Coding would be great but at the very least they need to be proficient in various software, hardware and social networks. According to Laird Malamed, who has helped design top games at Activision and teaches at USC:

Learning computer programming is more than the process of learning code words. In fact, many of the undergraduate computer science programs do not focus on learning a language, but instead the focus

is on the logic, the use cases and the system. This systems thinking is
great priming for kids at any age. In fact, the process of writing an
essay is very similar to a computer program. You set out to achieve
something (a thesis or code task) and then support that (with evidence
or programming modules). Plus learning to program is fun and gives
kids a sense of mastery.
LAIRD MALAMED

Active thinkers and learners follow a process which James Paul Gee, in *What Video Games Have to Teach Us About Literacy and Learning*, terms as automation, adaption, new learning and then more automation. Essentially, skills learned become unconscious, thus automated. These unconscious skills need to be brought back into the conscious realm so that they can be applied to other problems, thus reinforcing the learning. Technology, and video games, train children in this process. Gee states:

In any case, I have already made my own position clear: passive learn-
ing – rather than active, critical learning – will not lead to much power
and empowerment in the contemporary world, however much it may
suit one for a low-level service job. Mastering literacy or math as a set of
routinized procedures without being able to use these procedures proac-
tively within activities that one understands and for the accomplishment
of one's own goals will not lead to learners who can learn quickly and
well as they face new semiotic domains throughout their lives.

Indeed, video games specifically but also along with other technologies, teach literacy beyond the standard print based reality we all know. Instead, such learning expands into what Gee terms, "semantic domains" which involve symbolic representational understanding, often intermingled with print, and more relevant in our technology based and global world. According to Gee,

Semiotic domains are human cultural and historical creations that
are designed to engage and manipulate people in certain ways. They

attempt through their content and social practices to recruit people to think, act, interact, value, and feel in certain specific ways.

Or, people need to learn in systems not just language.

And technology doesn't just mean electronics and extends to providing a key to the jobs of the future. Software programs are increasingly substituting in automating all repetitive tasks including things like writing (written by employed software engineers). Advances in sciences are continuing to speed up, as technology enables previously unimagined advances such as decoding DNA. From space, to medical devices, to drugs, to neuroscience and beyond we depend on technology. Even manufacturing jobs now require extensive knowledge and skills in this competency. Basic online search is a fundamental required skill. Content, historical and current, is now often best found online and children need to master its order. Ideally, they will also learn networks and device management.

To me, understanding what technology my children should be learning is one of the hardest areas to evaluate which is in part complicated by how little technology they use in school, making this area more media than education in my mind.

Already computer literate, as with most children, mine take to technology like fish in water. They can YouTube and Google search like pros, understand Wikipedia (I taught that to my son by looking up his favorite Mario Brothers characters on the site and he was sold) and prefer word processing to handwriting class. Both work iPads and smart phones, games and game consoles, remotes and radios easily. That isn't traditional "education".

I read today an almost joke article on one of my technology industry blogs about the one non-programming CEO of a start-up (inferring that the rest all code). How high do you want your child to go? This question isn't flippant. I pay a lot of money to get my web work done yet am sure some of what they're doing isn't that hard. No, let me correct, I watched a picture get added to one of my website backgrounds then resized and the whole process took less than two minutes, mostly perfectionist resizing. My answer to that reality was to hire someone a few times a month to teach my son basic programming, video making (with a Flip camera) and video game design.

Today we can raise money online with Kickstarter (crowdsourcing with video required). Our whole history can be researched online. If someone does a search for your name what do they find? Your children will eventually need to address that issue as well. That digital record should to be more than a few silly pictures on a social media site. As I addressed above in discussing our children's world many of them are creating websites including blogs. Some are starting companies online, usually though not always parent directed.

Social networks are marketing as much as they are interacting with friends. Recently we heard a big outcry about some potential employers wanting Facebook passwords to research job applicants. For now that request has been discredited. But I've been asked by a potential business contact for a Facebook – not Linkedin – friend request before they'd even speak with me. What do you think they did with that request? (Answer – checked out who I really am, not who I say I am). Children need to eventually use these networks to build a contact base and presence, potentially even for marketing themselves or their products.

Children who growing up playing video games all Saturday and put computers together, component-by-component, often got very good jobs when they grew up and some started companies and got rich. Technology is a career not just entertainment and getting hired requires depth in that commitment.

The full package is required to work at a place like Activision. Passion, ability to speak and write, clear specialness that shines through. It's sort of like what the top schools like for in freshman applicants. Often, the referrals are key because they can talk to these points better than an interview can. However, project work - in school or other work - really helps. I'm amazed when candidates come in and cannot explain why a game they made turned out how it did. Where is the introspection? And I've had ones who had not played our biggest games before the interview.

I would tell my own kid to be passionate about something. In many ways, it does not matter what. However, to work in games, they

have to be a key part for sure. Passion not just about something but
about doing something. So, when you see a comic fan dress up for a
convention, sure that can be seen as nerdy, but it is also engagement. I
bet that kid can write 20 pages about the latest plot of the Avengers
better than they can explain Moby-Dick.
LAIRD MALAMED

Thus I put together two lists: one includes the technology children must master and the second adds in those technologies that children headed into a more tech savvy career path should add (or really, honestly, all).

The technologies children need to learn before college

1. Computer mastery not simple ability to use a computer. They need to be familiar with numerous programs such as Word, Excel, PowerPoint and the list of Google options (maps, search, docs or whatever it morphs into). Dropbox is also useful. Being able to effectively search and research a topic is key.
2. Mac familiarity, not just PC. I'd add iMovie personally.
3. Video making. Pick your camera and pick your editing and compression technology (Adobe, Apple, Microsoft for compression).
4. Skype; Facetime (iPad calls on camera).
5. Tablets and smartphones. Textbooks are already migrating there and they are so very simple.
6. They should be able to make Powerpoint presentations.
7. Simple social networking skills are key. With a simple email address your children can get on most related sites and set up a profile. They need to be counseled, as with sex education, before they get in trouble not after. I'm shocked at how trusting my children can be, even after warnings, with respect to the Internet. Facebook, Twitter and all other social networks are personal brands and children should treat them that way. They provide an amazing ability for teenagers to begin establishing who they are in life, what they stand for and

to begin building networks. Some of my early Twitter follows and followers have vast numbers of followers merely because they were on the service early. I'm a pretty good networker but the options available for children today will enable my kids (and yours) to leave me in the dust. Don't fear the technology, help them.

The other technologies children should learn before college

1. Basic programming is something I think all children to learn. With all due respect to The Algebra Project and its assertion that algebra is a gatekeeper to literacy today I will venture that in a few years it will be computer programming...if we are to be a knowledge-based economy. Computer programming follows the simple logic of math, being symbol or at least not always plain language based, and building each successive step logically on the last. Computer literacy is key and increasingly other children are learning programming so they see digital possibilities differently, practically speaking.
2. At the urging of my son's digital coach I'll add Adobe's Creative Suite. If you want your child to create online this software is intuitive, easy to use and great. Unlike early computer interfaces most of what is available for the consumer market is easily grasped by children (who can then teach you). Online exploration in creation is empowering and allows for ongoing experimentation and low risk failure. I love watching how fearless children can be learning online and how much more like "play" it is than offline learning.
3. Instagram and other manipulation tools? Probably not, but watching my daughter and her friends I added it anyway.

Resources

For learning about programming numerous websites offer wonderful tutorials including: www.codeacademy.com and teach the net on YouTube.

Both Apple, through their stores, and Adobe, through www.tv.adobe.com, offer great tutorials.

Using www.gamestarmechanic.com children can create games and enter contests to win prizes.

www.scratch.mit.edu offers an extensive range of options for children to create and share such media as games and music.

If you can't afford a computer search out school or library computer labs and ensure that your child spends time exploring these resources. Or, a better use of funds than a smart phone with its monthly plan is to get an inexpensive computer. Monthly DSL Internet access is a nominal additional cost if you already have a phone.

CFY, formally, Computers For Youth (www.cfy.org) and Computer Corps (www.computercorps.org) are both non-profit organizations that provide children with free computers should the family qualify. Both are limited in geographic reach and school penetration but parents should pursue these options should they apply.

WORLD FOCUS AND GLOBALIZATION

The 20th Century was the century of Aviation and the century of Globalization. The next century will be the century of Space.
WILSON GREATBATCH

Okay, the above quote isn't entirely fair, in that space truly is the next frontier (meaning it might not scale) while globalization is here to stay. But the deeper meaning rings true in that none of us can fight true change, and the world will continue to move faster than our brains or plans can keep up. The mass media and Internet have torn down the last barriers that kept information and societies isolated, and world trade is a given. Money flows across borders in an instant and we can Skype anywhere for free.

How global a focus do American's have? Not very overall.

We haven't had to look outwards for a long time as our country has not only held superpower status it also crafted much of the world's mainstream media. Our movies are the biggest in global box office receipts, some topping a billion dollars. Our books, newspapers and magazines are bestsellers globally, and online, and adhere to respected and professional expectations, garnering prestigious awards. Musically, the Black Eyed Peas of the world are heard and shared in most countries, even those we'd think of as remote. And English is the language of diplomacy and business, spoken by the educated across the world. Thus Americans, with their mostly strong dollar and protected shores coasted in social and intellectual isolation for a very long time.

In his book, *Strategic Vision: America and the Crisis of Global Power*, Zbigniew Brzezinski quotes two National Geographic studies from 2002. In the first, a higher percentage of 18 to 24 year olds in France, Japan, Mexico, Sweden and Canada could find and identify the United States than could their American counterparts. In another, young adults from in Sweden, Italy, France, Sweden, Greece, Japan, the UK and Canada had a better grasp of current events. The Americans beat out only the youth from Mexico in the latter study.

The world around us hasn't stood still.

> *The speed of light does not merely transform the world.*
> *It becomes the world. Globalization is the speed of light.*
> **PAUL VIRILIO**

Indeed, for years we have accepted many talented foreign students into our college and graduate schools, providing jobs for them upon their graduation and thus increasing our highly educated pool of talent. Current policies and shifting economic storms are leading many of them to return home for better opportunities, thus we lose that talent permanently. Meanwhile, these foreign students are taking the majority of our engineering and science degrees abroad, leaving us lacking in the expertise needed to build the strategic industries that will ensure our future prosperity. Sense any opportunities in that dynamic?

Most school systems abroad teach English to all students; our foreign language programs have been cut or don't exist in many schools thus few of our students graduate proficient in more than one language (unless they grew up speaking another language at home).

We've been consuming en mass and as of 2010 about 30 percent of our debt is held by foreigners. While half the world's population doesn't have enough water, our population, 5 percent of the world total, consumes one-third of the world's resources. How are we going to pay for that consumption, especially when only 2 percent of our budget is available for education, the means for producing from quality workers (earners) in the future?

Meanwhile, our strategic industries are left to develop alone, whether that means operating domestically or aiming to cut costs by opening offices abroad. Countries such as China, Russia and Brazil invest in or own vast swaths of the companies in strategic industries that include: energy, utilities, telecom, financials, industrials and materials. Our government spends instead on entitlement programs, not developing industry, allocating to consumption not production and job creation. Perhaps your child is interested in one of these industries.

Long term many developing countries present a real challenge to our own population, forced to compete on this new global playing field. The emerging powers have growing consumer markets, an educated professional workforce, natural resources, access to capital and a rule of law (needed to encourage investment), a large and growing population and a healthy manufacturing sector. Add to that an elite educated in the United States with a solid grasp of American business practices, English proficiency and global connections and your children are facing serious competition for opportunities.

Americans do have some advantages in the race of globalization. Living in California we're perhaps more blessed with a diverse population of influences, which increases our overall perspective. Our local economy is also massive. Los Angeles is rich with Mexicans, South and Central Americans, Persians, Europeans from all such countries, ditto with Asia and Africa, Australians and New Zealanders and even a smattering of smaller nations. Unfortunately, on a day-to-day basis most of us are exposed to a much narrower range of influences.

It's never been easier to expand our perspective.

Travel, and immerse yourself in local culture. If you can't travel get online and learn. Read newspaper headlines as a family, or follow such organizations on Twitter. Watch foreign movies and read bestsellers from abroad aloud. Read foreign fairy tales or folk stories. Look through the front-page section of the New York Times daily as a family. Buy a Rosetta Stone course in a foreign language.

My father travelled a lot for work and he'd return with foreign comic books or dolls. The pictures and costumes spiked my curiosity and led me to travel when in college each summer. Children have wonderful imaginations and an endless capacity for wonder. Awaken that curiosity and introduce them to that magical place that is their world. Read books about your own family's country of origins and if you have related stories or pictures to share do so.

Learning about the world is not only crucial to becoming a competitive worker of the future it also helps children learn to discover their own passion. Ideally, they find that area which will grab their imagination and lead to a true professional fit not just mere job acceptance. Any interest can become a job, which will take them out of drudgery and into a mission (the latter being vastly more fulfilling). We all work hard, whether as a bum looking for sustenance food and a safe place to sleep at night, to a manual worker, to a CEO who juggles the fate of thousands of people and billions of dollars. Help them find passion that will turn work into a mission, thus less of a burden. Opening their horizons is a first step to achieving that goal.

Resources

Read a lot. Newspapers such as the *New York Times*. Magazines such as *Time*, *Newsweek* or the *Economist*. Even travel magazines. Read fairy tales or comic books from around the world, even if sometimes you're stuck understanding only the pictures. Discuss what you read.

Listen to music from around the world. Putumayu has a wonderful selection a www.putumayu.com.

Travel if you can. If you can't, travel online or through the Discovery Channel.

The resources in this topic require more creativity than do many other areas.

ARTS AND MUSIC

After silence, that which comes nearest to expressing the inexpressible is music.
ALDOUS HUXLEY

Arts and music programs have been decimated in many school systems throughout the United States. Are they merely unimportant electives, which granted, make a person's experience of life richer and more nuanced? Or, do they impart a deeper meaning to our existence, foster creativity and the understanding of valuable patterns that repeat importantly throughout life?

During the 2010 to 2011 elementary school spending on the arts went up marginally, while middle and high school were cut, around 10 percent each overall since the 2004-2005 school year. And the small increase for elementary schools was in staff, with art supply spending down about 80 percent over five years (art teachers can teach other classes and still be considered part of art spending). Only 54 percent of schools meet state requirements for art education.

Not testable or often asked for in a job description (baring related fields) art and music have long been treated as mere light electives, though some schools make them the centerpiece and develop children for the performing or other arts. As noted earlier, such schools tend to do an excellent job educating children perhaps because they impart discipline, the patience to achieve your best and routine. Art and music can be repetitive but also enhance learning!

To me the most important aspect of both music and art is that they are both areas where a child is on equal footing and expertise with adults. And, equally important, a child can teach an adult or other children. And oftentimes, children teach and share both art and music better among themselves. Far too few disciplines allow for this great equalizer, empowering to the child and teaching confidence in a skill they can master. Who sings with more passion than a child or can get so engrossed in a few tins of paint and a blank piece of paper?

Art enables us to find ourselves and lose ourselves at the same time.
THOMAS MERTON

Art and music are magical, taking us closer to the divine and allowing for an un-judged expression of emotion. They link us to the past and sometimes the future, conjuring up worlds unknown but still possible to experience. They also provide context to historical places and literature, filling out missing pieces of how people lived at a given time and illustrating the different realities. Art and music are mythology come to life.

Who can forget Venus emerging from Botticelli's shell, her hair whipping in long blonde tresses around her shapely limbs, the sea a vast backdrop? Who doesn't remember hearing the lilting lightness of early Mozart? Traditions and cultures find their voice through the great works of art that memorialized them. Early history and epics were originally sung to the community long before the written word came into widespread usage and turned them into texts. People would gather together to listen rapt as a singer told of bravery or deception, and all could gasp at the storylines as a community. Art and music unite.

These disciplines also provide perspectives about different cultures and time periods, along with religions. Indeed, centuries ago art was often created for the worship of God alone. The Sistine Chapel is a lovely cascading array of story lines and people scattered masterfully across a massive ceiling. It recounts the Bible in bright, vivid imagery. Johannes Sebastian Bach wrote many pieces for specific sermons, such as Good Friday.

Art and music are also disciplines, following set patterns and rules. In music anyone serious about mastery must learn the scales and how the sounds interact together. The rules of form are precise and ordered. Constant repetition and practice is necessary to get better and play a piece well. Indeed, only hours upon hours of such work will produce a decent result.

Art likewise corresponds to patterns. Certain ratios exist throughout nature and it is only someone especially creative, such as Pablo Picasso, who can tweak those patterns effectively. Much as math and science preach the importance of order so does art. Drawing is all about getting the proportions right, based on recurring absolutes that cut across nature. To draw a face one starts by first drawing a horizontal then vertical line through the middle of a piece of paper then symmetrically aligning proportions based on these guidelines.

Art and music are also creative and fun. We can all yield a maraca or marker. Given a safe environment in which to explore their imagination children can surprise, be it by utilizing video game influences or pairing unicorns with zombies. Indeed, most kids haven't yet learned to temper their art, the way us more inhabited adults do. This abandon is quickly stifled in most courses where there is a right answer and way of doing things. Art and music allow for free expression and exploration across boundaries with little risk.

Art and music are solace and take us back to familiar times or places, conjuring up depth and emotion. My children play music incessantly, a never-ending stream of songs that speak to them with hidden meanings and some not so hidden. We all engage in the present with those words that strike our heart and somehow music delivers them so much better than just words in poetry (compare the popularity of the two). Music can also cross cultures and languages. People around the world listen to Shakira and Justin Bieber.

A picture is worth a thousand words
ICONIC BUT ULTIMATELY UNKNOWN

And thus it is that generations and cultures can hold on to an image above all else sometimes, children being no exception. Pictures are simply more memorable and touching. Instagram was a year old company that sold itself for a billion dollars built on manipulating and sharing images. Lauren is on Instagram compulsively (in her mom's opinion) sharing and commenting. Less interested in digital conversations, her and her friends pass pictures back and forth on end. Art.

And then I'll harken back to Steve Jobs and his memorable Stanford Commencement Address (well worth watching: http://www.youtube.com/watch?v=UF8uR6Z6KLc&feature=g-logo). In it, he ties his success back to a calligraphy class he crashed right after dropping out of college. It was learning to appreciate the deliberate aesthetics of the lines that helped him design the Apple interface. Artists see the world differently, able to discern those simple elements that matter most throughout life. Jobs saw the simplicity of fewer lines on a blank space.

Will your child become a musician or artist? As stated earlier, at best tens of thousands of people earn a living directly from actually creating or performing in such professions. But it's possible, and nowhere more so than in Los Angeles. Laird Malamed as mentioned earlier and who headed production for games at Activision, clarified that art, science and math were pre-requisite skills for video game design. Jason wants to be a video game designer and now takes his skills with markers and crayons as seriously as his multiplication tables; and he's right to do so. We can all define ourselves through creativity.

Check your school for its arts and music program. The complaint most heard from children while interviewing for this book was the lack of resources dedicated to art and music. If your school doesn't have much of a program the online resources are vast. Create magic for your children.

And don't ignore drama if your children are interested. Being on stage develops presence and the ability to connect with an audience. Taking on a persona is something we'll all need to do sometimes in life. Drama teaches that skill.

Resources

Create family playlists on: Pandora, Spotify, iTunes or MOG. Listen to their season or event specific lists.

Decorate your house with child created art. Keep supplies around and work on projects both independently and together.

Sign your child up to learn an instrument or art class. Go to a concert or art museum or view them online! iTunes has amazing concerts in its store, and often for free. Many museums now post their collections and limited time exhibits online. Some notable examples include: http://www.metmuseum.org/, http://www.lacma.org/, http://www.louvre.fr/en. Listed were the sites for the Metropolitan Museum in New York, LACMA (Los Angeles County Museum of Art) and the Louvre Paris. The latter offers online briefs on learning about art.

Apply to get JamStudio free in your children's school: http://www.jamstudio.com/Studio/index.htm. JamStudio allows children to learn to write their own music. It's an inexpensive tool which can also be used at home should your school not be interested.

Apps are great in this area. Drawsomething, an app, recently popped up in a confirmatory email, thanks to my kids' download.

LEADERSHIP AND A CIVIC MIND (RIGHT PURPOSE)

We're all being judged, constantly and throughout our lives and we also judge ourselves, oftentimes more harshly than do others. Each individual decides with every thought and action what sort of person they'll be. While often there's time to repent or change, practically speaking we're still followed by the lingering reputations our pasts built. A good name once sullied is hard to refurbish to a true luster.

We live on an island surrounded by a sea of ignorance. As our island of knowledge grows, so does the shore of our ignorance.
JOHN ARCHIBALD WHEELER

Parents form a child's earliest conceptions of the world and its rules, both unspoken and articulated. Later, peers and life itself will further shape the being we nurtured but no influence is as ingrained and deeply held as what a child learned at home. Children watch how we live our lives and interact with others. They see how we treat ourselves and whether our rewards are healthy or not. They learn judgment, character, ethics, beliefs, faith and love.

Daunting as a parent, thinking that our actions have such an impact on the small people we love, these influences also provide our children with strength and values when things in their life invariably go wrong. When lost, we all need a foundation from which to draw the absolutes around which we base our lives.

This section thus discusses leadership, ethics and a civic mind. It also has some invaluable advice I've received over the years and a pointer on presentation. We are both what people see and what they don't.

Leadership isn't a passing of the baton but rather embracing it. No one accomplishes much by running away.

Why are there so few leadership books aimed at children? Much as we bemoan the lack of leadership in the United States when have we focused on teaching it? Leadership classes aren't a regular part of the American curriculum though we do learn about leaders, yet mostly in the context of another subject. But shouldn't this topic at least be introduced to our young, not as a byproduct but as a possibility or even an expectation?

True leadership is a hard and lonely battle, full of responsibility with little glory, at least at any given moment. For a true leader deflects praise, supporting those who helped him instead. In failure he takes the full blame. How to explain to a child that taking the right path, sometimes alone, is a painful and punishing process but mostly worth short-term pain for long-term gain?

The term leadership has attributes, theories, styles, approaches and even a history. It has been debated, defined and argued. Sometimes the definition depends more on the side of history of the person in question. But don't we all know instinctively what constitutes leadership and who we know that fits the definition of leader?

No one asks you to lead. Somehow true leaders step into that role and generally take on responsibilities (or more likely problems) that no one else wants. Leaders earn their followers. Is leadership an objective or subjective term? Or, to be literal is a leader simply someone who leads?

Leadership and learning are indispensable to each other.
JOHN F. KENNEDY

Can leadership be taught? I believe that for the most part it can; but only to those who want to learn. Leadership isn't for the faint of heart. Watching a group of ambitious people you can easily see the jostling for position and power, yet there is also too often a hesitation when tough positions or actions are required. Perhaps we like to be thought of as leaders yet hesitate when the opportunity presents itself, either through a lack of preparation or confidence (or character).

Yet those children who grow up to be the greatest successes will across the board be leaders. To leave a big footprint you must be willing to step into the mud, no matter how deep it looks.

Defined by many things in his life, my friend Richard (Dick) J. Riordan is nothing if not a leader. Starting his own law firm, two private equity firms, a few non-profits and being mayor of Los Angeles is plenty to meet the definition. He is also leading reforms in education and public pensions. Deeply intellectual, with a library of over 40,000 books, he's spent much time pondering what sets apart those who lead. The following are the leadership principles he teaches his students at UCLA's Anderson (MBA) School.

Dick starts with four axioms and two half axioms: courage; character; relentless pursuit of goals; and empowering others; followed by caring and a sense of humor.

Courage is the strength of mind that empowers someone to face difficulty, danger and fear. We all face challenges; leaders are defined by those who withstand the pressures compared with those who don't. People who aspire to leadership are typically very action oriented. Yet sometimes the greatest amount of courage is demonstrated by listening. Only then can you hear when facts don't support your position or that the tide is currently against you. Surviving a blow or loss can be the ultimate form of courage.

All leaders need the courage to take risks. Sometimes, when you risk you lose. Taking action doesn't always lead to the expected outcome (law of unintended consequences). And, too often action is required in a vortex of information or certainty. Leaders learn from their mistakes and use that added judgment the next time.

Sometimes courage is getting out of the bed in the morning and facing the dark light of dawn. When the Northridge Earthquake struck Los Angeles the last thing Dick wanted to do was get out of his safe, warm bed and face the devastation of Los Angeles, including possible deaths, debilitating infrastructure challenges and a broken communications system. But he did it because he was in charge of the city and its people.

And the city was eerie, dark with the normally omnipresent street lights out. Otherworldly lone car lights would punctuate the blackness, while car alarms continued to sound in the distance. He had the courage to do it anyway.

If you have no character to lose, people will have no faith in you
MAHATMA GHANDI

Character defines you and smart people will figure out yours surprisingly quickly. Looking up a definition of character one will find "traits or features that form a person; ethical and moral qualities" which is perfect.

What makes for a solid character?

First, one must be reliable, whether that means showing up when you say you will or doing an action as promised. Honoring your commitments should also be paired with trustworthiness. The two together allow people to rely on you, knowing that you will be a solid ally.

Working hard is the next element. We'd all like to be out playing football or lying on the beach on a warm, summer day, when our friends beckon. This book was written on many such a sunny Sunday and it wouldn't have gotten finished otherwise. A corollary is self-control, or discipline. Watching television is always easier, as is eating that extra brownie. Saying no takes strength, or character.

Loyalty and respect for others are also key factors in defining someone's character. The undercurrent of these principles is that who you are is defined by how you treat others. Would Jesus have spawned a new religion had he not advocated for the downtrodden and the poor? Respect is a fading quality but it always reflects well on anyone who practices it.

Much as how you treat others and the quality of what you do reflect character so does your impact on the world around you. When we watch people we look for the details. Do they throw their trash away? Do they do what they said they will? Do they serve themselves food first? Sometimes in an effort to look strong or in control people ignore those around them. Lots of words could define this concept from caring to friendship to citizenship (the last will be discussed below).

Provide your child with the support and guidance for them to build their own character. Discuss actions, especially those situations involving conflict or ethical choices, focusing on why certain decisions and resulting actions were more admirable than others.

If your actions inspire others to dream more,
learn more, do more and become more, you are a leader.
JOHN QUINCY ADAMS

Empowering others means giving people the tools, leeway, trust and support to get their job done. And, inherent in that definition is providing a clear vision of that end goal yet also letting them interpret a better end goal, if possible.

Ask those you lead, "How can I help you succeed?" Then support them.

Leading isn't about getting credit or "me". Leading is about empowering others and letting them revel in the accolades when there is success but accepting blame when there is failure.

Vision is an element of empowering others. People work harder for causes into which they've bought or believe to be important. Asking someone to fill out a form is requiring rote work. But assigning them the job of helping an impoverished, illiterate single mother with five children and no home successfully fill out a shelter application form to get off skid row (with it's drugs, violence and rats) will usually get a rapid and impassioned buy in.

> *Leaders aren't born, they are made. And they are made just like anything else, through hard work. And that's the price we'll have to pay to achieve that goal, or any goal.*
> **VINCE LOMBARDI**

The plain fact is that real accomplishment is rarely easy. There is luck but those who are repeatedly lucky tend to work harder than their competitors. Perhaps animals have an advantage with this axiom; they don't waste time with their insecurities, questions or lack of purpose. They just do things. When Dick's golden doodle dog, Billy, wants someone to throw him a ball he makes sure they know, usually by knocking them over, ball in mouth, or sitting on them. No matter how often he's pushed off or harshly pointed elsewhere he tries again. Then comes the stare, the whine and the paw. He never gives up but eventually his target does. If only we all had that single minded purpose and clear vision of achieving our goals.

First, teach your children to set a goal then support them to relentlessly achieve it. Goals can be simple or hard to define. Importantly, if you don't know what you are trying to achieve in life getting there might happen but will you ever be sure? Much is possible for those who don't give up.

And a word on failure. Don't let it be final. Rather get up and keep going. You haven't actually failed until you quit and the line between failure and success is often a very fine one. Be relentless.

> *If you don't know where you are going, any road will get you there*
> **LEWIS CARROLL**

It's hard to be leader without caring for others. Empathy gives our actions depth. No one builds anything of value alone. Caring also takes our goals and actions out of self-serving and into inspiration. Seeking to maximize our own opportunities and situations is hardly something anyone deserves praise for doing. Leaders act for benefits beyond themselves thus the universal impact they can have. It's when you can see past yourself to the greater good that you become a leader.

Is a sense of humor important in a leader? Probably. Those with a sense of humor can engage better with people thus impact them more deeply, gaining support and increased effort toward a common goal. We need to somehow cross those difficult divides that can exist between people if we're to impact them. While a wonderful vision can inspire too often it falls on deaf ears. Humor destroys defenses, especially among children who open up like flowers when engaged in laughter. Watch a child laugh.

All people are capable of leadership and our country has a long history of people great and small who stepped up to the plate when the time came to stand up for what is right or drive change. Leaders can include a small woman, Rosa Parks, who refused to give up her seat on a bus. Or, it encompasses the (almost) faceless Navy Seal team who dealt with Osama Bin Laden. No company founder waited for someone else to find an idea and begin building. Leaders not only benefit themselves they benefit society.

Teach your children these principles and read them this section.

Resources

Michael Josephson's book called *Parenting to Build Character in Your Teen*. The book is a quick and accessible read.

The Seven Habits of Highly Effective Teens, by Sean Covey, Stephen Covey's son. The book is likewise an easy read and is appropriate for younger children than the title suggests (and will likely lose older teens). The main focus is developing the qualities that will help a teen get ahead in life, including leadership.

Read the newspaper together and discuss a story of a bad or stellar leader. Explore what actions by that person led to your conclusion.

Discuss the American founding fathers and what made them such leaders.

Read *Zen Shorts*, by Jon Muth. A picture book, it elegantly elaborates on perspective and character.

Ethics

A strong ethical system is one of the most valuable characteristics a parent can teach their children. Nothing in life is potentially more impactful to their long-term success and happiness than doing what is right, and knowing how to recognize and avoid doing what is wrong. Almost any book or movie on those people who inspire others makes clear that ethics, which form a large part of character, were a driving force in shaping the importance of that person.

In the US we have a strong sense of justice, fairness and doing what's right. Our Puritan forefathers and our equality seeking founding fathers steeped our nation deeply in such ideology and it continues to shape political debate and national opinion. And others punish those they don't trust or think are unethical, and often won't work with or hire them. Deeply unethical people often end up in jail.

Yet watch how we often shape our children. The main reason young children lie is to avoid getting in trouble. Even early on, they try to minimize punishment yet don't have the maturity to make certain ethical or even safety related judgment calls. Parents often perpetuate this conflict by putting the role of confessor on a child's shoulder, encouraging them to lie. Instead of asking if your child did something bad discuss what would be the best resolution or punishment for one who did the action. The truth will become clear quickly, and is more likely to do so than directly confronting the child.

This conflict is pretty universal. One bit of advice I heard was cautioning children to answer, "I don't know" to any potentially trouble related question asked by an adult. Funny or not?

Each parent must negotiate this slippery slope based on their own value system and personal set of ethics. Just remember that avoiding conflicts now will only create greater problems down the line as by not providing an open dialogue on conflict ridden issues we don't support children with the guidance and guidelines for handling difficult ethical issues.

Fairy tales and myths are actually one of the best ways for children to begin to grasp ethical dilemmas and issues. Often the main character is placed in in a morally conflicted position and must navigate a resolution, often at great risk to himself or others. These tales provide insight into societal norms and the related implications of our actions.

Resources

Read fairy tales and myths to your child. Some good ones include: *The Grasshopper and the Ant*; Anything about the Trojan War; *Cinderella*; *King Solomon*; *The Princess and the Pea*.

Walt Disney movies are also great at addressing ethical issues, as is Charles Dickens, *The Hunger Games*, and an assortment of biographies (of leaders).

A Civic Mind

A civic mind is one that gets engaged in the world around them. We live in a democracy, the success of which is reliant on its citizens getting thus involved. At the most basic level we should all be voters, but more importantly informed voters. You are raising your children to assume this monumental responsibility, one many people have died to protect while others today are risking their lives, goods and families to achieve.

Perhaps that statement above seems extreme but I don't think so. Our country holds a privileged position globally and part of its ongoing success on a relative basis is due to our form of government. Because of one person, one vote foundation of representative government we get both the government we earn and the one we deserve.

The best argument against democracy is a
five-minute conversation with the average voter.
WINSTON CHURCHILL

And America was founded with the idea of citizen rule, a democracy, which has less flatteringly been called mob rule. Get your children engaged and encourage them to assume their share of that burden and great legacy both.

Teach them about our balance of powers, with the executive, legislative and judicial branch (each with its own function). The executive branch executes the laws, the legislative makes them and the judicial explains and applies the laws. Due to the concept of checks and balances each branch of government has oversight over the others. Their powers are articulated in the Constitution but have been clarified over the years through laws, regulations and court case rulings.

Our President is elected to a four-year term of which he can serve twice. The legislature is composed of the Senate, with two senators from each state serving six year terms, and the House of Representatives comprised of 435 representative serving two year terms. Our Supreme Court justices are appointed for life by the President as vacancies arise. They constitute the final form of review but choose what cases they want to hear, usually preferring issues relevant to constitutional law. They are the third level of review for the federal courts. State courts exist to hear issues having to do with state and not federal law.

Each state has it's own government roughly modeled on the federal one and based on their distinctive state constitution. All powers not reserved to the federal government belong to the states, which can lead to much confusion. Sometimes the distinction can be unclear.

Our democracy is an ever-evolving one. Teach your children to become engaged in the political process so that they can assume their role as citizens. Being engaged is more empowering than just watching the government's actions as they impact you. One person can and often does make a difference.

Resources

Supreme Court Justice Sandra Day O'Connor helped develop a website to teach children about our government. It's at: www.icivics.org. The site has games and other resources, including a great list of other web sites and resources. It's also a little quirky and still not perfected in my opinion.

Go to the White House's webpage: www.whitehouse.gov. Much of the content isn't child focused but they have a picture of the day, picture gallery and videos of musical or other performances. The site is a great way to engage your children and draw them into their government.

Encourage your child to submit and essay to Citizenship Counts about why they value being an American citizen: http://citizenship-counts.org/index.php/program/students/essay-contest/http://citizenshipcounts.org/index.php/program/students/essay-contest/. The site itself has other resources promoting and teaching citizenship. I'm a big fan of contests as they encourage real critical thinking, initiative and a goal orientation.

Each year two high school students from each state spend a week in Washington DC learning about government: http://www.ussenateyouth.org/. A US Senate Resolution established the program in 1962, granting these students a trip to see major leaders in action.

Life Lessons, or Some Little Things I've Learned Along the Way

Sometimes in life it's the details that matter; those little things which betray an added sensibility, maturity or understanding. Yet no schools offer classes in these subtleties. Rather they're picked up from observing those around us or from quiet tips. Knowing how to relate with others and project the right qualities helps people differentiate you and view you more favorably.

A man's manners are a mirror in which he shows his portrait.
JOHANN WOLFGANG VON GOETHE

What every child should be told:

1. Mentors matter. Perhaps no other factor will distinguish those who reach great success from those who do less well. Pursue mentors aggressively and reward them by doing well.
2. Smart people will test you, always and forever. Live up to your best at all times.
3. Character counts.
4. Sleep eight hours each night; nothing good happens after midnight.
5. Read daily. Learn for the rest of your life.
6. If it won't matter in 100 years it isn't worth worrying about too much. If you can't change it likewise don't worry much; instead focus your efforts on things you can impact.
7. Taking no action is an action and a decision in itself.
8. Money matters a lot but people matter more.
9. Perceived power can matter as much as real power.
10. All passes.
11. Luck favors the prepared, those who work hard and never give up.
12. As Winston Churchill stated, never give up.
13. People equal money and jobs. If you need to raise some or get a job start meeting with people.
14. No one owes you anything.
15. Life passes quickly and speeds up as you get older.
16. There isn't always time to fix things; embrace those you love.
17. Everyone feels overwhelmed.
18. Be polite. You are judged by your manners and the company you keep.
19. You get credit for what you've done not what you say you'll do.
20. It's better to ask forgiveness than permission.

21. Presentation matters. Dress well and conservatively in business.

*"Either one learns politeness at home," Dick said, "or the world teaches
it to you with a whip and you may get hurt in the process."*
F. SCOTT FITZGERALD IN *TENDER IS THE NIGHT*

Resources

*How Children Succeed: Grit, Curiosity and the Hidden Power of
Character*, by Paul Tough. Opinions on the author's arguments con-
tained herein vary widely. Having said that, the book presents a compelling argument that success is based upon more than academics
(and looks to personal characteristics such as character). Anyone with
any common sense will need to agree at least in part.

BALANCED PERSON

*Let us resume our inquiry and state, in view of the fact that all
knowledge and every pursuit aims at some good, what it is that we say
political science aims at and what is the highest of all goods achievable
by action. Verbally there is very general agreement; for both the general
run of men and people of superior refinement say that it is happiness,
and identify living well and doing well with being happy; but with
regard to what happiness is they differ, and the many do not give the
same account as the wise.*
ARISTOTLE

Success often comes to those who aren't balanced because they put so much
effort and focus on accomplishing a directed outcome. Rarely does anyone create or succeed at something great without personal sacrifices,
whether it's from working long hours to suffering persecution from
those who don't want you to succeed. Some people get lucky and others
inherit but most work for their success, and make choices along the way.

But does material success equal happiness? I think those that say no are being idealistic. Success or affluence is a start and take away certain concerns such as how to pay rent. Successful people also tend to have more control over their daily life and tasks, the latter of which tend to be more interesting and mentally challenging than are more rote ones. But it also increases other stresses, hence the high divorce rate you can see among top performers in any field, and time becomes an enigma. People should strive for balance, and living well. For part of what makes life so vivid and momentous are those moments of friendship and enjoyment, be it laughing with friends, playing tennis or reading a good book.

Success comes in a lot of ways, but it doesn't come with money and it doesn't come with fame. It comes from having a meaning in your life, doing what you love and being passionate about what you do. That's having a life of success. When you have the ability to do what you love, love what you do and have the ability to impact people. That's having a life of success. That's what having a life of meaning is.

TIM TEBOW

When I started writing this book a lot of people mentioned that giving back to the community was important for all kids to fit into their schedule – to get into college and because it's the right thing to do. A friend handed over information to a program that for thousands of dollars takes children abroad on public service projects to help pad their resumes. Giving back and appreciating what we have are important, but to make us better people, not just to get into college. Most people reading these pages are doing so as much from the luck of being born at the right place and time as from their own efforts (though let's not discount that some people regardless of birth are proactively reading these sorts of books to improve their life while others aren't). Teach compassion for those with less, because we really are happier when we care for others and don't just evaluate what they can do for us.

How does one remember to engage in all that makes life rich? First start with cherishing your body, the temple we're all blessed to own and one when not healthy extracts a huge toll on our quality of life.

Resources

Mentioned earlier in the book is the J.K. Livin Foundation founded by Matthew McConaughey and Camila Alves will provide an easy to use curriculum for teachers and/or schools to help guide children to make better choices with respect to health, emotional wellness and good decision making. Encourage your school or favorite teacher to reach out to the organization, even if it hasn't expanded to your geographic region and adopt their program. Their website is www.jklivinfoundation.org.

Health and Wellness

Our bodies impact everything we do in life and should be treated with respect. Too often society focuses on outward appearances without providing ongoing support for efforts in improving our overall health. Even medical insurance tends to pay only when things go wrong and not for preventative care. Different people have different bodies but none function well with bad food and too little exercise. Even the brain is negatively impacted by too little exercise.

Parents should be providing their children with good physical habits and not just mental ones. Your kids will mirror what they see you do.

In Los Angeles as estimated 40 percent of children are overweight. Nationwide the number is estimated to be about 33 percent. Being overweight is directly correlated with diabetes and, later on, heart and other chronic disease. Over 24 million Americans have Type 2 diabetes and the number is estimated to double by 2025. The fatty buildup of arterial plaque is now known to begin accumulating during childhood, increasing later risk of serious heart disease, the top cause of death in the United States.

We should all be making active choices about what we eat and ensuring that it serves its basic purpose, to make us strong and healthy (not to nourish us emotionally). Our society has food issues, from supersizing to extreme diets, and this mindset passes on to our children. Lost too often is the idea of enjoying as opposed to feeding, and the social aspects of a meal. We should eat out of hunger not emotional need. But we should enjoy that food as a family, taking time to relax and talk about our day. Moderation and balanced diets are much less likely to lead to obesity, eating disorders or food hoarding.

Eating without conversation is only stoking.
MARCELENE COX

In *How To Get Kids To Eat*, author Ellyn Satter tells the story of two children on the heavy side. One set of parents nags the child, and deprives him. The child grows up feeling unloved and punished, and continues to gain weight over time. Food is love and nurturing; accept it. Never starve or stuff a child. The second child is likewise heavy but the parents don't make the weight an issue and as a family continue to enjoy balanced meals together, with perhaps just an added focus on healthy and less calorie dense offerings (but never cutting out the ice cream; no one should ever be forced to give up ice cream unless they make that choice for themselves!, Satter states). By late teens the child is at normal weight. When food becomes an issue you cannot win.

Exercise is the next component in creating good health.

A recent CDC study showed that only about 35 percent of high school students got an adequate level of exercise. Only 70 percent of such students attended regular physical education classes.

Physical education also has tremendous benefits on learning and stress control, along with helping maintain health and staying slim. Exercise to set a healthy role model and include your child, for example take walks as a family. Note the local plants or birds. Discuss your day. Recent studies published show that sitting for even two hours a day takes a few years off your life. If nothing else, get your kids moving.

Sleep is also essential. Eight hours a night or longer during growth spurts matters. Children's growth occurs mainly while they're sleeping.

Resources

Spark: The Revolutionary New Science of Exercise and the Brain, by John Ratey and Eric Hagerman. This book provides important insight into the academic (and fitness) results seen by adding challenging exercise programs into schools.

How To Get Your Child To Eat...But Not Too Much by Ellyn Satter is a common sense resource by a practitioner on eating issues.

Lots of websites provide related information on health and fitness but this section really isn't defined by online games or videos. Read labels when you shop as a family or at home if easier. Swim, walk and play tag. Try meat free Mondays or a new fruit or vegetable a meal. Health and fitness is defined by the actions you take, not just the decisions you make.

Faith and Spirituality

A faith is a necessity to a man. Woe to him who believes in nothing.
VICTOR HUGO

Everyone needs to believe in something. Faith and spirituality have a long history of importance in the lives of people and communities. For me I always gravitate back to one God and the idea that there's something else beyond our worldly and daily existence. The idea of the "church" is a conflicted notion for many, and perhaps there are just too many churches for those stricken with a broken faith. Still, most people believe in something.

My background is somewhat typical, half Catholic and half Anglican, conflicting ideologies that founded a religious battle, and then I wrote about Islam. Believing in a constant God I've personally never really felt much religious conflict though I have felt cultural ones.

A spiritual faith provides a context in a larger order, beyond our daily travails and questions about what happens before and most importantly after our own life. It's solace and guidance on bigger issues that transcend the merely physical. When lost, hearing inspiring words that whisper of absolute universal truths helps nudge us along the twisted path of life. I find comfort not only in words but also in stepping back from coping and just sensing. People can self-balance with the right dealing mechanisms as we possess an internal barometer echoing words of wisdom.

And I'm not alone in needing a higher power next to me on my tougher days, when nothing is going right and I feel alone. Throughout time, people have yearned to believe in something vaster thus almost all cultures have a faith in a God or higher power. Life is too random for individuals to not eventually feel driven to defer to an other or we lose all sense of reason. God's wisdom shows across time not in day-to-day life. Even if you believe in no God don't you want your child to have faith? Perhaps not, but bad things happen and they will need a coping mechanism to process fate. Take it outside God if need be.

Thus I won't preach the importance of choosing a specific God or church. Ultimately, most people follow the religion of their parents so spiritual decisions are often deeply ingrained from our earliest experiences. As noted earlier, Catholic schools do much better for their children than the schools surrounding them most probably due to the values and community they build, even embracing those of different faiths.

The values and traditions inherent in faith are key in shaping people, providing identity and community. As in my earlier points about literature, religions are generally based upon books of narrative, or stories, not just concepts. Children learn about reacting when faced with a moral dilemma independent of immediate peer feedback, or even that of society as a whole. Ultimately, the person we can never escape or leave behind is us thus we need a guiding moral compass. And morality is often learned through religion. Moses had to face God on the mountain even though he didn't like everything he heard. But he delivered the Ten Commandments, or the law, to his people as instructed. Most of us still live by those pronouncements in various forms, from the prohibition against killing to the stigma that comes with theft.

While the great holy books of each major religion do use narratives to express eternal conflicts, providing universal guidelines to follow even when we're pressured to do otherwise, their purpose is more sophisticated than that of simple story. I'm a huge believer in pre-analyzing all possible outcomes when dealing with issues, challenges or opportunities but still life sometimes surprises. When the latter happens, we need deeply rooted beliefs, absolutes that focus our decisions and ability to handle the repercussions of those related responses.

And, let's not forget the importance of structure and ritual, especially to children. I read that holidays are often more important to children from divorced families because they signify more. A child from a broken home needs and respects the ritual and custom that forms their newer sense of family. Most religions likewise have customs and rituals providing familiarity and comfort to those who feel vulnerable or alone. Even if not running a single parent household we mostly trample through family time and ritual these days, in the quest of productivity or even coping.

Faith in a religion with the resulting traditions and customs can provide this grounding but so can less organized forms of spirituality. Today I was dealing with a major personal conflict and went to yoga. On arrival at the studio I didn't feel strong enough to face the people I know from attending the same class regularly or to go through the series of poses. But I stayed. And as I started following the familiar progression I began to feel more grounded and at peace, even though my problems weren't solved. The class and studio has been there for me during happy times and sad. We all need a safe place. Indeed, I staggered in one day during the lowest moment of my divorce and my teacher, Steve Ross, smiled at the sadness in my eyes and whispered, "breathe". So I did and began to feel better. Nothing like faith or even spirituality can provide that grounding. Give such a blessing to your child, in whatever form most fits your family.

Yoga and Meditation

Purity of heart is to want one thing only.
KIERKEGAARD

I doubt I'd be alive without yoga. And I may be the world's worst meditator (but I still try). Most books on educating children don't address these two topics but I'm going to do otherwise. Faith and spirituality address both the conscious and unconscious mind; yoga and meditation likewise address the less controllable unconscious.

Sometimes in our day we'd all benefit from stopping whatever we're doing and becoming conscious of our breath. Closing our eyes and focusing on that simple in and out motion separates our controllable inner being from the chaos of the world. Yoga and meditation bring us back to our own being, separate and more controllable than everything surrounding. If one can't be alone with his own mind and body he can never be comfortable in the larger world.

Yoga came into my life as my marriage was falling apart and I was trying to escape into denial. But each time I stood on my mat my feet found their grounding and my body aspired to the poses, succeeding. The structure of the poses gave me discipline in a disintegrating world. I felt like a person and I accomplished something when I finished class.

At the time I was mostly going to classes with Tom Morley at Maha Yoga, though I'd also begun taking from the studio founder, Steve Ross, a legend. Tom has blonde curls and a ready smile for all. He engages and listens. Steve forces you to face yourself and find the answers within, though with a gentle nudge and guiding hand. They centered me with only a few words but more a stable practice.

Yoga and meditation take us from the discordant voice in our head which comments critically on every movement. The poses are perfect no matter what your level, the most important aspect is to do finish them to our own best ability. Indeed, a beginner must try harder thus is doing poses with more effort and gets that credit. If we can't do a pose then breathing is all that's required. Yoga's original purpose was to prepare the body for meditation not movement.

My kids have taken yoga classes with varying success. Teachers who talk too much seem to lose their attention but each child may be different. I recommend trying a series of simple poses for your whole family. Perhaps in following a succession together you can bond and re-center at the same time. If nothing else, watching each other fall is a bit like the silliness and fun of Twister and you can laugh together.

Meditation is a bit of a challenge for me as I'm action driven like most westerners. The theory behind mediation is that you reduce stress and reorient your brain to respond differently, basically reconfiguring the neurons to cope better. Numerous studies have hooked wires up to meditating monks' brains then watched the effect of meditation on their neural pathways and it's profound.

In their book, *Destructive Emotions*, a personal favorite, by the Dalai Lama and Daniel Goleman, the authors note the impact on one monk's highly trained brain as he meditates. The monk identified is Oser, not his real name, and he's hooked up to an MRI machine with all sorts of wires spouting. The impact on his brain is to be studied as he does various sorts of meditation. Oser was chosen based on his over 30 years of spiritual and meditation training, including time spent in individual reflection. A westerner who embraced Eastern mysticism Oser walks a fine path between the two realities.

A beginner may think of meditation as centering on one point, focusing. Yet mediation encompasses a vast array of points for the brain as it narrows. Oser suggests meditations on six states, including "open state" and devotion. He also meditates on fearlessness, which includes "bringing to mind a fearless certainty, a deep confidence that nothing can unsettle – decisive and firm, without hesitating, where you're not adverse to anything." In essence, a meditation on openness, in contrast to our more generalized world of people who close off, frozen to new experiences, traumatized by the bad experiences that have come before in their lives. Oser often senses past teachers in his meditations, as they play a key role in his understanding of gratitude. Compassion excludes no one, yet try it, meditation on the giving emotion often rewards you with a flood of warmth and kindness.

MRIs offer a graphically detailed picture of a brain's structures. Oser was hooked up to an fMRi, which offers the architecture in video covering various regions of the brain with change based on stimulus offered at a given moment. Going past pure structure, fMRis show how structure interacts in motion.

Interestingly, meditation on compassion, fearlessness and devotion, areas one might expect to produce similar brain functions, varied. Yet in all meditations, Oser's MRI responses showed that the brain displayed a concentration of action in the left middle part of the brain as Oser meditated, the part of the brain that controls feelings of happiness, joy, energy and enthusiasm. Also shown was a decrease in the right pre-frontal regions that control negative emotions. Seemingly, the more Oser focused on positive responses the more he directed his brain to those regions, directly benefiting his own mood. According to the study, our thoughts do control our mood, irrespective of the other differing impact from different meditations. Such efforts can get us to rewire and trigger our brain in positive ways.

But how to take our chaotic lifestyles and "find" that certitude!

I learned a new absolute from Steve that helped me breach the impossible moat for my unquiet mind into the realm of the meditator. He told me that when we begin we shouldn't always aim for a quiet mind, which must come later. Rather, we've such a mass of collected thoughts in our head that we sometimes must just accept them running wild as we try to still our mind. Only when all of those thoughts have been released and expressed can we find the silence.

My mind can be a mess. I scatter, then need to find all of the lost pieces and try to put them back together like Humpty Dumpty (a literary reference!). An all too common mental state in our too busy world. It's worth the effort.

Meditation is peace. Sit your child down and teach him to relax.

Resources

Meditation in a New York Minute by Mark Thornton

Happy Yoga by Steve Ross

Various yoga videos targeted at children. I have yet to find one I love.

GIFTED CHILDREN

Gifted children's performance has stagnated over the past ten years as resources were diverted to special education (for those with handicaps or other disabilities) and teaching to mandated tests. Our school system is also not directed by learning but rather by instructing which doesn't speak to the enthusiastic curiosity of gifted children.

Most schools have programs that seek to identify gifted children, whether through testing such as IQ tests or observation. My children's school tests children on their level of competency in certain subjects then put those that score on the high end in special groups designated to move faster and at a higher complexity. But my daughter went from the highest reading group one year, to almost the lowest, then to the highest again (my way of pointing our that these systems aren't flawless but they do have some reason to them).

Look out for your children if you think they're gifted. Test them, push their schools for additional resources and supplement their education. The latter options are vast, from tutoring services to videos I'll recommend in the resources section of this book. Get them to the library reading!

A gifted child is – clinically - one who scores 130 or above on an IQ test. But that definition isn't sufficient. For, a child can be gifted in one area and not others. Moreover, some gifted children are so perfectionistic or analytical they stall their way through an IQ test not wanting to pick a wrong answer. Identifying gifted children can be difficult and many teachers aren't trained in doing so. Sometimes a gifted child is the one acting up in class because they're bored with the lesson and frustrated as a result. Others might be quiet and unwilling to speak up. Many schools don't even begin identifying them until second or third grade; by which time a lot of learning time has been lost (and it's foundational learning).

Gifted children are a product of both environments and genetics. Early influences on the children such as reading to them, speaking with a broad vocabulary, appropriate stimulation and even adequate nutrition have an impact. Some experts believe that gifted children can process information faster.

Billions of neurons, or brain cells constitute the complex structure that is our brain. These neurons communicate by releasing and accepting chemicals termed neurotransmitters. Traveling through root-looking structures named dendrites, these chemicals seek connections with synapses, or nearby neurons. The density of these connections constitutes our brainpower. Each area of the brain, and its related expertise, can develop at differing rates, leading to our complex set of competencies. Gifted children for whatever reason have built up extra intellectual capabilities relative to their peers.

So how do you identify a gifted child to ensure that they get the additional academic resources they need to fully reach their potential? And remember, when evaluating your child, that all gifted children are different. Albert Einstein learned to speak and read late relative to his peers.

Gifted Child?

1. Has your child reached language milestones early?
2. Do they learn new words quickly and have an extended vocabulary
3. Is your child curious? Inquisitive? Does he love to research his arcane (seemingly) areas of interest and then tell you all about them?
4. A self-taught reader?
5. Does he speak quickly?
6. Can they talk easily in adult conversations, moderating their comments differently than when they're speaking with peers? Do they pick up nuances?
7. Can your child handle multi-step directions?
8. Do they seem to have – relative to their peers – a deep knowledge base?
9. Do they like to learn and do they remember things/facts easily? Do they possess a great memory, insight, perspective and understanding?

10. Can they focus and concentrate?
11. Are they creative?
12. Speed is often an indicator of giftedness. Such children can't learn or speak fast enough. They love to learn and view it as fun. Additionally, their activity level can be high as they try to cram all of that learning into their day.
13. Gifted children are often natural leaders and show that competency early.
14. Such children also relate well to those older than themselves.
15. Does your child enjoy time alone? Art, music and natural beauty?

The above qualities are only a starting point. Gifted isn't something that happens early on and doesn't progress. Children proceed in life at their own pace. Sometimes shy kids get overlooked because no one listens to what they have to say. If you suspect your child is gifted get them evaluated and start paying attention to the above listed qualities. A mind is a terrible thing to waste.

Resources

Flash cards, work-books, the lists at each subject end or videos and books listed at the book end.

www.nagc.org The National Association for Gifted Children is a great starting point of resources.

Check with your school to find out if they can provide deeper resources. Outside tutors also help. Even a Rosetta Stone language course might be a fun option.

For those raising prodigies:

How To Raise A Prodigy: http://www.nytimes.com/2012/11/04/magazine/how-do-you-raise-a-prodigy.html?pagewanted=all : by Andrew Solomon.

FAILING OR THE THREAT OF IT

First, if you suspect that your child is having problems in school don't despair! The mere fact of recognizing the problem gives you an opportunity to address and fix it. With the proper attitude and dedication most school-based problems can be fixed.

Indeed, the biggest risk most children face is that their problems are not recognized and diagnosed, thus escalate to the point they can no longer be ignored. By then, the child is defensive, scared and probably wary of adult involvement (will they get in trouble?).

Recognizing a struggling child checklist

1. Empathize and don't accuse. Children will try to protect themselves from punishment or disappointing a parent. Before you do anything reassure your child that you are there to help them resolve any issues and that you love them enough not to assign blame.
2. Some signs of a child in trouble are behavior, sleep or eating changes. A little sullenness can be normal; hiding and being depressed regularly are not.
3. Identify the real issue. Regardless of age, all of us deal with denial. Sometimes what looks like one thing is actually another. Acting out in class might be frustration with a lack of reading skills. Feeling ill in the morning might be fear of facing a bully or a math class the child doesn't understand. And children very often do manifest stress by feeling ill (so it isn't all in their head or avoidance).
4. Get help. Teachers and administrators are there for you and your child. You may encounter some that won't help but don't start with that assumption. Once you suspect a problem set up an appointment with your child's teacher to get their thoughts, suggestions and inputs. They see your child in class. Ask what resources the school has to deal with the problem.

5. Talk to other faculty at the school: the principal, past teachers, coaches, anyone you can identify who can provide insight into the real issue.

6. Sit your child down and ask for their thoughts and suggestions. How you phrase the conversation is key. Right now is not the time for arguments and blame but rather to be a parent and listen. Problems are solvable with communication; don't drive your child away.

7. Assess all that you heard and assign a category of issue: academic and perhaps behind in a class or many classes; a learning disability such as dyslexia or ADD (attention deficit disorder); a social problem such as a bully; boredom; a bad teacher or dysfunctional school; hearing or vision problems; conflict at home; hunger or lack of sleep (my son at six actually had a problem latter; he decided he only needed four hours of sleep at night; after about two weeks the school called me!) or something you can't identify?

8. Get outside help! Many schools will have resources to help, ranging from special education programs to psychologists. They can also recommend outside specialists who are worth the cost to test your child and set them on the right path. This group includes your pediatrician, a psychologist, speech therapist, tutor and a variety of other specialists.

9. Get involved. A struggling child needs your support and can't fix the problem alone. Set up a place for them to do homework, help them with it when necessary or at least check it, make sure it's in their backpack when done, buy them the supplies they need and ask. Make sure they eat well and ask about their day. Joke, to lighten the mood (they are kids and in no way have destroyed their life yet! Most problems now are still fixable).

10. Reassess the situation often and keep the school and teachers informed. Only a rare problem is solved alone so keep those who care invested in finding a solution.

11. Add your own resources from this book, be they videos, books or websites. Learning should be fun; social issues are about finding constructive coping methods.

12. Discipline and desire are important differentiators. Set clear goals, rules, guidelines and expectations. Children can't perform to standards that aren't clearly set and enforced.

Sometimes a problem has been allowed to build for too long, or spirals out of control quickly. Of the interviews I did for this book my questions on this topic were hardest for the adults involved. One of the women who runs my children's school addressed the suicides of two children she'd known since they were five. My pediatrician discussed the heroin addiction of a child he'd met at under a day old. My dentist survived a divorce that left him with almost sole custody of his three daughters, thrived and then watched his family got torn apart as his oldest daughter struggled with life threatening anorexia for years. Children, like the rest of us, fail. As parents watching that happen is devastating. What to do?

First, shore up your own strength in whatever way works for you. There is truth in that old adage that you can't help others unless you're strong. Then, get realistic. Anyone bent on destruction of themselves will win. I struggled for years with an eating disorder and I always knew that I ultimately made the decision as to whether or not I got better. But when I asked for help I didn't get it - which had negative repercussions (so listen! Most people aren't as self-destructive as they seem they just don't know how to ask for help).

Next, if a child is past simple intervention you still have options. A GED isn't the same as a great education but it's better than nothing and very often the first step in turning a life around. Make sure your child can at least read and do basic math. Sit down with them, hire a tutor or send them to a remedial class or camp.

Find a mentor, someone with whom your child can bond. Ish teaches yoga at my local, favorite studio, Maha Yoga. Tall, dignified and so mellow I've only ever seen him calm and smiling, he's also the guy who dealt with children coming out of jail (still called parole officer with children) until his recent retirement. The kids who got him are lucky; this man is so accepting and loving I'd open my heart to him even if scared. Children speak differently, and everything matters more in their worlds. If they won't talk to you, the parents with whom they've become embroiled in a power struggle, let go and find them someone else.

Hospitals, military schools or those for troubled children, detox, tutors, doctors, teachers and the list goes on. You aren't imagining things. The scope of answers is too long for this book but don't ignore the issues you identify, resolve to fix them, keeping yourself grounded first.

And check online for blogs or support groups of parents addressing the same issues. None of us need face such problems alone and those who've gone before us have constructive comments regarding what works and what doesn't.

BULLIES AND MEAN GIRLS

Sometimes the world is difficult, and children don't always have the maturity to cope effectively. I'd like to quickly run through a few key issues though the complexity of each really deserves their own book. Each of the below issues can escalate and thus should all be taken seriously. If you suspect that your child is in trouble now is the time to step up, leave the denial and blame behind and get the needed help (specific to each situation). Bad behavior, either done by your child or to them, often doesn't resolve itself.

Bullies

Both girls and boys can be subject to bullying but it happens more often between boys. Anyone watching boys from the time they first take that initial brave step to when they start climbing and then begin raising their fists can attest to the impact testosterone has on little boys' bodies and minds. Testosterone is correlated with high self-esteem, psychological dominance and physicality, a mixed blessing.

Testosterone occurs in both men and women, though only a small amount in females while it determines maleness in large part. First

showing up six or seven weeks after conception it begins to differentiate the boy fetus from the girls. Dr. James Dobson in his book, *Bringing
Up Boys*, states that a huge surge of the hormone actually damages their
developing brains, altering its structure. According to Dobson discussing the brain during this process, *even its color changes. The corpus cal-
losum, which is the rope of nerve fibers that connects the two hemispheres,
is made less efficient. That limits the number of electrical transmissions
than can flow from one side of the brain to the other, which will have lifelong implications. Later, a man will have to think longer about what he
believes – especially about something with an emotional component.*

Language development is also impacted, being more concentrated
in the left part of the brain for a right handed boy, with women's language skills being more balanced between right and left.

Testosterone also strikes the boy again in adolescence with a surge
that develops him into a man, deepening his voice and creating larger
muscles. The boy will also develop facial and body hair, possibly acne
and that infamous teenage behavior. During this time period a typical
boy has 15 times the amount of testosterone as does a girl.

High testosterone has also been correlated with aggressive behavior with Dobson citing a study of 700 prisoners in which the ones with
the highest testosterone were more likely to engage in unprovoked
violent behavior and get in trouble. He notes that testosterone is *a
facilitator of risk – physical, criminal, personal.*

But hormones alone don't account for all of the bullying or violence
among boys or even girls. Children will behave as they've been taught
or modeled and boys tend to communicate physically. They jostle and
fight, with girls more likely to use words or complex social interactions. Different forms of parenting or discipline at home or in school
can have a direct impact on how they treat others. We've personally
witnessed parents admonishing the child their own child attacked
(witnessed by all). Violence in discipline won't discourage violence in
your child's behavior but setting limits will. Then, some children are
just more physical, regardless of the firm hand of adults.

The CDC tracks bullying. According to their surveys, about 20 percent of students are bullied on school grounds each year with about 5

percent saying they missed school due to a fear of violence either at school or on their commute. Almost 8 percent say that over the previous year they were either threatened or injured with a weapon at school. In 2009, 11 percent of those in grades 9 through 12 were in a physical fight. Those under 18 constituted 16 percent of violent crime arrests (murder, rape, aggravated assault and robbery) and 26 percent of property crime arrests (burglary, larceny and auto theft). During 2008, 1,280 juveniles were arrested for murder, 56,000 for aggravated assault and 3,340 for rape.

Most boys have been bullied or witnessed it; 75 percent of children report having been bullied. Obviously, certain kids are more a target, with the smaller and less popular boys especially at risk. A deep pool of loyal friends helps, but isn't a saving panacea. Most kids don't feel comfortable discussing this topic, either as a participant, witness or victim. Often a strong social code of not "telling" exists. Stay vigilant, and don't be afraid to follow up if you suspect bullying behavior. But discuss the issue with your child in depth first as going behind his back could sometimes make the situation worse, not better.

Bullies are often acting for attention or to feel powerful. Sometimes they come from homes where aggressive, belittling behavior is acceptable and don't know better. Bullies vary, boy or girl, realizing that they're doing harm or not. Often they will pick children over whom they think they can easily assert control because they assume the person is meek or won't otherwise stick up for themselves. New kids are always at risk.

Girl bullies are less likely to physically hurt your daughter but, being less direct, will resort to emotional taunts. Harassment and reputation destruction are also frequent methods.. This ongoing activity can actually be very aggressive in its own way and very painful.

One further note, cyber bullying is a constantly growing and very serious threat, having led to teens committing suicide as a result. Only you can decide at what age to let your children online to social networking sites without knowing their password and monitoring interactions, but that decision and power is ultimately in your hands.

Signs a child is being bullied from the Oprah website:
1. *Acts withdrawn*
2. *Has unexplained injuries*
3. *Clothing is torn*
4. *Fears going to school*
5. *Has trouble sleeping*
6. *Mood changes*
7. *Stops talking about school*
8. *Finds excuses to miss school*
9. *Has new friends*
10. *Displays aggressive behavior at home (Sometimes if your child is being bullied, he or she will take it out on a sibling.)*

www.oprah.com/relationships/How-to-Deal-with-Bullies/3#ixzz 21TqkAC3Z0

If your child is being bullied never minimize or discount what they say or how they feel. Bullying is serious. Then, you'll need to navigate your way delicately through the related minefields, especially if the bullying child's parents or school don't support you and your child. Discuss notifying the school with your child, who is likely to be resistant and rightly so. Explain to them that this one step is crucial in stopping the problem. If you feel the other child's parents might be helpful contact them as well. Then, protect your child and his self esteem as much as possible. Provide a safe escape and home. If the bullying has a physical risk then you need to push hard for support from the school. Most importantly, listen, don't judge and empathize.

If your child is a bully then you have a different problem. Boys learn not to express emotions and phrases like "boys don't cry" only reinforce their reticence. I once heard an adult former mean girl confess and say that she did it because her home life was so bad and she had no other outlet. Boys likewise act out aggressively too often when tension at home rises. Depressed clinically or just not dealing well with home or other problems, bullies are created somewhere in that inability to express emotions. Get past your own issues, accept that something going on at home might be contributing and start listening to your child. Punish, but with a constructive purpose and not just to show you're in control.

Resources

Bringing Up Boys by Dr. James Dobson

The movie *The Fight Club*, if your children are old enough to see the violence. Otherwise, *The Breakfast Club*.

Mean Girls

Mean girls are everywhere.

You don't have to listen to those mean girls. They're just there to make you upset and make you feel bad about yourself. And you know, inside, they feel bad about themselves too. But they don't wanna admit it to anybody.
AMANDA SEYFRIED

No girl will escape school girls unscathed in some way, whether as victim, perpetrator, enabler or witness. Women are very often indirect in how they relate, which causes many social complications. And being indirect can often be a huge liability, inciting negative reactions in other girls.

I recall one conversation with a woman, who called me, the mother of a girl with whom my daughter had been struggling. I had online proof that the woman's daughter was harassing my own yet she called to accuse my daughter of being the mean girl. As I told Lauren, she might have been contributing (how was I to know for sure without direct evidence...when girls are wily and not direct?) but if I had evidence that the other girl was behaving badly I wasn't going to fall on the family sword and let Lauren take all the blame.

To make a long story short, the moms never resolved the conflict; the girls a few months later became friends. I add the story because it's illustrative that girls will be girls, at all ages, and we need to approach their interactions with a healthy dose of skepticism.

Girls can also be brutally mean and destructive, falling into the bully or mean girl category or, for the high achievers, both. There are numerous movies made on the topic including one titled *Mean Girls*.

In her excellent book, *Queen Bees and Wannabes*, Rosalind Wiseman, addresses the different roles girls adopt as they angle for power.

The **Queen Bee** is the girl *whose popularity is based on fear and control, think of a combination of the Queen of Hearts in Alice in Wonderland and Barbie.* This girl walks into school blessed with a combination of looks, money, charisma, will and perhaps intelligence or at least a strong sense in manipulation. These girls tend to be mean but to do well impressing adults. They dictate other's behavior.

The **Sidekick** is the closest mirror to the Queen Bee and derives her power from that of her more powerful counterpoint. More likely to moderate her behavior than the Queen Bee she's often also easily replaced.

The **Banker** keeps tabs on everyone and this information is her power. Often meek and seemingly well behaved the Banker has almost as much power as the Queen Bee.

The **Floater** is the idealized girl that too many parents convince themselves is theirs. Able to mix among groups, the Floater is strong in a lot of areas but not too much of anything. She's pretty, but not too, and on. Able to stand up to the Queen Bee, she has strong self-esteem and doesn't need to be mean to others (thus is widely liked). I'm not saying it doesn't happen and if you're daughter does fall into this category then congratulations. But it's a tentative balance to manage over the years and most girls aren't mature enough before a certain age.

The **Torn Bystander** feels torn, whether to be loyal to her clique or to do what's right. This girl may not be as socially savvy or ruthless as some, or is perhaps conflicted by her tomboy tendencies which may her more comfortable with boys, but whatever the issue she isn't sure how to handle it.

The **Pleaser/Wannabe/Messenger** fits her name. At the border of a clique, she does what's needed to stay in their good graces. Anyone who tries hard always lets it show. All or at least most girls occasionally veer into this category.

The **Target** is the one set up by other girls to be humiliated or victimized. The Target might be in or outside of the clique but most often is chosen because she has in some way challenged the Queen Bee or the clique, thus is usually far from being the weakest one in sight (unlike with the target of bullies). Targets are isolated and often not supported, except by perhaps a few close friends. This role is a tough one to navigate.

All girls will be subject to mean girl behavior. The above is meant as primer to instruct on the basics. The response of a parent has to be carefully targeted to the situation. Some kids are savvier than others at navigating the complications and severity differs. Listen and support your daughter but don't accept her version of events at face value.

Resources

Queen Bees and Wananabees by Rosalind Wiseman

Read or watch *Cinderella* and *Snow White* by the Brothers Grimm or Disney

Watch the movies *Mean Girls, Heathers, You Again* and *Legally Blonde.*

DRUGS, ALCOHOL, SEX, PREGNANCY, CRIME AND EVEN GANGS

Alcohol and Drugs

Children get into the darnedest things. At two they're digging through your kitchen cabinets and scattering your pots around the floor. Later they're going through your bathroom and slipping prescriptions or condoms in their pocket. And if you have a gun that might end up in their possession as well.

The numbers are brutal from a parent's perspective. Alcohol kills 6.5 times more teenagers than do all other drugs combined. Traffic accidents (about 45 percent are alcohol related) are the highest cause of death for people between 6 and 33. By eighth grade 52 percent of kids have smoked cigarettes, 20 percent have used marijuana and 52 percent have drunk alcohol. Kids who drink alcohol are fifty times more likely to try cocaine. One estimate puts the cost to the United of States of underage drinking at $58 billion a year. About 40 percent of those who begin drinking at 13 or younger develop alcohol dependency at some point in their life, with 10 percent of those who began drinking after 17 developing such dependency. And well over 60 percent of teens who drink say they got their first alcohol from their home or that of friends. By senior year in high school 80 percent of kids have had a drink, and not just one. More than a third have done so by eighth grade. During the past month an estimated 26 percent of people aged 12 to 20 used alcohol, with binge drinking being at 17 percent.

Surveys range, but about 60 percent of children consistently say that drugs are available in their schools, and that includes in middle school, across all demographics. Illicit drug use has declined but prescription drugs use has grown. Indeed, 15 percent of high school seniors reported using a prescription drug in the past year; most were from friends or family who often didn't know they had taken them. Crystal Meth use is more concentrated in small towns, where kids between the age of 12 and 14 are 104 times more likely to use it than kids in larger towns. An estimated 27 percent of teens know a classmate who has used ecstasy and 17 percent know more than one. Ten percent of teens claim to have attended a rave, at which ecstasy or other drugs were available at about 65 percent of them. By eighth grade 20 percent of kids have tried marijuana. By tenth grade 15 percent have used amphetamines. An estimated 1.8 million kids (0.8 percent) of kids twelve and older currently use cocaine.

And teen arrestees often test positive for drugs. The National institute of Justices Arrestee and Drug Monitoring System stated that about 66 percent of underage boys arrested tested positive for marijuana.

Signs of drug or alcohol abuse (or use)
1. Disrupted habits including sleep, eating or school attendance.
2. Your child smells like alcohol or has dilated eyes. Be up when they come home late and feel free to check.
3. They have begun wearing drug or alcohol related shirts, keep props like shot glasses or bongs around or hang up related posters.
4. They lock you out of their room, keep it well aired regardless of weather and won't let you in their car if they have one.

Ready for a drink yet (see how pervasive intoxicants are in our society...we joke about them). A note of hope for parents is that those teens whose parents speak to them regularly about the dangers of drugs are 42 percent less likely to use them but only about 25 percent of these kids say their parents initiate such conversations.

Sex

Alcohol or drugs make youths more likely to have sex. According to the CDC, in 2009 about 46 percent of high school students had sex. Almost 14 percent had already had four or more partners. Before having sex, 27 percent used drugs or alcohol and only about 40 percent used a condom. Also according to the CDC, in 2006 an estimated 5,259 Americans between the ages of 13 and 24 were diagnosed with HIV/AIDS. About 19 million sexually transmitted disease (STD) infections occur each year with almost half occurring among those aged 15 to 24.

The United States has the highest teen pregnancy and births rate in the western industrialized world, which is estimated to cost our country $7 billion a year. While teen pregnancy has been declining, that follows years of high growth (between 1986 and 1991 the rise was 23 percent). About 34 percent of women under 20 become pregnant, or about 820,000 per year. Eight in ten are accidents and 79 percent of the teens are unmarried.

African-American and Hispanic teens get pregnant at a higher rate than other ethnicities, with Hispanics now having the highest rates.

The younger a girl is when she first has sex the higher the likelihood that the sex was unwanted or even not voluntary (intoxication for example). Almost 4 out of 10 girls who had sex first at 13 or 14 fell into this category.

Girls who become pregnant and keep the baby find their lives inalterably impacted. Only one-third end up receiving a high school diploma with only 1.5 percent earning a college degree. Not surprisingly almost 80 percent of them end up on welfare. Children of teen girls typically have lower birth weights and tend to do worse in school. Daughters of teen girls have a 22 percent higher chance of ending up a teen mom, while sons have a 13 percent higher chance of ending up in prison.

Reproductive/sex education is now taught in most schools but too often it focuses on birth control, not judgment. Abstinence is sometimes explained as an option, but only as an option. Our media, especially the music and movie industries, sell a message of glamorous promiscuity and fun. Above a certain age your child will make whatever decision they want but until then you should address sex in a direct conversation. Judgment need not come into play but your child needs to be informed of the consequences and risks. As with drugs and alcohol, too many parents choose not to have these conversations, leaving their child left asking for their (immature) friends understanding and input. And remember to tell them that sex isn't just physical gratification or a means of keeping a boyfriend. Deep emotions come into play that are also hormonally, or physically, driven. Sex is a serious issue, even if our society doesn't always treat it as such.

Serious Acts with Serious Consequences

When a child spirals seriously out of control you can only protect them so much from the consequences of their actions. But that is also the time when your parental role is the most important.

I discussed this issue with Simon Gee, who handles child-based programs at Hathaway-Sycamores. This non-profit delivers many needed services for families and children in crisis, dealing with issues such as loss of home, violence and gangs. The first point he made was that a parent must never give up on a child, especially one who is in serious trouble. At that point he said parents must reorient their priorities toward their child, being there after school or finding programs that can fill in and address the particular crisis. At that point, parents have an obligation to step outside their own anger and resentment for the moment and help. As a society and as a person, we do owe children something. Luckily, with some effort parents can find a support structure and program to aid in resolving just about any crisis. If you are having a hard time go to a local church or your child's school and ask.

Typically, a child rarely ends up in serious trouble alone. Your contribution might simply be that you were carrying a crushing workload to support your family. Get past blame and anger and make every effort to reach your child, regardless of how your relationship might have deteriorated or how defensive they are.

But whatever you do, also explain to them that there are consequences to their actions. We can only shelter them to a point, then they need to carry their own burden. Punishment and a loss of privileges are to be expected as they've shown that they can't behave responsibly.

Get help. This too shall pass.

A Quick Note on Psychopaths

Psychopaths form about 1 percent of our population but are responsible for somewhere between 15 to 25 percent of those in prison, while also being the perpetrators of a disproportionate number of murders and violent crimes. No matter how badly your child behaves he's not likely to be diagnosed a clinical psychopath.

But, I'm including this note because the disorder is now increasingly being studied among the young, with some experts saying that psychopaths can be diagnosed as early as 5 and others disagreeing.

As historically the disorder couldn't be treated others don't want to unfairly label un-fully developed young. Children however do show some change with treatment.

A clinical psychopath basically has no empathy and feels little to no guilt. They are also able to coldly calculate how to get what they want. So, for example, most young children provoked will strike back immediately in anger and feel remorse for their action later. A child psychopath will wait until the right moment to strike back, showing un-childlike restraint, and feel no remorse. Narcissism and impulsivity can also be related traits but are too much a part of children's makeup to be a reasonable test.

Thus, no matter how badly behaved, your child likely isn't a psychopath. But, if he is, increasingly you can now get a diagnosis and help.

Resources

Trouble, Age 8, Jennifer Khan, The New York Times Magazine, May 13, 2012.

In Home Violence

To my knowledge my children don't go to bed scared. They don't wake up fearing for their life and well being as they leave our house heading to school. They don't confront physical violence in their homes or out of it. No palms slap them and no guns ring out as they cower under their pillows. Not all children are so safe and my heart goes out to kids whose realities are different. To those families I'll say one thing first, know that you can escape violence and you deserve better.

No abuse is acceptable. Adults can chose to stay or leave an abusive situation but children can't. They're stuck with the fists and guns, the violent neighborhoods and even gangs. The mental abuse can be worse and some children grow up being taunted, threatened and chastised for just being alive. Violence and emotional abuse don't only affect the poor.

I want to touch on this subject because it's so important but it's far vaster than a chapter in a book. If violence is an ongoing and recurring reality the first bit of counsel I'd have would be to recognize that you've done nothing to deserve it. Mostly, children and victims get blamed by their aggressors. Children tend to blame themselves. Violence is never justified regardless of how you've behaved (the problem NEVER lies in you when someone else resorts to violence).

I have a wonderful parenting book from the 1950s called *Time is the Piper*. One big point of the book is tying parental action to something a child can understand. Punishing doesn't necessarily lead to better behavior but can rather feel disconnected from a child's reality if they can't tie their actions to their parent's reaction. Violence falls into that category, as does emotional abuse. We're given these small, precious, defenseless lives, entrusted to our care and guidance. A parent can do almost anything to a child who cannot assert much in response.

Protect your children. Cherish them. Don't hit or criticize unnecessarily. If you or your children are in a dangerous situation, be it neighborhood or a person, explain that life won't always be this way. Where there is breath there is hope. And there are people to help. Taking a child from a home? Morally repulsive to me but sometimes it's for best. There are people who will help even if the first one you ask won't. Schools, churches, homeless shelters and centers for the abused.

In downtown Los Angeles we have a wonderful place called Union Rescue Mission. Andy Bales runs the center and he quotes a recent, recession-based number of homeless kids under 18 as making up 40 percent of our current local homeless number. The absolute doesn't matter as it changes but the core message, of how vulnerable are women and families with children, resonates. He takes them in and houses all. The mentally unbalanced are separated from families but he embraces everyone, as his mission before his own God and he never judges.

Union Rescue Mission aims to get the families off Skid Row and into a community of families, where they can learn self-respect and to feel normal. Shamed are the eyes of children living in abuse or on the street.

His story is so simple. Working late one night he refused to share his sandwich with a man in need. Going in to teach the next day he chastised some children for not being inclusive then realized he was no different.

He then devoted his life to those most in need and he's had an impact. His father was also a homeless child during the Great Depression.

Finding a place to escape abuse might be hard but they exist. Search and someone will help.

COLLEGE: GETTING IN AND PAYING FOR IT

College is a goal all children should have, whether it's to attend an Ivy League school or a less ambitious goal of a vocational program at a community college. Various charter and Catholic schools have shown that most children can make it to some form of college and graduate. For the ambitious or especially bright the only analysis is which college and whether or not to attend graduate school after. Without college kids are facing life at a great disadvantage career wise and are less likely to get a job let alone a good one.

But how to pay for college with the annual costs now totaling over $50,000 at many private schools (and no longer being under $10,000 per year at many state schools)?

According to the Department of Education, 94 percent of students earning a bachelor's degree borrow to pay for it, up from 45 percent in 1993. In 2011 the average debt for all borrowers was $23,300. But 10 percent owed over $54,000 and 3 percent more than $100,000. At elite universities which have larger endowments the average loans can range under $10,000

According to a Wall Street Journal and accompanying study, upper middle class families (with income between $94,535 and $205, 335) had the biggest jump in percentage of student debt between 2007 to 2010. In 2010 about 25.6 percent of such families took on such debt, up from 19.5 percent in 2007, with what they owe jumping from $26,639 to $32,869 during that period, after adjusting for inflation.

Currently, over three million households owe $50,000 or more of college debt, up from 794,000 in 2001 and 300,000 in 1989.

Meanwhile, according to a study by the Center for Labor Market Studies at Northeastern University, during 2011 about 54 percent of all under 25 year old bachelor degree holders were under-employed or jobless, a total of 1.5 million young people.

In my (originating) discipline of law, just 55 percent of 2011 law school graduates (43,735 was the total number of all graduates) had law related jobs nine months after graduation, with 28 percent being unemployed or underemployed. Looking at the range, of the 20 top schools in employment 83 percent had legal jobs while at the bottom 20 only 31 percent were working as lawyers. A report by Brian Tamanaha states that private law school tuition rose from an average of $7, 526 in 1985 to $35,743 by 2009. The growth in public law schools for the same time period was $2,006 to $18,472.

John Schnapp covered the challenge for newly minted doctors in the Wall Street Journal, July 20, 2012, in an article titled *Doctor Pay and Social Priorities*. He looked at graduating doctors from Harvard, of which only 3 percent of applicants were privileged to get accepted. Their four-year studies average $200,000 and a sizable number graduated with over $100,000 in debt after financial aid. Starting salaries averaged $50,000 escalating to $60,000 within the years after graduation. Many will need to fund specialist training.

Young people not surprisingly are having a hard time paying off this debt. Department of Education data also states that only 38 percent of college loans are current (meaning the borrower is current on repayment) down from 46 percent in 2006. Balances are unpaid for a number of reasons, including that the borrower is still in school, has postponed paying or just stopped. Eight percent of these loans are currently in default and almost 1 in 9 borrowers who started repayment in 2009 defaulted within two years, about double the rate of default in 2005.

These trends are unsustainable and have been getting increasing and well-deserved media coverage. We can all agree, based on cold hard data, both that college creates better lifelong opportunities for our children but it's also almost cripplingly expensive.

With careful, long-term planning any family can plan and find scholarships and other forms of financial aid so that the burden isn't quite as bad. Most kids are taking on loans, but how much varies dramatically. Below are recommended some detailed resources with information specific to most colleges and financial aid packages, of which there are many. Also included is a basic checklist which you should read not near the end of your child's high school career but at the very beginning. College is a big event and these days requires extensive planning, from class selection, to SAT prep classes, to meeting very specific requirements for certain programs or financial aid.

> *I'm a man of leisure. That's because I have an*
> *English degree and can't get a job.*
> **Jarod Kintz, *At even one penny, this book would be overpriced. In***
> ***fact, free is too expensive, because you'd still waste time by reading it.***

And a note on majors, in an earlier section of this book we discussed the jobs of the future and the skills, or majors, required to fill them. Anyone talented enough in a discipline, who works hard and makes good decisions will prosper. Anyone less focused might not. A recent news article stated that Library and Information Arts was currently the worst major as judged by employment outcomes and pay. While everyone should follow their passion they should check beforehand if that dedication will result in a job, and at the very least minimize loans if they decide to pursue such a major regardless. Engineering, most sciences, math and the disciplines that lead to jobs caring for people, such as nursing, show long term job prospects.

Financial Aid

Financial aid covers all forms of aid to pay for college including loans, while scholarships and grants typically are awarded under a specific program and do not need to be paid back.

The major forms of financial aid are:

Government grants, both state and federal
Pell grants

Merit scholarships, from schools and a variety of other organizations and businesses

Need based scholarships from schools and a variety of non and for profit organizations

Loans

Prizes and awards

Government Resources

Federal grant programs require a FAFSA application, which is a Free Application for Federal Student Aid. This form is necessary to be considered for any and all federal grant programs.

Pell grants are federally provided funds for low-income students. Obviously, your family is evaluated, not just the child, and the factors include: cost of attendance, whether your child is in a full or part time program, expected family contribution and length of study. The Federal Supplemental Educational Opportunity Grant (FSEOG) is a campus-based aid program for those Pell Grant recipients that are the most financially impaired. Apply early as this grant is campus based thus very limited. Other well-known grants for low-income students include Academic Competitive Grants and National Science and Mathematics Access to Retain Talent (SMART) Grants.

Other federal grant programs include such varied areas as those to small businesses or for women who study in fields in which they are under-represented, such as science.

States each have a website that covers what they provide. Grants and scholarships are offered for a wide range of individuals, including minority or need based or for those studying a subject for which there is a need in the state, such as nursing.

Merit Scholarships

Merit scholarships are awarded for something, and these are those funds we here when a child gets money because they'll be a starter on a sports team. Included are areas such as athletic, arts, ROTC, academics and music/drama. They're also awarded for good grades or to fund study in a certain discipline. They are not required to be repaid. All students should research those available at their college of choice and apply for those that fit. As noted, those schools with large endowments often have a much deeper pool of such financial resources.

Some businesses or organizations also offer such scholarships. Below are some resources which can help you find a broad array of such funds. Each of these applications is specific to the requirements of the scholarship or grant thus extensive research and careful reading of the requirements might make a difference between getting the grant or nothing.

Need Based Scholarships

Need based scholarships can come from schools, non-profit organizations and even businesses. Some, such as from the Gates Foundation, cover costs beyond bare tuition. Below are resources to help you identify some of the resources that might apply to your situation.

Need is also a relative term. According to Christopher Drew in the New York Times, *Help For The Not So Needy*, last year families earning between $180,000 to $200,000 received on average $23,750 in need based aid from Princeton. He notes that Harvard is almost as generous.

On the low end only about 1 percent of entering freshman get merit aid at Boston College, Johns Hopkins and Skidmore.

Loans

As noted above, most college students are now taking out loans to fund their education. These funds can be arranged through your college financial aid office but remember to ask what the expected payment amount and terms will be. Do not take on more debt than you can service and analyze before applying to colleges that you can afford. Certain majors or professions are also more likely lead to better paying jobs thus can perhaps support a higher debt load. College should still be a time for discovery and fun but the cost for that carefree time has become more burdensome for today's students. Also consider if your child might want to work during college to help cover some costs and limit the debt required. As a parent that thought doesn't stir my heart but in today's world, where a college education is increasingly unaffordable to middle class families, it's an economic reality.

Prizes and Awards

Contests can be great fun though the chance of winning is never great. Below are some resources that can point you to current options.

College Plans

College today requires extensive planning starting freshman year in high school or before. A clear sense of realistic goals and a game plan for reaching them is crucial. Learn as much as you can about what your schools of choice value in applicants, be it extensive community service or sports strength. Some schools favor those in private schools while many state funded schools do not. With a clear goal and understanding of how to reach it, not only will your child get into an appropriate school you'll have a better chance of funding it with a minimum amount of debt.

For those aiming high, the Ivy Leagues or equivalent, a solid game plan is even more essential. Kids around me are building their resumes in grade school and have parents driving them to such activities on a daily basis: instruments, sports, art, language and community service. Some of it is overkill, but your child not only needs good grades he needs something to set him apart. Most kids that go to highly competitive schools are in the top 30 percent (or for some schools much higher) of their class and are good at something outside of school. Certain guidance counselors have stated that niche expertise is easier, such as tuba players since so many schools need to fill a band. Perhaps a better approach, and one I prefer, is to expose your children to many interests and passions early on so they can follow the one that strikes their fancy. The encourage and support them, be it through classes, a tutor or learning about it as well and doing it together. Ask every guidance counselor you can find what they recommend for your actual child; each of them is so different.

Checklist for college planning

1. Have an honest and detailed conversation about college when your child has just begun high school. Overbearing? No! College today requires extensive planning and opportunities will be missed if not pursued on their timetable and not that of your family or child.
2. Identify the path your child is on, wants to stay on and intends to follow. While they don't need to know their desired major or preferred school even a general inkling makes a huge difference.
3. Find out what classes will be required to attend those programs. As pointed out, locally a very small number of students are graduating with the pre-requisites to attend our California state colleges or universities. Thus the kids need to take classes after high school graduation to be a part of these schools' classes.
4. Does your path require advanced placement classes or even supplemental education from a community college curriculum? If your child wants to eventually attend a vocational program are there local schools that offer internships while in high school?
5. Does your child belong in a magnet or other specialized school, such as for science or the arts?
6. What sets your child apart and will distinguish them on their college applications? Some schools are looking for balanced students while others want one that excels in a specific area. Check which is preferred at your child's school of choice. If your child isn't a fit, reevaluate goals or refocus extracurricular efforts. Community

service and student offices do look attractive to many admissions directors.

7. Don't forget the grades! This factor is key. Get a tutor if your child is struggling in any subject.
8. Look into financial aid, both specific to your preferred colleges and also with respect to what scholarships and grants might be a fit. These days the financial aid options are so vast just about everyone qualifies for something.
9. Don't assume you don't qualify for need based aid; all schools calculate it differently.
10. Know your deadlines.
11. Fill out state and federal government aid applications.
12. Remember that special circumstances matter, from health issues, job loss, supporting extended family, divorce to military service.
13. Sign your child up for SAT prep courses as recommended by your school. The test judges many things, one of which is how well prepared kids are for that specific test and the type of questions it asks.
14. Meet with your school's college guidance counselor. While they may vary in quality always use whatever resources your school provides.
15. Don't panic and don't pressure. Your child can be all right even if the stars don't all align as your family hopes.
16. As college gets closer honestly reassess what you can afford.
17. Plan a reasonable budget for the first year and stick with it.
18. Have a great last summer together before your child goes away to school

Resources

Each year Edward Fiske puts out a book called *The Fiske Guide to College*. It's a comprehensive guide to over 300 American colleges. Included are both academic and non-academic insights. Princeton Review, the College Board, Barrons and the Yale Daily News Staff also put out useful books on the same topic.

The College Board also puts out yearly book on scholarships and financial aid. The book is excellent. It contains detailed information on most American schools and on the financial aid landscape, in all its complexity.

www.collegeconfidential.com is a useful website targeted at those headed for college. It creates a community so many questions, for example, are answered by individuals not the site, thus can't be relied on 100 percent (but may be more honest).

www.collegescholarships.org is a website which explains and walks you through the application for many federal government scholarships. They also have links to each state's respective page for like state information and some overview information about other forms of financial aid.

www.ed.gov is the Department of Education's web site. The site offers a comprehensive overview of applying for financial aid including an eligibility estimate and required forms.

www.scholarships.com provides a huge list of varied types of scholarships, including contests.

Posse Foundation at www.possefoundation.org. Posse bills itself as a college access and youth leadership development organization. Essentially what they do is identify promising children in less ideal economic circumstances. These children are then placed in groups of 10, the "posses", who support each other at the partner college. Each child is given a full tuition scholarship for four years.

www.collegenet.com allows kids to write on topics and participate in online forums to win scholarship money.

Each year numerous articles come out detailing which schools top the merit based scholarship pool, meant to incent smart children to attend their schools. A recent article in the New York Times was entitled *Help For The Not So Needy* by Christopher Drew and dated July 22, 2012. In his article the University of Miami topped the rankings giving an average merit aid of $23,208 with 24 percent of freshman getting merit aid.

But remember that not all children need to go to college. If they don't, they might need vocational school or to start a company (the latter being the course of many famous billionaires). Accept your child's decision; you ultimately have little practical choice but to do so.

Community and for profit vocational programs

The Old College Try? No Way by Alex Williams in the New York Times: http://www.nytimes.com/2012/12/02/fashion/saying-no-to-college.html?pagewanted=all . This article provides support and resources for kids choosing a faster career start to the expense and time of college. Uncollege, MIT, Stanford and so many other online free courses can provide knowledge though as of writing no degree or certificate.

Callie

Callie is eighteen with long dark tresses and intense dark brown eyes. With her love of horses and dance, and a delicate frame, Callie is a willowy vision. She recently graduated from an all girls middle and high school, moving on to a large eastern college.

Her previous campus is located in a stately white stucco building with a red tile roof and expansive grassy front lawn. Each graduating class presents a small group of girls dressed in flowing white dresses with flowers in their hair. Parents watch, proud and involved, as their children move on to less protected environments and a broader reality.

Callie had always wanted to attend the girls' school and chose it over another option that she knew many of her childhood friends would pick. The school provided a close community in which girls were encouraged to gain their own voice, absent that of the opposite sex on a day-to-day basis. This social void empowered them to soar as confident leaders but also set them up for daily comparisons with respect to other girls. Callie felt that the girls were able to break out of their shells and the school, and find their true purpose and passion, despite any conflicts.

Her dad works in the music industry and her mom is a designer. Callie's older brother skipped college to immediately begin touring globally with his band. Her brother is her best friend and vastly different in temperament and interests. Callie is the driven one, who would dance and ride horses until 7:00 or 8:00 each evening then do homework sometimes until 3:00 a.m., juggling numerous advanced placement classes. Most of the academic pressure she felt was self-imposed. Yet she also supported her brother's very different path, finding his courage inspiring as he chased his passion.

Her social circle has mostly evolved around her brother and her friends from her earlier schools.

Los Angeles is different, she stated, essentially meaning that her community of friends came from a broad range of social sources, and wasn't just school based, unlike that of many students she's met at her new school. Indeed, at the girls' school she had friends across all classes, especially as she was head of the peer support program. Under the program she essentially spoke to other classmates or organized support programs for them. The biggest issues she faced had to do with her classmates' relationship issues, be they from family, school or boys. Serious ones were transitioned quickly to trained adults. But the experience helped her make friendships across the school, while her own class wasn't so close. Relationships were also strengthened online, as is so often the case today. Boys, while not present daily in school, were socially a regular part of her life.

She also has two younger sisters, much younger, who are still busy with school.

The family lives in a modern, window-strewn house on a hillside above the beach. Their Saint Bernard dashes in and out open doors (but behind gates) and the family likewise in always on the move in and out the busy household, which has just seen its second member move out into adulthood.

Callie chose her college seeking a new experience as she'd always been wary of leaving home. Originally she'd wanted to attend USC so she could stay closely tied to her existing life and still has every intention of moving back to Los Angeles upon graduation. Then, she decided to branch out and experience something vastly different, choosing a college in a cooler climate and with a vast depth of sports teams and the school spirit missing at her girl's school.

Eventually, Callie wants to go into the fashion industry with her dream being to work at Vogue or Chanel. Her role model has long been Coco Chanel who freed women from the constraints of restrictive clothing and let them shine as individuals. Callie has studied Chanel extensively, viewing movies, reading books and engaging with the array of fashions. In part her choice of vision comes from wanting to break the stereotype of a girl in an all girls' school as being perhaps more needy for men, and even slutty, to create a more elegant and classic self image. But Callie is also sophisticated in that she sets a high standard for herself and works hard to achieve that vision.

As well, her mother is stylish and extremely fit, an example in a city that aspires likewise to look good. Escaping those expectations, in appearance conscious Los Angeles, has been an ongoing struggle. Callie has thus juggled both her own rigorous self-standards with an accepting family who supports their children whether aiming to master school or to escape it and pursue a separate passion. Her local social structures send conflicting messages but mostly end up being supportive in that they are deeply rooted in a shared path and mutual interests.

Twenty years from now Callie will doubtless be running fashion shows or designing her own line of clothing should she decide to continue along that path. Ever responsible and disciplined, with a solid support structure and accepting family, Callie is making her own choices.

PART THREE

TECHNOLOGY AND THE FUTURE OF EDUCATION

It's hard to see a revolution when you're in it
TERRY MOE, THE HOOVER INSTITUTE

EDUCATION IS A MEDIA BUSINESS, PLAIN AND SIMPLE. I SOMETIMES get push back when I say that as if academia is really so different from printing newspapers or making movies. They're all industries based on created content, an oligopoly of dominant companies that control that content and an expensive and tightly controlled distribution network. K-12 education just has a forced audience while those attending college are paying an increasingly high premium for their credited content. Not only is their audience forced it's also funded in that the companies know from where their audience is coming and who is paying for their content.

Except an interesting shift has been an ongoing tsunami in the media world over the past ten to fifteen years. Technology opened up a floodgate of cheaper and sometimes better, or at least fresh and new, options. The music industry was the first to be impacted, they denied the impact and watched their audience decamp to cheaper or even free content. Young musicians now build an audience via YouTube and Facebook and sell on iTunes or their own websites without studio contracts. We've watched the movie, television and publishing industries likewise evolve or grasp to hang on.

What about education? Seemingly, it's the last media industry so impacted. Perhaps no one can break the stranglehold of the US school system? Or is it that the content hasn't yet evolved to meet teachers and students needs? Overseas and in supplemental education the realities are different, with technology being embraced. As Terry Moe kindly pointed out to me, K-12 education is controlled politically and thus even the most obvious advances in our own country are met with gridlock (I'm taking liberties in interpreting his comment but the underlying insight is his).

Terry Moe is at the Hoover Institute and has written numerous books on education, including a favorite of mine titled *Liberating Learning*, in which he and his co-author John Chubb dissect schools and the impact of technology on their future. Brilliant, he's truly thought through the future of education, and is more optimistic regarding higher education as it's more competitive, thus evolving faster. His concerns are real. With K-12 education being government controlled and heavily influenced by unions and other interest groups, any of the below innovations is easily possible today but their actual implementation is unsure both in actuality and timing. I tend to believe that the free market forces around the schools will exert pressure as parents increasingly exercise options and pull their children out of the public school system as has happened here in Los Angeles with charter schools.

A trickle down of innovation? Intelligent minds differ on how long any such effect will happen due to the lack of free market forces in K-12. I asked Moe about this issue, one he's studied extensively, and he expressed concern with how long the powers against real reform can continue to scuttle broad innovation. I'm hopeful that parents will increasingly empower themselves with resources such as this book and bypass any institutional barriers to getting their children the best modern education possible.

Arthur Levine, interviewed earlier and like Moe an expert on higher education, summarized this evolution well. He said that this current younger generation drives digital culture. They are already accessing online educational content and thus change is happening. What he couldn't predict was whether there would be a Berlin Wall moment or whether the creep would look more like the adoption of television or the telephone. In the latter case the shift looked sudden but was a long time in coming.

He also noted that most innovative change really does come from the periphery, where competitive challenges force new means or methods. Thus, many educational institutions such as for profit schools or community colleges are facing declining enrollment and must respond.

They will need to cut costs to stay solvent while still providing a decent education and keeping what students they can still attract. Technology can solve that conflict. He also noted that my state, California, faces the opposite challenge. We have too many students and not enough higher education slots along with severe budget shortfalls. My local system thus likewise will need to cut costs but with the added challenge of scaling to reach more students concurrently.

And thus real change has already begun coming, more at the college level but it's also starting to impact K-12. Not all efforts have been successful but let me quickly summarize what's going on and where I expect it will end.

Those on the periphery in K-12 education are creatively using like challenges to improve what they offer students on a cost effective basis. Numerous charter schools have been experimenting with different variations of blended learning, trying to bring technological advances into the classroom. By introducing software to customize learning, be it through the actual instruction or in the questions asked and feedback provided, new models are starting to emerge. Not fully scaled yet, these alternatives to a traditional lesson plan and way of learning have pushed change. Some schools, such as in Los Altos, CA, have flipped the day. Children now watch videos from The Khan Academy at night then discus them in class the next day. Innovators include: Rocketship Education, the Alliance, Carpe Diem, Collegiate High School and DC Prep.

Harvard, MIT and Cal Berkeley recently announced a $60 million partnership in online higher education called edX. These universities will offer free online courses jointly and globally, taught by some of their finest professors. While no related degree is anticipated, the classes work as prerequisites for other classes and eventually students will likely be able to pay a fee to get a certificate. Classes can also be atomized, or split, such that only various parts can be taken to meet other class or program requirements, allowing students to use their time more wisely. As Moe pointed out, lecture classes lose their value as they can now be viewed online; the geographic requirements of travelling to lower ranked schools becomes less necessary, other than for social reasons.

One early class, *Circuits and Electronics*, taught in an earlier effort through MIT by the first president of edEx, Anant Argawal, got an initial signup of 154,763 students with 7,157 completing the course. While the drop-off might seem high the class requires a background in complex math and engineering. Indeed, the class was chosen as an early test case because it was one Argawal already taught offline, and his regular class attracts about 200 students per session. In an interview he noted that one of the many surprises was how quickly students answered and commented on other students' questions – often correctly and when incorrect they were often quickly corrected by other students. He began to wait before adding input into these student forums and instructed his teaching assistants to do the same to allow for student interaction.

The final exam for *Circuits and Electronics* was the same for the online and offline students. Online students could track their real time grade both during the class from homework assignments and while taking the final exam. Some students reportedly dropped off the test once they achieved an A, even if they hadn't finished the exam. (Laird Malamed, mentioned and interviewed earlier in the book, took the class and knows Argawal).

Stanford already offers many classes online and while thus far students not accepted into the university don't get credit that option remains a possibility. YouTube recently started an education based offering. Khan Academy offers thousands of free instructional videos online, including a map detailing their recommended progression within disciplines and student specific feedback. I could go on.

Coursera is a for profit company founded by two Stanford professors which offers approximately 111 mainly introductory courses for the 2012 to 2013 school year (college level). The classes are free and offered globally. No credit will initially be given though local schools can do otherwise. The classes consist of lectures paused every ten minutes for a quiz (in its early stages, the classes may change as the program develops). Caltech, Duke, Johns Hopkins, University of Michigan and close to twenty other prestigious universities have signed on to the program (offering classes and support).

iTunes U has also updated its capabilities. On the iTunes store, it offers thousands of free courses and lectures. This open courseware is only different from edX in how the system around it supports efforts (with iTunes being less structured). Top universities post their lectures on iTunes and viewing them is free, on most any device.

Anyone globally with a computer and Internet connection can now get access to the best higher education content for free and learn anything they want. Currently, not only is music now free (Spotify, Pandora, etc.) so are some of the best courses. So why are college students taking on such massive debt for a degree when they can learn for nothing? Because as noted earlier, individuals with such degrees have been out-earning those without them, and the gap only continues to broaden even as the unemployment for those coming out of college grows (though less than for those without such an expensive credential).

A recent study by Ithaka S+R, a higher education non-profit think tank, found that students in online courses did as well as those in more traditional ones. The study looked at 605 undergraduates at six public universities in New York and Maryland who were randomly assigned to one of two groups. The first took traditional statistics course meeting three hours a week while the second was enrolled in a computer assisted class which met once a week and relied on an online course developed by Carnegie Mellon University's Online Learning Initiative. The online students did as well as the offline ones, sometimes better. Most experts do concede that online learning works better with the motivated.

The Carnegie and Gates Foundations are funding the Shared Learning Infrastructure (SLI) to help teachers better utilize online resources in the context of meeting common core standards. Content will be tagged to match with the common learning standards most states have adopted. The initiative is still in its early stages but shows great practical promise.

This advance raises numerous issues. Can this content continue to be free? If so, what's the incentive for providing it? Servers are no longer as expensive as they once were and while not costless are getting close. And, what about the conflict between credentials and knowledge? Do people attend college to learn or to get a degree that will help them get a job? This conflict is a real one and still unresolved. University costs have risen 5 percent above inflation for years and how long is that increase in costs sustainable? Let's ask here the basic question of what is a degree really worth when knowledge is essentially free? Moreover, the universities use tuitions to fund such expenses as research and salaries for vast administrations. Does that directly benefit their students? Perhaps the related prestige adds to the value of the degree; one can only hope.

Should the top universities decide to compete with the for-profit colleges that currently make up about 10 percent of the higher education market they could arguably offer a more prestigious credential at a competitive price. Already some of MIT and Stanford's online classes enroll over 10,000 students globally. The possible repercussions of these offerings are potentially staggering and are changing the higher education landscape drastically.

These courses are likewise available to students in the K-12 educational system and are being used, potentially shifting the market disruption into our public schools. Khan Academy videos have entered classrooms. Online instruction (during the K-12 years) from the top universities still isn't counted as college credit but some top universities are contemplating doing otherwise. At the very least, their free videos help children learn about topics in which they have an interest and develop a competitive edge. Use them.

Florida's virtual school is testing online learning statewide and as mentioned earlier, the Alliance Charter Schools are experimenting with different online learning models. With respect to the latter, the first year they shifted to their new model their biology teacher wrote his own online curriculum, as digital options are still limited. Numerous companies for years have provided a variety of digital curriculum and increasingly they're adding in gaming, avatars and customization. So what does the school of the future look like?

Schools will never replace teachers though they may need fewer of them to guide the class and resolve questions or children who are just stuck. Nor will the local school buildings disappear as they are community and socialization centers, providing those services as schools always have and as the community demands. Rather, what goes on in the classrooms will increasingly evolve based on how certain charter and other schools have trail blazed, along with the major universities and both technology and media companies. This change will be frustratingly slow in coming and parents/students/even teachers will need to be proactive in grasping at the newly developed resources to better educate.

Change won't happen overnight.

A lot of foundations and organizations are interested in change in education which is great. Exxon Mobil spent their entire marketing budget for The Masters golf tournament socializing how bad our system is versus the rest of the world. This suggests a full scale attack on our system from the middle. The problem is that little evidence suggests changes happen that way. Take cars. Cars and horses co-existed for many, many years. You can still see pictures from the Depression with horse drawn milk carts. That's only 80 years ago. The car was invented 30 before that and mass produced 25 before that. Yet, today's car dominated society took decades to happen. Lots had to happen - roads, fuel stations, financing, insurance. I think the same may happen in education; hopefully some of the fringe work is already in place. Smart phones are another example. Palm had smart phones out 12 years ago. It still took 6-7 years before they tipped into the masses with the iPhone and BlackBerries.
LAIRD MALAMED

All students, not just future technologists or those in progressive digital schools will need to acclimate to the digital realities of online classes and tracking frameworks. The world has already moved in that direction, now the schools are catching up. Below is a description of changes already being implemented or on the verge of being implemented in a school or many. While I wish we could say that these advances will come quickly they will likely follow the advance of many changes, building slowly until they crash down in a wave of change. The frameworks are being established.

The tools are available to turn the California schools around in less than a decade if the institutional barriers would just get out of the way.
FRANK BAXTER

Schools of the Future Will:

Still use teachers and most will be in a local building, if perhaps designed to be more interactive. Teachers will be better leveraged and won't need to adapt lesson plans to a class of diverse needs but will rather be able to address each child's individual needs. Teachers benefit from hybrid schools as much as children do. We've outsourced certain tasks to technology because doing so is cheaper, generally offloads work people don't want to do and does that job well (other than automated customer service lines). Labor heavy, the education world may be the last to benefit from advances of technology.

As Frank Baxter pointed out, teachers will evolve more into coaches, guiding the children who are used to navigating online worlds and interactive content. If classes don't stay engaging, children no longer need to go to school to learn and may drop out. This shift will continue redefining the role of a teacher, who now can respond more easily as tutor or customized coach based on each individual needs due to the more expansive resources and feedback available. Teachers will really be teaching!

Most parents don't want to replace teachers and the human response and feedback they provide, just as they favor a local school filled with neighborhood children. Humans are social. Indeed, in his book *The Social Animal*, David Brooks states: *The people in the executive suites believed that school existed to fulfill some socially productive process of information transmission – usually involving science projects on poster boards. But in reality of course, high school is a machine for social sorting. The purpose of high school is to give young people a sense of where they fit into the social structure.*

Even as technology encroaches into the classroom students will still worry about where they'll sit at lunch and whether or not their teacher likes them.

School buildings may eventually be designed to create a more inter-active and engaging experience, with larger and open spaces inside the classroom.

The value of degrees won't diminish but the related knowledge will get augmented. People, employers, judge. As the top schools con-tinue to get more selective, with increasingly more qualified global appli-cants applying, degrees will continue to retain significant value as they signify pre-screening and a certain level of achievement. But the prolif-eration of excellent free online content, both credentialed and non-cre-dentialed, will supplement prestigious degrees and the knowledge they connote. Added resources make the truly talented and hardworking bet-ter able to distinguish themselves: skills will be more easily identified. Some institutions will take advantage of these new markets and even crowd-sourced content (people not institution based) will proliferate.

Schools will be both device and teacher based. Children will use computers or tablets. Frank Baxter told me that at many Alliance schools children were already bringing their own variety of devices and doing homework on smartphones. Interfaces (or what the chil-dren see on a screen) will improve.

Paper textbooks costing $100 plus are obsolete. Yes, you can use them for a few years (in the subjects that don't need updating) and take notes if the school allows, which most don't. Digital books are much cheaper, though the publishers can and sometimes do set price irrespective of costs. Downloading them takes an instant and students can mark them up freely, add links and click through to videos or other embedded resources. A tablet or even a laptop weighs a fraction of what a stack of books does. Students can log into their respected school account and resources from any computer, at home or library, and with a password access their assignments, books, teacher updates, test scores and daily activity.

Educated members in our society work on computers. Why don't more students in the classroom?

The costs are nominal compared to the about $600 billion of gov-ernment, and not including private, money spent yearly on K-12 edu-cation. Consider the cost of one extra administrator, who now form a

50/50 ratio with teachers in our schools compared to being under 30 percent twenty years ago. At a cost of about $60,000 per year and more if benefits are added, how many $400 iPads could that salary fund? The answer is 150, and then multiply that by all the waste we have in our school system. Or just charge less for textbooks in digital form and you get the cost savings to fund the hardware.

They will be customized and more effective. Students can learn at their own pace. Another name for this capability is adaptive learning. Software is amazing and as hardware has progressed to process and store for a nominal cost and at a dizzying speed new possibilities continue to open up. Online learning can be fun, engaging and customized to a child's level. Technology is patient and non-judgmental yet it can also respond and adapt to feedback. Ever wonder why an online game can adapt to your level and provide both new and skilled players enough challenge and reward to keep coming back? Technology is adaptive in real time, and can tailor questions measuring a child's level, why they miss certain questions, which related skills they need to improve and what they need more detailed guidance to grasp.

Schools will provide detailed child specific feedback to the child and teacher. The same software that can customize learning also has the ability to tell both the teacher and the child the results of its analysis. This feedback is so important. A teacher will then know perhaps that a whole class is struggling with a concept or that only one child is being left behind and customize the next day's learning to make up for that discrepancy. Likewise, a child gets both a possible reward or a disappointing heads up that they are falling behind. I remember in school not really knowing until test time if I really understood what the teacher was telling me. Homework was actually a poor predictor as I could look back in my textbook until I found a way to do any problem or exercise that stumped me and use it as a crutch, whether or not I understood its principles.

Software is so sophisticated today. Companies use it to get minute feedback on consumers or to provide rewards and incentives to use their goods or services. Even digital badges or stars are motivating.

The costs to add these services range from a few thousand dollars to millions but since they are digital scale at a very low cost. Why haven't these effective tools made their way into school systems yet?

Let children know how they're doing and share that information with their teachers, and perhaps parents. How can they improve if they don't have ongoing and real time data telling them what they need to spend time on?

Incentive programs will make their way into online school content, allowing for better engagement and monitoring of student behavior. Harkening back to the aforementioned conversation with Kris Duggan, founder of Badgeville, like programs are still generally more difficult to implement in schools than in a large corporation. Required are resources, such as a sophisticated technology department to implement these solutions on a network of some sort. Meanwhile, our many of public schools are not generally interconnected thus don't have the dedicated staff and hardware to implement these solutions, even though their sophisticated engagement and monitoring on a real time basis is quite simple to use but sophisticated in related returns.

Guided frameworks for learning will develop and follow students. Duggan also pointed out that the ability to guide students to maximize their learning options and the actual understanding of their related studies exists, though it isn't widely used. We sometimes cringe at the thought of how our digital lives can now be monitored and tracked. Yet the reality is that such a framework exists across all demographics and ages and regardless of our career path. As parents we need to be mindful of shaping and not falling victim to online and digital profiles created of our child. We can either worry about pictures of them with lampshades on their heads or help craft a sophisticated learning record and personal profile. The depth of the tools and options continues to expand quickly. They also provide feedback and choices with guidance today expanding beyond the profile and have the ability to guide sophisticated learning and track results. An online class can lead to fulfilling, at an A level, all prerequisites for a sophisticated college program at a prestigious university and perhaps even a scholarship. Credits can be tracked, classes tied to Linkedin profiles, school or other status rankings shared, efforts rewarded and class-work noted.

And platforms are getting linked. This platform is also portable, interactive and reflects status. Participate and help your child take advantage of these advances, either as they trickle into his school or other areas. Schools may be the last frontier when it comes to indus-tries being impacted by technology; digital changes already impact your child.

Globally, digital experiences are getting humanized as psychology meets technology, for example in Facebook. As we humanize digital experiences they will increasingly become how things are expected to be, forcing schools to adopt their methods. Facebook is a good example illustrating how people interact with software, and how their expecta-tions evolve as a result. People now expect such visual digital feedback and cues increasingly from other sites and sectors. Things are being done differently; less so (still) in schools.

Individual teachers and schools are also pioneering to provide digi-tal tools to their students. These examples will provide active roll mod-els for other such innovators. Be proactive in this area.

The content and content quality will be better. I don't under-stand why some of the educational content is of such bad visual quality. For years, the content was mostly textbooks and there weren't many possible differentiators visually. As content increasingly moves online that reality has changed. The argument that Disney or Activision can spend tens (or hundreds) of millions on developing a movie or game is less persuasive than it used to be as YouTube and social games eat away at their business. No, the production quality is not equal but the content is very often witty, engaging and even magical.

Schools will be more project based and will foster group or child directed learning. People learn by doing. Repetition only gets you so far and doesn't foster a solid understanding in a topic. Applying the principles that you've heard in actual application tests your knowl-edge and forces you to think through and question the core concepts. Groups further foster cooperative learning as does being forced to teach someone else (if you can't explain it, you can't teach it and you don't understand it).

I love watching children teach each other and it doesn't matter if I'm watching my children or someone else's (referred to as peer to peer learning). They explain things so simply, relying on basic concepts and examples. They motivate and are less threatening than adults. And they're more patient.

My son one day came to me and asked me to check his handwriting homework, his least favorite subject and one that has driven both of my children to tears. It's the only course to do so. My daughter saw that I was working and offered to check it for me. We all agreed. She turned to him and asked, "Is this your best work?" He stared at her for a minute then shook his head no. She told him, "You always need to do your best work. I'll only check it when you've done your best work." He agreed then returned when he'd done his best work, she asked her questions again then checked it after he confirmed that the work truly was his best. He'd done perfect work this time.

Children know how to talk to each other and mostly, they trust each other when tasked with a mutual project.

Schools will be interactive. Schools can now do more than passively deliver information and wait for a response (should they actually get one). Interactive learning engages and requires feedback from the child, from which people learn better than when passively consuming content.

Schools will be less lecture based and perhaps allow for viewing the lecture at home in the evenings or using expert professors. Flipped learning happens when the lecture is watched at home and the classroom time is used for discussion, exercises or other more interactive options. The idea behind this concept is that children can get almost as much from a taped lecture (and unfortunately certain credible research backs up this premise even when the lecturers are from the top schools) as they can from one in a classroom. Thus the teacher is freed up to really engage children and address both their issues and their enthusiasm in active learning.

Lectures may not be the best way to impart knowledge anyway.

Schools will include more videos and eventually, game based learning. While the transition from traditional classrooms and resources has been gradual at best, sophisticated companies have raised massive amounts of funding to develop quality video content and to innovate in using engaging gaming concepts to better teach. Games as discussed earlier are especially good at engaging their users to want to learn as they master a game.

According to James Paul Gee, quoted earlier, games are good at triggering the steps needed to learn. The risk of engagement is low yet people are motivated to put in effort. Thus they can often observe a meaningful achievement from that effort, especially relative to the risk taken (for example, no bad grade attaches). Success is inspiring.

I tell my students that games are social activities. Like sitting around a fire telling stories, games have almost always created an opportunity for players to interact with each other, learn cultural traits and socialize. In fact, our perception of games as solitary activities is only due to recent history of computer games being mostly player vs. machine. I feel this is why multiplayer and social games continue to rise in popularity. From the early records of games in Egypt to now, games have been about playing together. Sometimes that is competition (friendly or otherwise) but often it is collaborative. Play is seen in a number of species on the planet and often it is around teaching and engaging.

LAIRD MALAMED

They will allow children to learn more and not be limited to tested subjects or budget constraints. Learning content is already being decoupled from the institutions we call schools. While the shift is happening much quicker at the higher education level that massive transformation is already trickling down. Indeed, much content is available though not always in an organized or usable format. The quality also varies greatly and no one company provides a comprehensive solution for parents or children (or even teachers). But if a child has an interest and doesn't have the access or means to develop it offline a good probability exists that they can do so online.

Schools will foster actual skills, decoupling credentials from learning to a certain extent. If I were to predict the one innovation that will get the most push back from a variety of sources this one would top the list. Top university content is now available online. Anyone can now learn from the best professors and across a sophisticated range of coursework. Is a college degree from a lesser institution now worth in upwards of $200,000 when graduation doesn't guarantee a job (needed to pay back the loans most kids must take out to fund that expense)? Now, in the long run we can only guess if the prestigious universities that are going online will offer varying degree programs, beyond a Harvard, Stanford or MIT traditional credential but the possibility does exist. But at the very least high school, college and later stage students can brush up on their knowledge and skills sets.

When working full time I would occasionally take classes through UCLA Extension one night a week and typically in downtown Los Angeles. Staying until 10:00 pm, driving home and then reporting for work the next day was brutal. It's all migrating online now, and UCLA is one of the schools who started early, though they still charge for their classes (and offer credit for them). No one needs to drive home late anymore.

Schools will be more cost effective. The current system is unsustainable. I am going to ignore higher education here because we've all seen that argument (it can't grow cost wise at 5 percent above inflation, leading to massive student debt, forever) and focus on K-12. One night I was studying numbers from government reports and couldn't get them to make sense. Why does the department of education have K-12 education spending growing over 20 percent from 2010 to 2015 (with a dip! In 2011) while the US Census report has only nominal student growth during that time period? We are spending too much and seeing our results decline. And the country faces a lack of funds going forward. Meanwhile media costs (meaning access to it) have plummeted as technology enables massive distribution of a quality product. The costs have to come down.

Schools will also be more accountable. They will get more ongoing feedback on what they're doing that works and what doesn't so they can fix a problem before it becomes a crisis. Here in Los Angeles *The Los Angeles Times* got a firestorm of attention for publishing teacher results and rankings. We already know that our students as a whole are underperforming their peers globally; let's figure out why. The trend in life is for greater accountability with the increased access of information. This tide is coming so that parents and students can monitor their own results even if schools and teachers refuse to. Technology requirements aren't complex.

Schools can customize their programs to serve higher risk or needier students. The related changes discussed above will hopefully level the opportunity playing field and allow at risk or poorer children better long-term opportunities.

Already new programs are being created to leverage technology to benefit at risk kids.

David Dwyer looks professorial, with a beard and humble manner and he is a distinguished one, at USC with a prestigious chair, the Katzman-Ernst Chair in Education Entrepreneurship, Technology and Innovation. USC is a lovely enclave just outside downtown Los Angeles. With its graceful Spanish style architecture and vast open space in the middle of campus while there it's hard to remember that the surrounding neighborhood houses numerous gangs and lower income families living humbly.

Prior to USC, Dwyer has headed Apple's efforts in education and designed online K-12 curriculum. He's now focusing his efforts on a project titled USC Hybrid High School (HHS), which has vastly extended hours. Required are 35 hours per week per student, with a goal of offering more than 75 hours per week (up to 12 hours a day, Monday through Friday, 8 hours on Saturday and 6 on Sunday afternoons). The school is open 300 days a year and seven days a week; essentially doubling the time students can access curriculum. He's addressing the problem that about 30 percent of kids who drop out of school do so because of scheduling conflicts. Around 10 to 20 percent of the children who drop out are gifted or talented. Imagine that in our country we have high school students, even the brightest ones, stopping their education because they need to work or care for family members. Dwyer is navigating complex government regulations on attendance and classwork that boggles the mind, luckily with USC support, as he aims to help children stay in and graduate high school.

Much of his curriculum will be online as teachers just can't otherwise cost-effectively meet the scheduling demands of HHS. However, this model isn't just distance learning or providing computers with content. Rather the teachers are available to the students, overcoming the difficulty many students have in completing such programs alone. Work is done at the school and real time feedback data provides insight into each child's progress.

Dwyer still had 400 applicants for seven teaching positions. Such an engaging project draws interest. Dwyer also recognize the importance of social-emotional development and has an extensive advisory program that addresses social and personal skill development for all students. The program even has a Ph.D therapist counselor on staff and is working toward a partnership with USC's School of Social Work to engage more resources for students.

What intrigues me about his program is its scalability and practicality. Like any new effort he's taking a risk that the children who drop out, smart or not, don't have social problems that prevent them from sticking to even a flexible schedule and the progressive ways of digital learning. But do we really want to give up on those kids without trying?

More important, Dwyer is, at a high school level, decoupling actual learning from a structured, standard curriculum model to meet the student part way, instead of mandating an outdated delivery system that just doesn't always work. I'd like to see USC scale HHS and funnel those same students into a cheaper, and perhaps less comprehensive but still useful degree program for those who can't schedule or cost wise attend a four-year traditional institution, which is my projection and not related or attributed to USC in any way.

Schools will also offer more choice and more options. Technology reduces the cost of content, in education and in all forms. I'm excited to see the new options for learning that are snowballing in availability. This trend is only at its most nascent stages.

The digital divide and education gap will continue to grow. Speaking with a number of teachers in financially challenged schools they all concurred that the technology in their school was minimal. For example, one high school in Venice, California has one computer lab with about 40 computers for around 2,000 students. Budget cuts were seemingly hitting technology early in the process, with teachers not being even able to print documents or make copies in some instances.

Our poorly performing schools overall are not making much progress improving, as has been widely and well documented. Engaged and affluent parents will continue to seek out resources and ensure that their children are technologically literate and well educated. Our strapped public resources are likely to lead to further cuts in most services, including schools. Teachers can only do so much and parents will need to be proactive or their children will not get an adequate modern education.

But hope exists for parents regardless of demographics.

Free content is already widely available online. All children and all schools will be impacted, whether in the classroom or because children can now learn and explore on their own. Whether a child is a future CEO or factory worker, the competitive dynamics of individuals have changed. This makes the importance of internet and computer access crucial.

LAIRD MALAMED

Resources

www.edx.org is the website for edX classes.

www.khanacademy.org The Khan Academy offers a great selection of free video classes.

www. oli.cmu.edu is the website for Carnegie Mellon's open learning initiative.

PART FOUR

INTRODUCTION

IN THIS LAST PART OF THE BOOK I'LL PRESENT SOME PRACTICAL daily advice for helping your child thrive. All children can benefit from developing study skills and discipline in their daily practices.

I'll also offer a conclusion and further resources, including a list of books and video sites recommended for children. And for busy parents who don't have time to read each page I offer a summary of numbered points that, if you take nothing else from this book, can make an impact on your child's educational future and life opportunities.

DAILY PRACTICE

Homework

Helping our children with their homework can't be the top activity on most parents' lists of desired to dos. Sitting with them not only brings up memories of a world we've moved beyond, our kids are often frustrated or even panicked. By the end of a day many of us are just plain tired and don't relish correcting fractions.

This book in part arose from a frustration of not finding enough online resources to resolve homework crisis's and figuring out what a dangling participle is ("you write books how can you not know?").

But homework is much greater than just a few pages supplementing our kids' daily work and not done correctly or with real understanding can lead to a child falling behind, which is much harder for a parent to fix. As with all activities that must be done regularly, treating homework with consistency will make a long-term positive difference.

Thus, below are some simple and self-explanatory rules for your family to adopt in the homework battles.

Homework rules

1. Establish a consistent time and place to do homework. If your family schedule is complicated and ever changing with sports, work and extracurriculars set up a schedule for each day, and if you don't always match it just ignore that one day's breach (but finish the homework!) and get back on schedule next time. Trying to do homework in the same place adds for habit reasons but also helps with focus.
2. If one schedule attempt proves difficult, try to figure out a better or more realistic time and place.
3. Don't do your child's homework for them; do be present or have someone present for questions.
4. Check their work; answer questions; below are some resources for finding quick online answers but also establish a like network of parents willing to answer the phone to provide tips and feedback if needed. Don't abuse that network and answer all related panicked texts quickly.
5. Minimize television, video games, the Internet and even novels until homework is done. Winding down for 30 minutes after school is great; attempting the whole Harry Potter series isn't.
6. Don't assume you aren't supposed to be involved, or that you're supposed to do the work. Ask the school. My son had a homework assignment in second grade sent home because his lines weren't straight enough. I thought I was letting him do his own work; his teacher thought I should have been more involved. Ask.
7. Put up a board with long-term assignments. Try to let your child organize shorter ones if possible; if that doesn't work add the short term ones to the board until your child learns to self organize.
8. Setting a time and place to do homework should release you from having to follow up as to whether or not your child is doing such

work. But if you don't see your child doing their homework as expected then ask!

9. Together go over returned homework with errors. Taking time to follow this step is the quickest way to ensure your child isn't falling behind and struggling with a subject. It also shows real commitment to your child's success.

10. Find a tutor if your child is struggling with a subject, or ask the teacher if they can donate some extra child to help your child master it. Few problems recognized and addressed are impossible to fix.

11. Many parents mention that their child has little homework. Should that be the case I'd worry. Not perhaps in first or second grade but after those early years. Other kids are taking work home, some a few hours each night. Your child will be competing with those children for jobs one day. If nothing else, make your child read each night, even if for as little as 20 minutes. Balance the books between fiction and non-fiction, classic and newer contemporary ones. Pick a topic in this book and explore the related resources in the back of each section.

12. Teachers make mistakes and error judgments. Stay involved.

Resources
www.google.com, www.dictionary.com, www.wikipedia.org

Study Skills

Telling children that they're smart has often led to worse results than complimenting them for putting effort into something. The first, that they're smart takes the control of their results out of their own hands, leading to a fear of failure. The last shows them that hard work is recognized and gets deserved results.

Don't ever, ever, believe anyone who tells you that you can just get by, by doing the easiest thing possible. Because there's always somebody

behind you who really wants to do what you're doing. And they're going
to work harder than you if you're not working hard.
MARIA BARTIROMO

Doing a quick search for hard work and success stories online comes up with a long string of anecdotes tying the two together. You only have so much control over your child's intelligence, personality or interests but you can instill a work ethic. Effort absolutely matters, and there is no substitute for hard work. In the long run, the one who works the hardest for something finds a way to get it.

Study skills are an integral first step in teaching a strong work ethic. And study skills often either save time or get better results, if not both. Wasted effort in the wrong direction or on the wrong task won't get your child to the top.

Schoolwork isn't always interesting, and sometimes it might seem like mindless repetition. But repetition can be the only way to learn something like multiplication tables. Other topics require the ability to analyze and not just repeat back the obvious, such as in essay writing. Practice with your child and try to spot their natural learning styles and inclinations and teach them others.

Study skills basics

1. Discipline is key. Follow the guidelines for doing homework listed above.
2. Take time to sit with your child and note how they focus their attention. We all favor certain types of work, which we tend to do better. Help identify weaknesses and strengths.
3. Study regularly but also add in breaks. Children often learn best in small chunks and need to clear their mind and body without being forced to sit for too long.
4. Help your child learn to take notes. If you don't feel comfortable advising on lectures (the key names, dates and places; the key points; anything pivotal or that changed direction of something; anything the

teacher names as important or the subject of the lecture) take a text or other book and read through a chapter together, letting your child point out what they think is important and providing feedback. If you both have a hard time buy a book and the related Cliff Notes and view them side-by-side. No one identifies the important points better.

5. Set up a study session in your home with a few of your child's friends. Let them teach each other (but monitor them so they aren't just goofing off). Children very often teach and learn better among peers. Sometimes the best way to learn is to teach.

6. Review your child's notes with them.

7. Teach your child to outline a text (again, Cliff Notes is the best resource).

8. Show your child how to make charts or diagrams that explain the context of a complicated issue or the ties/relationships among factors.

9. Together find examples online for issues your child is having a hard time grasping. Let them take over doing so once they understand the process.

10. Teach online search and resources such as Wikipedia, Google and Dictionary.com.

11. Teach your child to identify common themes that cross examples in the same discipline or others. One key thing on which American children are scoring poorly is being able to draw inferences and apply data in other contexts; these skills are key to future high-level jobs.

12. Show your child how to outline or otherwise organize points in a logical order before writing an essay.

13. Have your child take practice tests if the teacher or school makes them available.

14. End the homework at a reasonable hour whenever possible so your child is well rested. This rule is especially crucial the night before an important test, when it's most likely to be ignored.

Standardized Tests

Only a few people like tests but such types do exist. Tests are meant to periodically evaluate how children are doing in school and practically speaking begins to funnel children into different paths from an early age. Tests are but one of the many ways children will be judged in life.

Standardized tests are a slightly different breed of test. As mentioned earlier all children are now tested at year-end under the No Child Left Behind law, using standardized tests. Nationwide our children are thus tested and graded on a relative basis (with a test like PISA comparing internationally). Thus any score is comparative and not absolute. As our nationwide grade point averages have gone up (not so long ago the top possible was a 4.0, now with advanced placement many kids have left that number in the dust) our children have done worse on an international basis.

Standardized test tools and methods are taught in the schools, hence the charge that the teachers of today are only teaching "to the test" meaning repetition of the actual question types as opposed to understanding the core concepts underlying the query. Your children need to learn both. While different tests are composed of different question types certain variables remain consistent, for example most have confusing multiple-choice questions. A child who understands the basic subject will likely do well on such a test but perhaps not as well as one who's done more practice tests and understand the subject less.

Test preparation books or classes help, and most are made up of many practices tests and an explanation of what the preparers are doing with respect to question phrasing and type.

From tests that pre-evaluate so a school can target curriculum to a class all the way through the SAT for college acceptance (and into college and graduate school) your child will be evaluated based on their standardized test results. Ensure that they learn how to test well.

Resources

Kaplan, Princeton Review and Revolution Prep all offer extensive test preparation resources and can be found online. Many local tutoring companies fill a community focused need. Each test has different options thus a quick online search of the test itself will get you the most targeted help.

Summers

Summer learning loss is a phenomena that has its own Wikipedia page and numerous studies documenting its impact. Essentially, repeated studies by numerous experts show a loss of learning by children over the summers as they transition to less academic time uses. Generally, lower income students lose about 3 months of grade level equivalency while other students lose around 1. Other estimates show a 2.6 month loss in math, a 2 month lost in reading for lower income students only and about a 1 month learning loss over most subjects. Children in middle class homes actually increase their reading level a bit over the summer. Two-thirds of the long-term reading and language gaps among various students are thought to occur due to this summer loss and the differing impact on students.

Almost all children, irrespective of income, lose proficiency in more factual based disciplines like math, with the respective loss varying more widely in subjects like reading, where lower income children do much worse.

Of our roughly 48 million children enrolled in K-12 schools only about 9 percent attend summer school (or a form of). Our original school calendar came into being when roughly 85 percent of our population was engaged in agriculture and children were needed to help out over the summer months. Now, we have developed this huge related achievement gap in our country tied to this break and the difference in how children use their time.

Urge your children to read over the summer; most private schools already have extensive required reading lists. Engage them in some form of factual based study, even if only flash cards or math games.

Resources

A reading list is provided at the end of this book

Please see the resources provided at the end of the math and science sections above.

Bad Schools

This topic is a tough one to address because it's all too prevalent today, be it a bad school or just a bad teacher. As previously stated, our schools are underperforming on an international basis and while they tend to be worse in poor areas they are still often suboptimal elsewhere. Then, regardless of how good is your child's school they might suffer through a bad teacher or two, which can have a big impact on long-term learning and how they view school.

Should you find yourself in that situation you should attempt to take action quickly. Too many parents don't believe that the system will do much to help them so they don't take the steps that are available. First, there is little accountability in the public school system (more in most private, charter or religious schools). Complaining is likely to have little impact and may lead to subtle retaliation against your child. We hate to write that previous statement but let's just face the real world for a second and not advise on an idealized problem resolution strategy.

If you are stuck with a poor teacher, delicately ask for a new one, focusing less on blame than a bad mix of teaching/learning styles. If you are rebuffed, and you very likely will be, supplement your child's education that year using the resources suggested in this book or with a tutor. Time is a huge issue for all parents; recognize that even a half hour a day during the week will make a tremendous difference for your child's long-term education. Or, hold "tutoring" sessions on the weekend and make them fun. Hopefully next year your child will get a better teacher.

If you're stuck in a poor or failing school get out if possible. Research local charter or magnet schools. Check out Catholic or other religious schools and organizations which help fund their tuition. All public school districts allow for a transfer to a better school should space be available. A woman locally here in Los Angeles recounted horror stories she'd lived through as her local school district took such parents to court in an attempt to stop them from following through on such transfers (the district lost but did manage to intimidate some parents who kept their child in the local, suing school). The woman herself succeeded in getting a transfer for her child.

If you are stuck in a bad school regardless, then supplement your child's education. Ideal? No, but if it's the only solution available to you then accept it and focus your efforts on your child. As your kid gets older they can often even take classes at local community colleges or online.

That we as a society accept poor schools on such a wide level is the topic of another book, and many exist. The lost futures of too many children are at risk in our country. Don't let your child be one of them.

Resources

www.greatschools.org is a parent focused website that offers (limited) feedback and rankings on nationwide K-12 schools and deep content to empower parents. My issue with the site is that the parent feedback is very self-selecting and limited in depth. But the site is nonetheless useful.

www.cfy.org offers an online platform of curated educational resources called Power My Learning (www.powermylearning.com). On the site parents (teachers and children can find videos and interactive content that is pre-screened and classified. They can also get detailed feedback with respect to their child's performance and use of the site.

www.knowmia.com has a range of excellent online educational videos offered for free and organized by subject.

Helicopter Moms, Tiger Mothers and the Price of Prosperity

Living in a more affluent community, all around me I see involved parents and the resulting mixed results of their offspring. Some kids do go on to excel at the ivy leagues and get great jobs. Others end up suffering from burnout and stress, resorting to unhealthy coping mechanisms such as substance abuse or eating disorders. *One in 5 American teens and children show symptoms of a mental disorder and 1 in 10 suffers from mental illness severe enough to result in significant functional impairment*, according to Judith Warner in her book, *Teach Your Children Well*. Often these children are from affluent neighborhoods with the better schools, deeper resources and more involved parents. Warner defined and discussed this crisis in her earlier book, *The Price of Prosperity*, as she cites numerous studies supporting her position.

So what's going on?

Warner points to increased pressure to perform, or excel, and isolation from parents who can be more self involved and goal oriented for their offspring than actually present.

So let's take a step back and go to the power of the word chosen to describe a phenomenon. Children should be **guided**, not **pushed**. But sometimes they should be **forced** as they need to learn not to get their own way but rather discipline and following through on their commitments. They should not be forced to do things that only gratify their parents' needs, goals, aspirations and interests, with no respect given to their own. And even children have **obligations** and need to learn to be respectful members of society, no matter how affluent or poor. Responsibility runs across all demographics and children need to develop an appreciation for it.

But around us we see the extreme of programmed children. In defense of the parents, for a minute, they are doing what they know in an effort to maximize their children's opportunities. Many affluent parents followed a safe and predictable path. They were team sports players who littered their own personal resumes with student offices, the right extracurricular activities and worked hard to get good grades. Then they followed a traditional path to a good school and perhaps graduate school, accepting the right prestigious job at graduation. The path was tracked, didn't require a lot of creative thought or planning and used to offer a stable, if not dynamic career. That was before our recent spat of massive layoffs and global competition even for thought –based jobs.

Is the real pressing issue whether or not we need to decide sooner to be the generalist of the past or the specialist of the future? For what the parents mentioned above are doing is trying to create great generalist children who can put off making a decision about whether to specialize. Or is it that status conscious parents push their values over their children's reality?

And who's to say that such a path guarantees a great future for the next generation? This book has already quoted information leading to a different conclusion, at least for many of today's kids. And if everyone (or most) are doing the same thing in certain communities do you want to follow the same cookie cutter path? Always ask, what sets my child apart?

Yet perhaps we do want to create those generalist children. Because for some that path is the right one and they aren't the ones being cited by Warner in her excellent book. The children who are being forced to follow a path dictated by their parents' beliefs and goals are likely more negatively impacted by stress than those who choose it on their own. Warner is a therapist who sees these overstressed and poorly (emotionally) thriving kids and has responded to their cries for help. A local acupuncturist to the stars told me that he likewise sees the same crisis. Many overstressed teenagers end up on his pricey tables with needles sticking out of their bodies to cope with their realities, including from his own children's school. His kids meanwhile aren't similarly stressed! Nor are many of their friends.

Let's define stress. It is the body's fight-or-flight reaction meant to work as a warning that you're in danger. At the perception of a threat your hypothalamus, in the base of your brain, triggers a response to the stimulus. The nervous and hormonal systems both respond, prompting the adrenal glands to release hormones such as adrenaline and cortisol. The former sets the body in motion, elevating your blood pressure, boosting energy and increasing your heart rate. The latter is the main stress hormone, and increases the glucose in your blood, along with the brain's utility of these sugars, and makes more available the substances used for tissue repair.

Unfortunately, cortisol also cuts the activities not needed during a crisis, such as those of the immune, digestive and reproductive systems and growth processes. The brain areas controlling motivation, mood and fear are also affected.

Chronic stress arises when that reaction never ceases because you don't escape what's triggering it. According to the Mayo Clinic website, the more perceived control you have over the stressors and the less certainty you have over them the more likely you are to experience chronic stress. Your body disrupted, we, or our kids, become at risk for sleep and digestive problems, depression, heart disease, obesity, memory impairment and bad skin.

Children who choose their electives and desired paths simply feel more in control, and they're right. Are you letting your child's goals and interests determine their path or are you doing it all for them? Are you making those decisions as an excuse not to spend time together, justifying that "caring" by saying *we're all so busy*? For busy families might look productive but are they nurturing, guiding and maximizing or rather just rigid?

I don't have the answers to such questions for your family but see a like situation around me daily. Programmed children are being led to a pre-programmed and hopefully stable career of doing what's expected. They won't soar into the heights of a Steve Jobs or J.K. Rowling because they're not being trained to follow a creative and new path but rather to follow what's perceived today as a safer one.

Having watched a number of friends reassess that track when their child begged to be let off, I think the points of Warner and other related thought leaders are important for any family really pushing their child to excel. I'm also more optimistic in that I've watched families respond positively to their child's pleas to set their own course. Get to know your child before setting their course or taking them off one and listen.

But don't excuse a child from learning tenacity and self-discipline with some complaining. A little work (or a lot) is good for us. You're the parent and need to weigh the evidence to guide your (hopefully) less mature child.

Indeed, a doctor friend educated in India stated that she was shocked that children in even the toughest of schools in the United States didn't work harder, like her cousin's children in India. All is relative. Amy Chau, in her book *Battle Hymn of the Tiger Mother*, is actually a great case study in this conflict.

For those who haven't read the book, Chau describes her parenting style with respect to education. Not only are her two girls expected to get straight As, they must also master an instrument, juggle other electives, be well behaved, not do play dates or slumber parties, and on, and on. Chau's first daughter, the responsible older child, does all as expected. Her younger one fights back. The book relates Chau's dramatic struggles including tears, threats, missed dinners and hours-long violin practice, with mom in attendance. Eventually this younger daughter, Lulu, starts acting disrespectful and refusing to do as she's told.

Chau gets angry. At this point, the broad criticism begins to fall on Chau's shoulders. To her credit, she eventually relents and lets Lulu channel her passions into tennis, at which she not surprisingly excels. But let's analyze the story further.

Chau talks about rushing from work to pick up her daughter, then rushing back after she's dropped Lulu at practice, working for 30 minutes and then rushing to get her daughter again, casting work aside. She discusses cashing out her 401K to fund her daughter's activities. She begs, pleads, researches and follows through to get the best for her children. The ensuing fights are full of tears and emotion. Her daughters defend her after the book comes out. And why wouldn't they? For all her sometimes heavy handed tactics Chau is there for her girls, regardless of whether they ask her to be or not. She forces, as parents sometimes must do in this increasingly competitive world, but she's their biggest advocate.

Guide. Support. But stay flexible.

Like Chau I want my children to have solid interests. Unlike many parents I adamantly don't want to choose them. Of all the interviews I did for this book one bit of advice was consistent. All interviewees advise their children to find their passion and turn it into a career. I want that for my kids.

CONCLUSIONS

The willingness to learn new skills is very high.
ANGELA MERKEL

Don't prejudge your children. Let them soar but give them wings. Risk is a part of life much as we try to shelter our offspring from its harsher side. We won't succeed and coddling them creates weakness and dependency not success. Focus on the big picture, lasting skills and ability to "pivot". The world will continue to evolve at a fast pace and good advice today will get outdated.

I am always ready to learn although I do not always like being taught.
WINSTON CHURCHILL

Children are born perfect. We mess them up. Recognize the distinctive beauty of your unique child and nurture their strengths and interests and not those you'd like to see them have.

Join our online community at www.laernn.com and use other parents as resources. While it used to take a village to raise a child, with the Internet we all now have access to the world. And relax, enjoy and recognize that before you know it your child will be grown.

17 THINGS YOU SHOULD TAKE FROM THIS BOOK (IF NOTHING ELSE)

1. Read to your child; encourage them to read and from a wide variety of sources.
2. Ensure that your child learns to perform well on standardized tests.

3. Get involved; the quality of your child's teachers and friends will have a huge impact on how well they do in school in life. Research your school and teachers. Talk to your child's friends and about your child's friends.

4. Focus on the whole child, a strong family and building a supportive community. Parents bear a tremendous burden with respect to their children and the overburdened school system...but they don't need to assume that burden alone and should tap all possible support structures.

5. Take time to know your child and advise them on a personalized not institutional basis. Get an IQ test, talk to them and their teachers, evaluate your resources and decide on a course of action. Pivot (a Silicon Valley term for "failure" and a new direction) when common sense dictates you do so.

6. Get online. Check out Khan Academy, YouTube videos discussed here, educational games, Wikipedia and even simple entertainment. Digital literacy is a must.

7. Push math, science, collaboration, creativity, starting something, resilience, life long learning (lead by example), history, a global perspective and the arts. Pick one "subject" to study as a family each weekend. Nurture your child's interests.

8. Research local school options.

9. Discuss jobs and the stock market, even if not in depth.

10. Write a silly story with your child.

11. Check out college web sites and explore financial aid options. Track deadlines.

12. Don't hover. Let your child fail and take responsibility.

13. Work with your child's teacher. They almost always went into the profession for the right reason but are now overburdened. Good school or not, the world is changing faster than the people in it. They see your child everyday and can make a difference.

14. Start something together. Teach entrepreneurship. I pay my kids (nominally) for business ideas.

15. Do an art project, listen to music, see a concert or show, visit a museum or beach. Discuss politics or current affairs. Broaden your child's horizon and perspective.

16. Read about a leader and discuss their leadership style.
17. Adopt a country or a child in another country.
18. Love your child. Relax. All will turn out just fine with enough love, listening and understanding.

The illiterate of the future will not be the person who cannot read. It will be the person who does not know how to learn.
ALVIN TOFFLER

AND 3 THINGS WHICH MATTER MOST

1. The earlier you can get involved in your child's education the better. Regardless of when you get involved you can make a difference. The schools cannot educate your child for the future so you must step in and supplement what they offer.
2. Broad knowledge and continuing to learn are only getting more important not less. Adaptability and creativity help too. Read, question and learn.
3. The jobs of the future are in entrepreneurship (creating your own job), math, science, services, computers and engineering, medicine and entertainment. Try to guide your child into a field in which he or she has the skills to be among the best; being the best is too hard but being among the best guarantees employment as long as the role exists. Many roles and professions will continue to disappear.

BOOKS TO READ BEFORE YOU'RE 18

Classics for All or Most Ages

Barrie, J.M; *Peter Pan*
Baum, Frank; *The Wizard of Oz*
Carroll, Lewis; *Alice's Adventure in Wonderland*
dePaola, Tomie; *Strega Nona*

Graham, Kenneth; *The Wind in the Willows*
Grimm Brothers; *Grimm's Fairy Tales*
Kellog, Steven; *Paul Bunyan*
Kipling, Rudyard; *The Just So Stories*
Lewis, C.S.; *The Chronicles of Narnia*
Milne, A.A; *Winnie the Pooh*
Potter, Beatrix; *Peter Rabbitt*
Stevenson, Robert L.: *A Child's Garden of Verses*
White, E.B.; *Charlotte's Web*

Younger Children

Bemelmans, Ludwig; *Madeline series*
Bosch, Pseudonymous; *The Name of This Book is Secret*
Brown, Jeff; Flat *Stanley series*
Cleary, Beverly; *Ramona series*
Dahl. Roald; *The Minpins*
Estes, Eleanor; *The Hundred Dresses*
Freeman, Don; *Corduroy*
Kinney, Jeff; Dia*ry of a Wimpy Kid series*
Leaf, Munro; *The Story of Ferdinand*
McDonald, Megan; *Judy Moody series*
Mosel, Arlene; *Tikki Tikki Tembo*
Muth, Jon; *Zen Shorts*
Osborne, Mary Pope; *Tales from the Odyssey; The Magic Tree House Series*
Parish, Peggy; *Amelia Bedelia series*

Older Children

Burnett, Frances; *The Secret Garden*
Carnegie, Dale; *How to Win Friends and Influence People*
Collins, Suzanne; *Hunger Games series*
DeFoe, Daniel; *Robinson Crusoe*
Fitzgerald, F. Scott; *The Great Gatsby*

Frank, Anne; *Anne Frank, The Diary of a Young Girl*
Funke, Cornelia; *Inkheart series*
Garci, Cami and Stohl, Margaret, *Beautiful Creatures* series.
Golding, William; *Lord of the Flies*
L'Engle, Madeline; *A Wrinkle in Time*
Lee, Harper; *To Kill a Mockingbird*
London, Jack; *The Call of the Wild*
Nesbit, E.; *The Enchanted Castle*
O'Dell, Scott; *Island of the Blue Dolphins*
Orwell, George; *Animal Farm*
Paolini, Christopher; *Eragon series*
Rawls, Wilson; *Where the Red Fern Grows*
Riordan, Rick; just about any of his series
Rowling, J.K.; *Harry Potter series*
Salinger, J.D.; *The Catcher in the Rye*
Stevenson, Robert Louis; *Kidnapped and Treasure Island*
Stewart, Trenton Lee; *The Mysterious Benedict Society*
Tolkien, J.R.R; *The Hobbit and Lord of the Rings*
Twain, Mark; *Tom Sawyer or any*

VIDEO SITES OR CHANNELS THAT TEACH

1. TedEd on YouTube
2. Discovery networks
3. The Khan Academy
4. UC Berkeley
5. Freesupplimentalmathvideos on YouTube
6. Edutopia videos
7. Jet Propulsion Lab Resources
8. Createthenet on YouTube
9. Mythbusters
10. Knowmia

Note: many of the above post videos both on YouTube and on their own site. The best way to find your preferred platform is a simple web search. Also look at The Great Courses (www.thegreatcourses.com) for classes for sale taught by top professors. They include many targeted at high school students but even younger children can benefit from watching those aimed much older, with discretion.

The www.laernn.com website offers deeper resources and guidance on how to craft learning to suit your child and circumstances. Anything is possible in life, especially for those with the right educational foundation and supportive adults. It's never too early or too late helping your child succeed and reach the top of whatever peak suits them.

SOURCES

Education is the ability to listen to almost anything
without losing your temper of self-confidence.
ROBERT FROST

THIS BOOK DRAWS FROM MANY SOURCES INCLUDING BOOKS, ARTICLES, REPORTS, INTERVIEWS, WEBSITES, PRESENTATIONS AND CONFERENCE MATERIALS. Where possible sources are cited. However, many points in the books are opinions and thus, if from an interview that source is likewise cited when possible.

Books

- Aristotle, Ethics from The Basic Works of Aristotle Edited by Richard McKean, The Modern Library, Random House, 1941
- Bennett, William J. with Finn, Chester E., Jr. and Cribb, John T. E., Jr., The Educated Child: A Parents Guide From Preschool Through Eighth Grade, Touchstone, 1999
- Bettelheim, Bruno, The Uses of Enchantment: The Meaning and Importance of Fairy Tales, Vintage Books, 1976
- Bronson, Po with Merryman, Ashley, Nurture Shock: New Thinking About Children, Twelve, 2009
- Brooks, David, The Social Animal: The Hidden Source of Love, Character and Achievement, Random House, 2011
- Brzezinski, Zbigniew, Strategic Vision: America and the Crisis of Global Power, Basic Books, 2012
- Christensen, Clayton M. with Horn, Michael B. and Johnson, Curtis W., Disrupting Class: How Disruptive Innovation Will Change the Way the World Learns, McGraw Hill, 2008
- Chua, Amy, Battle Hymn of the Tiger Mother, Penguin Books, 2011
- Dewey, John, Democracy and Education, Simon and Brown, 2011
- Dobson, Dr. James, Bringing Up Boys: Practical Advice and Encouragement For Those Shaping the Next Generation of Men, Tyndale House Publishers, Inc., 2001

- Fiske, Edward B., Guide to Colleges 2010 26th Edition, Source Books, Inc., 2009
- Flesch, Rudolf, Why Johnny Can't Read and What You Can Do About It, Harper and Brothers, Publishers, 1955
- Friedman, Thomas L. with Mandelbaum, Michael, That Used To Be Us: How America Fell Behind In The World It Invented and How We Can Come Back, Farrar, Straus and Giroux, 2011
- Gee, James Paul, What Video Games Have to Teach Us About Learning and Literacy, Palgrave Macmillan, 2007
- Hoffman, Reid with Casnocha, Ben, The Start Up of You, Crown Business, 2012
- Levine, Madeline Ph.D., The Price of Privilege: How Parental and Material Advantage are Creating a Generation of Disconnected and Unhappy Kids, Harper Collins Publishing, 2006
- Levine, Mel M.D., A Mind At A Time, Simon and Schuster, 2002
- Levitt, Steven D. with Dubner, Stephen J., Freakonomics, Harper Collins Publishers, 2005
- Levitt, Steven D. with Dubner, Stephen J., Super Freakonomics, Harper Collins Publishers, 2009
- McGonigal, Jane, Reality is Broken, The Penguin Press, 2011
- Moe, Terry M. with Chubb, John E., Liberating Learning, Jossey-Bass, 2009
- Moses, Robert P. with Cobb, Jr., Charles E., Radical Equations: Math, Literacy and Civil Rights
- Murray, Charles, Real Education, Three Rivers Press, 2008
- Nisbett, Richard E., Intelligence and How to Get It, W.W. Norton and Company, 2009
- Peterson, Paul E., Saving Schools, The Belknap Press of Havard University Press, 2010
- Pink, Daniel H., A Whole New Mind, Riverhead Books, 2005
- Satter, Ellyn, How To Get Your Child To Eat But Not Too Much, Bull Publishing Company, 1987
- Tapscott, Don, Growing Up Digital, McGraw Hill, 2009
- Wagner, Tony, The Global Achievement Gap, Basic Books, 2008

- Wiseman, Rosalind, Queen Bees and Wannabes, Crown Publishers, 2002
- College Board, Getting Financial Aid 2011 5th Edition, College Board, 2010

Articles

- Banchero, Stephanie, Top Schools Move to Offer Free Courses Online, Wall Street Journal, July 17, 2012
- Berkowitz, Peter, Why Colleges Don't Teach the Federalist Papers, Wall Street Journal, May 7, 2012
- Biggs, Andrew G., Gollege Grads Need Jobs Not a Lower Loan Rate, Wall Street Journal, May 4, 2012
- Blume, Howard, LAUSD Weighs Lower Bar for Grads, Los Angeles Times, April 18, 2012
- Brooks, David, The Creative Monopoly, New York Times, April 23, 2012
- Caplan, Lincoln, An Existential Crisis for Law Schools, New York Times, July 14, 2012
- Chubb, John and Moe, Terry, Higher Education's Online Revolution, Wall Street Journal, May 30, 2012
- Drew, Christopher, Help for the Not so Needy, New York Times, July 22, 2012
- Green, C. Shawn and Baveller, Daphne, Action Video Game Modifies Visual Selective Attention, Nature, May 29, 2003
- Hambrick, David Z., I.Q. Points for Sale, Cheap, New York Times, May 6, 2012
- Hennessy, John and Khan, Salman (quoted and interviewed by Walt Mossberg), Changing the Economics of Education, Wall Street Journal, June 4, 2012
- Holson, Laura M., That Wacky Silicon Valley, New York Times, July 1, 2012
- Hurley, Dan, The Quest to Make Ourselves Smarter, New York Times Magazine, April 22, 2012
- Kahn, Jennifer, When is a Problem Child Truly Dangerous?, New York Times Magazine, May 13, 2012

- Lewin, Tamar, One Course, 150,000 Students, New York Times, July 22, 2012
- McKay, Betsy and Winslow, Ron, AIDS Cure is Back on Agenda, Wall Street Journal, Juky 19, 2012
- Martin, Andrew and Lehren, Andrew W., A Generation Hobbled by College Drbt, New York Times, May 13, 2012
- Miller, Claire Cain, Drop Out, Start Up, New York Times, July 22, 2012
- New York Times opinion piece, The Vanishing Workers, May 5-6, 2012
- Pappano, Laura, Got the Next Great Idea?, New York Times, July 22, 2012
- Reynolds, Gretchen, A Fit Body and Better Brain, New York Times Magazine, April 22, 2012
- Schapp, John, Doctor Pay and Social Priorities, Wall Street Journal, July 20, 2012
- Shellenbarger, Sue, To Pay off Loans, Grads Put Off Marriage and Children, Wall Street Journal, April 17, 2012
- Simon, Ruth and Barry, Rob, College Dept Hits Well Off, Wall Street Journal, August 9, 2012
- Walker, Rob, Peace, Love and Tumblr, New York Times Magazine, July 15, 2012
- Weber, Lauren and Korn, Mellissa, For Most Graduates, Grueling Job Hunt awaits, Wall Street Journal, May 7, 2012
- Wessel, David, Tapping Tech to Cap Tuition, Wall Street Journal, July 19, 2012

Reports

- Benchmarking for Success: Ensuring U.S. Students Receive a World Class Education, National Governors Association and Council of Chief State School Officers, and Achieve, Inc, 2008
- Building 21st Century Catholic Learning Communities, Lexington Institute, 2012
- Degrees of Separation: Education, Employment, and the Great Recession in Metropolitan America, Metropolitan Policy Program at Brookings, 2010

- The Economic Impact of the Achievement Gap in America's Schools, McKinsey & Company, 2009
- Exploring Digital Media and Learning, MacArthur Foundation, March 2011
- How the Best-Performing School Systems Come Out on Top, McKinsey & Company, 2007
- Los Angeles Catholic Schools: Impact and Opportunity for Economically Disadvantaged Students, LMU/LA School of Education, 2011
- The OECD Programme for International Student Assessment (PISA), OECD 2010
- The Teenage Brain: What's Going On, Dr. Stan Kutcher, Martha Carmichael and Matthew Kutcher, The 2008 Open Mind Workshop Series, 2008
- A wide range of reports from the United States Department of Education.

Websites
- Center for Disease Control
- United States Department of Education
- Wikipedia